Philanthropy and Education

Marybeth Gasman, professor of Higher Education, Graduate School of Education, University of Pennsylvania

This series highlights first-rate scholarship related to education and philanthropy, attracting the top authors writing in the field. Philanthropy is broadly defined to include time, talent, and treasure. In addition to traditional forms and definitions of philanthropy, the series highlights philanthropy in communities of color as well as philanthropy among women and LGBT communities. Books in the series focus on fund-raising as it is an integral part of increasing philanthropy and has an ever-increasing market.

Philanthropy in Black Education: A Fateful Hour Creating the Atlanta University System
  By Vida L. Avery

Previous books by Vida L. Avery

Race, Gender, and Leadership in Nonprofit Organizations (2011)
By Marybeth Gasman, Noah Drezner, Edward Epstein, Tyrone Freeman, and Vida L. Avery.

Philanthropy in Black Higher Education

A Fateful Hour Creating the Atlanta University System

Vida L. Avery

PHILANTHROPY IN BLACK HIGHER EDUCATION
Copyright © Vida L. Avery, 2013.
All rights reserved.

First published in 2013 by
PALGRAVE MACMILLAN®
in the United States—a division of St. Martin's Press LLC,
175 Fifth Avenue, New York, NY 10010.

Where this book is distributed in the UK, Europe and the rest of the world, this is by Palgrave Macmillan, a division of Macmillan Publishers Limited, registered in England, company number 785998, of Houndmills, Basingstoke, Hampshire RG21 6XS.

Palgrave Macmillan is the global academic imprint of the above companies and has companies and representatives throughout the world.

Palgrave® and Macmillan® are registered trademarks in the United States, the United Kingdom, Europe and other countries.

ISBN: 978–1–137–28100–5

Library of Congress Cataloging-in-Publication Data

Avery, Vida L., 1962–
   Philanthropy in black higher education : a fateful hour creating the Atlanta University system / Vida L. Avery.
      pages cm.—(Philanthropy and education)
   ISBN 978–1–137–28100–5 (hardback)
    1. Institutional cooperation—Georgia—Atlanta. 2. Atlanta University Center (Ga.)—History. 3. Atlanta University Center (Ga.)—Endowments. 4. African Americans—Education (Higher)—Georgia—Atlanta—History. I. Title.
LC2781.8.A84 2013
378.758′231—dc23   2013002497

A catalogue record of the book is available from the British Library.

Design by Newgen Imaging Systems (P) Ltd., Chennai, India.

First edition: July 2013

10 9 8 7 6 5 4 3 2 1

I dedicate this book to my parents, Dr. Parnell and Gloria "Glorious" Avery, who encouraged my siblings and me to attend a historically black college and university.

This book is possible because of them.

Contents

List of Figures and Tables	ix
Preface	xi
Acknowledgments	xiii
Historical Timeline	xv
Introduction	1
1 Historical Backdrop	13
2 Mythical Phoenix and the Ashes It Spreads	47
3 John Hope: Hallmark of the Truest Greatness	77
4 Layers of Complexity	101
5 Creating the Atlanta University System	123
6 Germinating a Black Intelligentsia	149
7 Conclusion	175
Appendix A Other Strategic Locations for Cooperation among Black Institutions	183
Appendix B Letter: John Hope to Edwin Embree (Hope's Six-Year Plan)	189
Appendix C Notable Atlanta University System/ Center Alumnus(ae)	197

Notes	211
Bibliography	263
Index	271

Figures and Tables

Figures

1.1	Basement of Friendship Baptist Church	36
2.1	John D. Rockefeller Sr.	58
2.2	Laura Spelman Rockefeller	60
2.3	John D. Rockefeller Jr.	61
2.4	Officials of the General Education Board	66
3.1	John Hope and family	80
5.1	Presidents signing the affiliation	145
6.1	Trevor Arnett Library	167
6.2	President John Hope at Atlanta University	168
6.3	John Hope's memorial service at Atlanta University	170

Tables

4.1	Overlapping curricular structure	103
4.2	Summary of funding sources	111

Preface

Philanthropy in Black Higher Education is the first book in a new series on Philanthropy and Fund-Raising in Higher Education. Vida L. Avery draws upon the archives located in the Robert Woodruff Library at the Atlanta University Center and The Rockefeller Archive Center in Sleepy Hollow, New York to tell the story of Black higher education and White philanthropy. She brings to life the actions and leadership of John Hope, who spearheaded the center and held a vision for Black colleges in Atlanta. Avery also weaves the history of White philanthropy and its often-controlling nature throughout the narrative. She thoughtfully explores the Rockefeller-sponsored General Education Board and its role in propelling Black education forward and simultaneously holding it back.

Readers interested in Black colleges and philanthropy in general will enjoy reading *Philanthropy in Black Higher Education* as it uncovers the stories and perspectives of often-overlooked leaders and shapers of Black education. Avery's beautifully-crafted history of the Atlanta University Center is a fitting book to begin the series, which seeks to unearth rigorous research. With her work, we are off to a great start.

MARYBETH GASMAN,
University of Pennsylvania
Philanthropy and Education,
Series Editor

Acknowledgments

I thanked God for giving me the strength, ability, and perseverance to sustain such an endeavor when I first began research for this book, and I give thanks again now that I have finished it. I thank my parents, Dr. and Mrs. Parnell (Gloria) Avery, for always believing in my ability to complete this task, even when I doubted myself, and spending time in numerous discussions as to where I was in the process and how it was coming along. Thank you for giving me the love of history and reading, the foundation of my education, and the inquisitiveness that led me to know that those things of the past shape our future. I am especially thankful to my mother, who pushed me to go back to school for my doctorate; yet sadly by the time of this publication had passed away. I also thank other family members who aided in me achieving this goal. Sibyl Avery Jackson, my sister, thanks for reminding me that "we Averys can do anything we put in our minds to," for lighting a fire to get my mind back on writing when I got tired, and for knowing what it takes to pull ideas out of one's mind and to craft them onto the page to tell a story. Natalie (Sherry) Avery Webster, my sister, Toni Williams, my sister-in-law, Kimberly Clayborn and Blyss Lewis, my sisters of the heart, thank you for being excited about my endeavor to write this book and for understanding when I did not have time to socialize.

Much appreciation and adulation I give to Drs. Marybeth Gasman, Wayne J. Urban, and Philo Hutcheson, my early mentors and instructors who championed my research in black higher education and philanthropy, and especially to Marybeth again for believing in the importance of completing this book and the impact it would have in higher education and philanthropic studies. I could not have completed my research or this book without the much-needed help from archival departments and their staff. I thank Karen Jefferson, Andrea Jackson and the staff at the Atlanta University Center, Robert W. Woodruff Library, Archives Department, for assisting me with documents, finding images and providing permission letters. I thank Taronda Spencer from the Spelman College Archives Department for her assistance. I also thank the Rockefeller Archive Center for giving me the initial grant for my research, and the late Dr. Kenneth Rose and the staff at the center for assisting me during my visit to conduct research. Michele Hiltzik, thank you for assisting me with obtaining subsequent approvals for image use and answering last minute questions. Last, I thank the staff at Auburn Avenue Research Library for their assistance.

No one can make it through a research project and develop it into a book without an extremely good personal editor and the support of fellow colleagues and friends. I thank Patricia Smith for editing my chapters and being a sounding board for me to pull my thoughts together. I also thank Dr. Michael Bieze, my "collegiate soul mate", for always being there for me, lending a shoulder to cry on when I was trying to get it together, and for giving immeasurable advice and guidance. Additionally, I am grateful to my Spelman sister Rosalind ("Roz") Brewer for the much-needed assistance she provided during the early stages of my project, my god-sister, Fredi Pittman Brown, and god-brother, Santel Frazier, for continuing to encourage me to see it through to the end, and who understood the sacrifices I had to make in order to complete this project.

Historical Timeline

1839	b. John D. Rockefeller Sr.
1861	Civil War begins
1862	Morrill Act, creation of land-grant institutions
1865	Civil War ends
	Enactment of Jim Crow laws and Segregation
	State Constitution Amendments, public education for whites
	Atlanta University (AU) founded by Congregationalist and the Freedman's Bureau
1867	George Peabody establishes the George Peabody Fund
	Atlanta University incorporated
	Augusta Institute Seminary founded by American Baptist Association
1868	b. John Hope, Augusta, GA
	Establishment of Friendship Baptist Church
1869	AU creates Normal Department
1870	Blacks prohibited from attending University of Georgia
1872	AU opens College Department
1873	AU opens Scientific Preparatory
1874	AU opens Agricultural Department
1877	Gilded Age (*industrial, urban, and agricultural growth in the United States*)
1879	Augusta Institute relocates to Atlanta, GA, and incorporates as Atlanta Baptist Seminary
	AU creates Department of Industrial Training
1881	Atlanta Baptist Female Seminary founded by Sophia B. Pachard and Harriet E. Giles

1882	John F. Slater creates The Slater Fund
	Rockefeller Sr. endows $600,000 to University of Chicago
	Rockefeller Sr.'s first donation to Atlanta Baptist Female Seminary
1883	Atlanta Baptist Female Seminary opens College Department
1884	Atlanta Baptist Female Seminary changes name to Spelman Seminary
1885	Spelman Seminary and Atlanta Baptist Seminary—1st Commencement Exercise
1886	John Hope attends Worchester Academy in Massachusetts
	Rockefeller donation to Spelman Seminary, erection of Rockefeller Hall
1888	AMA establishes The Daniel Hand Education Fund for Colored People
	Spelman Seminary receives State Charter
1889	Carnegie's essays, "The Gospel of Wealth" and "The Best Fields of Philanthropy"
1890	Progressive Era *(time of eliminating corruption, prohibition, and achieving efficiency in every sector)*
	Sherman Anti-Trust Act, any monopoly in restraint of trade is illegal and prohibits business activities that reduced competition
	John Hope graduates from Worchester and enrolls at Brown University
1894	John Hope graduates from Brown University, starts teaching position at Roger Williams University (Nashville, TN)
	Atlanta University separates its Elementary School
1895	Booker T. Washington's speech, "Atlanta Compromise"
	Atlanta Cotton State Exposition
	Hope's speech, "The Need of a Liberal Education for Us"
1896	Andrew Carnegie creates Carnegie Institute of Pittsburgh
	Plessy v. Ferguson, doctrine of "separate but equal" racial status
1897	Atlanta Baptist Seminary amends charter; changes its name to Atlanta Baptist College

Historical Timeline

1898	John Hope hired as professor at Atlanta Baptist College
	W. E. B. Du Bois hired as professor at Atlanta University
1900	Andrew Carnegie creates Carnegie Technical School
	Negrophobia, beginning of race riots
1901	Rockefeller Sr. creates Rockefeller Institute for Medical Research
	Robert C. Odgen's "Millionaire's Special" train trips to the South
	W. E. B. Du Bois's study, "The College-Bred Negro"
1902	Ida Tarbell's exposé, *The History of Standard Oil*
	Rockefeller Sr. gives $1 million to create the General Education Board (GEB)
	Carnegie creates The Carnegie Institute of Washington
1903	GEB receives charter and incorporates
	Du Bois, *The Souls of Black Folks*
1905	Carnegie founds the Carnegie Foundation for the Advancement of Teachers
	Rockefeller Sr. endows $10 million to the GEB
	GEB receives funds from the Anne T. Jeanes Fund
1906	Congress passes *Hepburn Act*, regulating and imposing penalties for rebates in the business industry
	Race riots in Atlanta, GA
	John Hope elected president of Atlanta Baptist College
	Niagara Movement, Storrs College in Harpers Ferry
	GEB pledges $250,000 to Spelman Seminary
1909	Rockefeller Sr. creates Sanitary Commission for Eradication of the Hookworm Disease
	John Hope's funding request to Andrew Carnegie, Booker T. Washington intercedes for John Hope
	National Association for the Advancement of Colored People (NAACP) created
1910	Carnegie creates the Carnegie Endowment for International Peace
	Abraham Flexner's, *Medical Education in the United States and Canada*—later *The Flexner Report*, survey of medical schools

	Du Bois's Fifteenth Annual Conference at Atlanta University, *The College-Bred Negro American* Du Bois resigns from teaching position at Atlanta University The Great Black Migration to the North Julius Rosenwald creates the Julius Rosenwald Fund
1911	Catherine Phelps-Stokes's bequest of $1 million creates the Phelps-Stokes Fund Standard Oil dissolves into 38 separate and smaller companies Carnegie creates the Carnegie Corporation of New York
1912	Rockefeller Sr. creates The Rockefeller Foundation Jesse Jones's survey, *"Negro Education: A Study of the Private and Higher Schools for Colored People in the United States"*
1913	Wallace Buttrick's "Study of Black Colleges" Atlanta Baptist College changes name to Morehouse College
1914	World War I begins GEB begins appropriations to select black colleges and universities Bureau of Education conducts survey, "Report on Negro Education"
1915	GEB holds first Interracial Conference on Negro Education Harlem Renaissance, cultural "New Negro Movement"
1917	Rockefeller Sr. establishes The Laura Spelman Rockefeller Memorial Fund
1918	World War I ends
1918	W. T. B. Williams's *Study of Atlanta University* GEB appropriates conditional grants to black colleges GEB focuses on building up select black colleges and universities
1919	Atlanta mayor, William Hartsfield, successfully brings new southern airmail route through Atlanta Atlanta Chamber of Commerce launches "Forward Atlanta" campaign

1920	AU holds Interracial Student Meetings Black student protests begin Atlanta has the largest black population than any other city in the South
1924	Spelman Seminary changes its name to Spelman College Lucy Tapely, Spelman College's president, resigns
1926	John D. Rockefeller Jr. donates $175.000 to Spelman College to erect Sisters Chapel in memory of his mother (Laura Spelman Rockefeller) and aunt (Lucy Maria Spelman) John T. Tigert, Commissioner of Education, *Study on Negro Education*, conducted from 1926 to 1928
1927	Jackson Davis's study of all black colleges, *Recent Development in Negro Colleges and Schools* Florence Read elected Spelman College's new president Morehouse-Spelman Summer School
1928	GEB and Laura Spelman Rockefeller Foundation pledge $2.5 million toward Spelman's $3 million endowment campaign Arthur Klein's, *Survey of Negro Colleges and Universities*, sponsored by the Phelps-Stokes Foundation GEB pledges $300,000 toward Morehouse's $600,00 endowment campaign
1929	Stock market crashes Affiliation of Atlanta University, Morehouse College, and Spelman College creates the Atlanta University System Myron Adams, Atlanta University's president, resigns John Hope elected president of Atlanta University; continues as president of Morehouse College Atlanta University's Commencement, sixtieth year as an undergraduate institution Jackson Davis, *Survey of the Atlanta Institutions*, focuses on Clark and Morris Brown Colleges
1930	United States Great Depression John Hope's "Six-Year Plan" requires $6.4 million

GEB resolves $450,000 in appropriations to AU for the library and appropriates $600,000 for an endowment
Morehouse and Spelman elected to the Association of American Colleges, receives "Class B" rating
GEB grants $3.2 million toward Atlanta University's $6.4 million endowment for Hope's Six-Year Plan
Atlanta University awards its first master's degree
Spelman celebrates its fiftieth anniversary
Atlanta University, Morehouse, and Spelman Colleges receives "Class A" rating from the SACS
ABHMS severs ties with Morehouse College

1932 Trevor Arnett Library construction completed
Morris Brown College joins the affiliation
1936 John Hope dies
1941 Clark University changes name to Clark College and joins the affiliation
1953 Florence Read retires
Albert E. Manley becomes the first black and first male president of Spelman College
1957 The Atlanta University System changes name to The Atlanta University Center

Introduction

It was springtime in Atlanta, the beginning of April. The harsh climate and the chill of winter had retreated, and the temperature had grown warmer. Seeds planted in previous seasons now produced fruits, and blossoming flowers bore new life—a new beginning. April 1, 1929, marked a beginning and new life of a different kind.

President John Hope, Morehouse College, sat with pen in hand, in southwest Atlanta, and signed a "revolutionary educational undertaking" into history.[1] Standing behind Hope and watching this historic event were Presidents Florence M. Read and Myron W. Adams, Spelman College and Atlanta University respectively. This undertaking was the culmination of seeds planted over the past two decades that now bore the fruit of several individuals' labor to ensure higher education for blacks in the south, particularly in Atlanta, Georgia.

The decision to affiliate Atlanta University, Morehouse College, and Spelman College was, as John Hope later stated, "a fateful hour in the history of Negro higher education, with circumstances favoring cooperation that might not occur again for 100 years."[2] With a charter granted from the State of Georgia for this university plan, Atlanta University would provide graduate and professional courses, while Morehouse College and Spelman College would provide undergraduate courses that led to a bachelor's degree.[3]

As a Spelman alumna, I had read Spelman's institutional history, as all freshmen at the time I attended were required to, and knew of the affiliation signed in 1929. However, I did not fully comprehend the magnitude of its significance until I began my research for this book. I discovered just how monumental and historic the affiliation was, especially considering that it occurred during a tumultuous time in US history. First, despite Jim Crow laws and segregation, Atlanta University practiced social equality and educated black and white students together. From inception, each Atlanta University president stood firm on this principle of social equality and never wavered even in the wake of possible financial ruin. Second, rather than deny students broad cultural and intellectual exposure, Atlanta University created a venue for interaction between the races and the institution integrated all of its activities.[4] Wealthy northerners, distinguished scholars, and artists visited the institution to see how blacks were being educated, and to give speeches and musical performances. By the 1920s, groups of students organized interracial meetings on the campus of Atlanta University, though white campuses, such as Emory University or Agnes Scott College, took substantially more time for allowing such meetings. These meetings opened a path for serious dialogue and provided an opportunity to resolve misconceptions about each race during a time when students were in need of such developmental maturity.

Third, when the institutions affiliated, Atlanta University was the only black institution that focused solely on graduate studies. Fourth, the Atlanta University System was also a "trail-blazer" because of its cooperative arrangements with other American colleges, thus making it a model for higher education throughout the country. The only other place in the United States where a similar concept was put in practice was in California at the Claremont Colleges. Based on the Atlanta University System affiliation, the Rockefeller-founded General Education Board (GEB) attempted to establish another center in Georgia that included University of Georgia, Emory University, Georgia Institute of Technology, and Agnes Scott College. Although this affiliation with the white institutions never came to fruition, the Atlanta University System was nevertheless the model.

Last, when John Hope became president of Morehouse College, he was not only the first black president of the institution, but also the first black president of any of the American Baptists Home Missionary Society's institutions. Additionally, at the time of the affiliation, he was simultaneously the president of both Morehouse College and Atlanta University.

The impact of this affiliation also stretched beyond the world of academe and onto the national stage as it related to the social issue of race relations. US President Herbert Hoover commended Hope for his work and acknowledged the affiliation's importance in improving the relationship between blacks and whites. However, despite these record-breaking first events, most people are unfamiliar with the story behind the affiliation of the three institutions. Most people are also unfamiliar with John Hope and unaware of his involvement with the affiliation, and even less aware of the relationship he cultivated with white philanthropists, which allowed him to negotiate his terms and use funds acquired to further his vision of sustaining black higher education.

Several scholars and historians have advanced a variety of viewpoints and interpretations of philanthropists' involvement with black higher education during the early twentieth century. On one end of the spectrum, scholars analyze the relationship from the philanthropists' perspective by dichotomously limiting their descriptions of the motives of giving as being either manipulative or benevolent. Some portray industrial philanthropists as conspirators who were mainly interested in implementing an industrial education curriculum to keep blacks in a position to provide labor, and not interested in "bringing industrial progress and social harmony to the South." On the contrary, scholars explain that philanthropists were more interested in "a profit motive that was the driving force of black higher education." Further descriptions indicated that philanthropists had a political agenda to recreate the antebellum South after the Civil War. To do this, it was necessary for blacks to be "prepared ideologically and practically for their role in the new America."[5]

Other scholars perceive philanthropists as manipulators of black college presidents, implying there was no other type of relationship that existed between philanthropists and black college presidents, and that black leaders had no sense of agency.[6] However, I found that these accounts neglected to look at the full dynamics of the history of philanthropy and black education and neglected to acknowledge that black college leaders, such as John Hope, contradicted such claims. Hope clearly had a sense of agency, which not only shaped the conditions of his life, but also the lives of many other black people.

At the other end of the spectrum, there are scholars who view philanthropists' actions largely as benevolent. For these scholars, the difference in race and the segregated circumstances of the South created the initial need for the GEB to provide education (e.g., agricultural and vocational training rather than liberal arts and professional training) for blacks so as not to disrupt a racially-volatile environment. They also point out that over time, the GEB established "democracy by enlarging the opportunities of a social group previously excluded." Blacks in the South could not "afford to forget the foundations upon which colleges for [blacks] have been built," therefore, giving philanthropists credit, at least, for elevating them to an educational level that they would not have otherwise achieved.[7]

While conducting research at the Rockefeller Archives Center, I had the distinct pleasure of meeting Eric Anderson and Alfred A. Moss Jr., authors of *Dangerous Donations*, who were there conducting research for a project. Though some scholars view them as apologists, Anderson and Moss's study of philanthropy provided a different examination of industrial philanthropists that went beyond philanthropic motives. For Anderson and Moss, historians placed too much emphasis on the motives of philanthropists and too little emphasis on the outcome of their philanthropy. As they noted, almost from the beginning of industrial philanthropy, blacks were educated beyond an industrial curriculum. Members of my family, graduates from the Atlanta University System (Center), and I were, and are, a testament to this contention. At the beginning of my research, I was a fourth-generation educator, and neither my mother, grandmother nor great-grandmother received an industrial education. They attended a college and normal school that prepared them to become teachers and not laborers in a field.

Other viewpoints have since emerged that challenged how we view philanthropy. In *Uplifting a People,* Marybeth Gasman and Katherine Sedgwick discuss philanthropy by highlighting black philanthropy as a means of self-help among freed slaves and blacks, which included the support of education. For Gasman and Sedgwick, black philanthropy, or giving, was rooted in "efforts to overcome oppression," this type of black philanthropy has gone mostly unnoticed.[8]

However, philanthropy from blacks to other blacks often involves an additional dimension of giving; examining the words "endow" and "engender" demonstrates this dimension. On one hand, in giving money, philanthropists "endow"; in other words, they give money in order to provide income for the purchase and maintenance of things necessary for a better life. A school is an example. "Engender," on the other hand, means "to bring into being." Many black philanthropists in the past, and even today, not only "endowed" but also "engendered" by being living models of what a changed man could be.

John Hope, for example, both endowed and engendered. Hope was able to "engender" in other black people a new, positive vision of self, by living his life in the manner that he lived: dedicating himself to making intangible principles tangible. For many black people during his time, acquiring a positive view of self was a daunting task given the overwhelming negative view projected onto them from the dominant Jim Crow social order. John Hope "engendered" in other black people a new awareness of self, an ability to dissociate themselves from this negative viewpoint, as reflected by his own life.

Hope's philanthropy extended beyond being the chief financial officer or fundraiser for a college or university. He gave of his personal resources and of himself, a true example of black philanthropy that hardly gets much recognition. Hope "donated more money than he could actually afford to [black] organizations, institutions, and charities that he believed were worthy of his support." An example of this type of giving occurred during the endowment campaign at Morehouse. Hope and his two sons donated $2,000 that created the Lugenia Francis Fund to honor his wife and to contribute to Morehouse.[9]

Hope also managed to give of himself regardless of the position he held. He dedicated his life converting situations into vehicles for the betterment of other blacks. Hope's qualities "made him a leader on the campus, and in academic circles generally thrust him into positions of local, national, and international leadership in the field of human relations and race relations."[10] During World War I, Hope served under the auspices of the Young Men's Christian Association (YMCA). In this role, he made several trips to Europe to work with black soldiers to ensure their fair treatment. When the YMCA opened their black branch in Atlanta, Hope taught regularly in the night school.

When black soldiers returned from World War I, many Atlantans, including Hope, foresaw an increase in racial animosity. After much deliberation, a solution to defuse the racial tension was arrived at when Will W. Alexander, a white southerner and former Methodist minister, organized the Commission on Interracial Cooperation (CIC) in 1919, which consisted mostly of conservative whites and a few blacks. Although the CIC members questioned Hope's demeanor and friendship with W. E. B. Du Bois, he became a member "after the commission enacted the fulfillment of a promise to commit use of some of the funds from a bond issue for the construction of a public high school for Negroes."[11] The city of Atlanta had "floated a bond referendum to expand and upgrade its public schools"; however, blacks suspected that white schools would reap all the benefit. Hope was the chief spokesperson for the National Association for the Advancement of Colored People (NAACP) committee that "had helped organize black Atlantans to defeat the referendum." Hope later became the first black to serve as chairman of the CIC, and became its president in 1932.[12]

Both Hope and his wife, Lugenia Burns Hope, were humanitarians. The area between Morehouse and Spelman was "a general haven for Atlanta's criminals." Lugenia Hope was the first to do social work in this area, as well as other areas in Atlanta; consequently, Hope, his wife, and others "helped organize what eventually became the Atlanta School of Social Work (1922)."[13]

Over time, scholars have both vilified and justified industrial philanthropists' motives and challenged the notion that more attention and discourse in philanthropy should focus on the recipient's perspective. I too was presented with this same challenge. As I was developing and structuring the concept for this book, I was encouraged to consider adapting the material to address definitions of philanthropy that have arisen around issues regarding the relationship between philanthropists/donors and recipients. At first glance, it appeared, to some, that I was only considering philanthropists' perspectives and motives within my study because it examined their involvement in black higher education and their interaction with John Hope. However, in the end, my study analyzed how Hope and philanthropists discerned common interests; how his solicitation and use of philanthropic gifts allowed him to achieve his vision of higher education of blacks; and illustrated the balance of power from both perspectives. Despite this being the case, neither of these factors nor perspectives was the initial point of departure for this book. For me, it initially boiled down to two simple puzzling questions: Why did the three Atlanta institutions affiliate, and why has the story of the creation of the Atlanta University System never been told?

Because scrutiny of the philanthropists' motives relegates "the decisions of blacks to the background and margins of the story,"[14] and since historians generally omitted the story of the affiliation in discussions of black higher education, I wanted to find a different lens from which to view past events, black college leaders, and their interaction with philanthropists. I also wanted to analyze the circumstances of the past in more ways than the one-dimensional views previously portrayed. Therefore, as a starting point, I chose the approach of telling a historical account by focusing on a single event, not an individual or individuals. The single event is the affiliation of Atlanta University, Morehouse College, and Spelman College that took place in 1929 and created the Atlanta University System.[15]

Focusing closely on a single event and using a cultural and historical account allowed me to emphasize information and individuals that have been traditionally lost within the broader accounts of higher education, black higher education, philanthropy, and black college leaders. Using this approach, *A Fateful Hour* tells the story of the affiliation of Atlanta University, Morehouse, College and Spelman College while demonstrating how philanthropists, John Hope, and other individuals pooled their resources together to ensure higher education for blacks in the South.

A *Fateful Hour* also provides a different perspective from which to view philanthropic relationships that extend beyond the simple categories of benefactor and recipient, while preserving John Hope's legacy and the story of the creation of the Atlanta University System.

The following questions guided the research that I address in this book: Were philanthropists only interested in providing industrial education for blacks? Were college presidents, such as John Hope, pawns in the game of capitalism and industrialization, as practiced by philanthropists? Why did three higher education institutions for blacks form an affiliation when each was rich in its own history and merit?

In answering these questions, I was surprised to learn how instrumental John Hope was in shaping higher education for blacks and how he used his relationships with philanthropists to further his own agenda and vision. He not only upheld his position to the structure of the affiliated institutions by maintaining a liberal arts curricular focus, but also negotiated terms with philanthropists before the affiliation took place. After the affiliation, he drew up the blueprints for what the affiliation eventually evolved into, the Atlanta University Center.

Collecting the Data

Since I had moving pieces of a puzzle that intersected at different points, I gathered the pieces from various places; afterward, I had to figure out how they fit together. In order to understand all the pieces, my first step was to gain knowledge about the artifacts left behind, the habits of the players involved, and the three institutions that were eventually affiliated.[16] Because there was little to no information published regarding the first-hand accounts or the behind-the-scene negotiations of the affiliation, I relied heavily on primary sources from the historical records left by the philanthropists, members of the General Education Board (GEB), philanthropic organizations, and the presidents of the three respective institutions.

Knowing that John D. Rockefeller Sr. provided the funds to create and establish numerous foundations, particularly the GEB, and that he financially aided Spelman College in its early stages of establishment and became its largest benefactor, I conducted a large part of my research at the Rockefeller Archive Center in Sleepy Hollow, New York. I applied and received a grant-in-aid that enabled me to spend a week researching the records of John D. Rockefeller Sr. and Jr., other members of the GEB, and John Hope. The behind-the-scenes correspondence helped me understand philanthropists' mind-set and motives in forming the affiliation and provided the majority of the missing pieces that allowed me to tell the affiliation's story.

Next, I reviewed information from the GEB's organizational history, minutes from meetings, and correspondence between various members. These documents highlighted the GEB's general interest in the development of a comprehensive system of education in the United States in general, and specifically the rationale for aiding black institutions of higher education. I also reviewed the records of and correspondence between significant GEB trustees and presidents, such as Wallace Buttrick, Wickliffe Rose, Frederick Gates, Edwin Embree, and Trevor Arnett. From this material, I learned of the business and personal relationship that existed between the philanthropists and John Hope, as well as Hope's important role in the affiliation. Additionally, I used personal narratives and publications by industrial philanthropists, such as Andrew Carnegie and John D. Rockefeller Sr.[17]

In order to gain more in-depth information about each of the three institutions involved in the affiliation, I conducted research at the Atlanta University Center Robert W. Woodruff Library, Archives and Special Collections Department; the Spelman College Library, Special Collections, Archives Department housed in the Women's Research and Resource Center; and the Auburn Avenue Research Library on African-American Culture and History, Archives Department, in Atlanta, Georgia. Each collection contains material on the three institutions, the institutions' presidential papers, and the personal correspondence of important members of philanthropic organizations.

Since John Hope was heavily involved in the negotiations and establishment of the affiliation, and simultaneously was president of Morehouse College and Atlanta University after the affiliation took place, I drew upon information gathered from the *John Hope Presidential Records* housed at Atlanta University Center Robert W. Woodruff Library, Archives and Special Collections Department in Atlanta, Georgia. These papers shed light on the intricacies of forming the affiliation and the complexities of dealing with the philanthropists. Other pertinent information in this collection included material, such as board of trustees minutes, changes the institutions underwent, fundraising activities and efforts, financial papers, and correspondences between Hope and members of the GEB.

Florence M. Read served as president of Spelman College at the time of the affiliation, was the secretary of the Atlanta University board of trustees, and the interim president of Atlanta University after John Hope's death. I examined the *Florence Read Presidential Papers* at Spelman College Library, Special Collections, Archives Department housed in the Women's Research and Resource Center in Atlanta, Georgia. However, at the time of my research, access to her papers was limited, and the material was unprocessed.

W. E. B. Du Bois's prominence developed during the time of my study. He was not only a professor at Atlanta University, but also while on staff, he was instrumental in raising the nation's awareness of Atlanta University with his studies on blacks, and was a close friend to John Hope. I gathered information from the *W. E. B. Du Bois Papers* housed in the Archives Department of the Auburn Avenue Research Library in Atlanta, Georgia. The archives contain the complete Du Bois collection from the University of Massachusetts on microfilm.

John Hope never understood why "a person would reveal his inmost self to public gaze." He often wondered, "How much of a man [was] actually revealed in the many so-called autobiographies." Hope rather assumed that "a biography might come nearer being correct than an autobiography."[18] Following Hope's guidance, I collected information from secondary sources, such as intellectual biographies on philanthropists and John Hope,[19] scholarly literature that discussed philanthropy and philanthropic activities,[20] and scholarly literature that emphasized the education of blacks in the South during the late 1800s into the early 1900s.[21] Additionally, I used the institutional histories of Atlanta University, Morehouse College, and Spelman College to discover each institution's development before, during, and after the affiliation. Data collected from the histories helped me understand the duplication of curricular work and the scarcity of financial support, which were the catalysts for the affiliation.[22]

Structure of the Chapters

I structured the chapters chronologically to show how philanthropists, John Hope, and other individuals involved in the affiliation rose to prominence in a parallel manner. Yet in time, their paths and interests intersected and led them to create the Atlanta University System.

Although the story of the Atlanta institutions' affiliation is the point of departure, its creation did not occur in a vacuum. In order to appreciate the historic merit of the affiliation, philanthropic support, particularly from John D. Rockefeller Sr., John Hope's significant role in its formation and establishment, and his relationship with philanthropists, Chapter 1 provides a comprehensive historical backdrop for the story. It examines the contextual social matrix from which all involved in the affiliation emerged and operated. In doing so, I explain the flaws in American society that were the outgrowth from slavery. I also discuss John D. Rockefeller Sr. and John Hope and show how similarities in their background, upbringing, and religious convictions formed the foundation on which each ran his life. This chapter also discusses the early philanthropic groups, missionary and black societies, and the establishment and early beginnings of Atlanta University, Morehouse College, and Spelman College.

Chapter 2 examines the emergence of industrial philanthropists and the philanthropic foundations that provided financial support for black institutions during the late nineteenth and early twentieth centuries. Rockefeller Sr. sponsored the GEB, and it became a clearinghouse for many other foundations.

Therefore, another focus in this chapter is on the GEB's creation and its systematic involvement with education and higher education in the South.

Chapter 3 focuses on John Hope and his path to becoming an educational spokesperson and fundraiser for the missionary society, a racial activist, and college president. I also discuss the race riots in the early 1900s, Hope's involvement with the Niagara Movement and the NAACP, and his path that eventually intersected with wealthy white philanthropists. The chapter ends with a vignette highlighting Hope's attendance and participation at the GEB's first annually sponsored "Interracial Conference on Negro Education."

Since the catalyst for the affiliation was the Atlanta institutions' duplication of efforts and scarcity of funds, Chapter 4 focuses on Atlanta University, Morehouse College, and Spelman College and examines the layers of complexity behind the overlapping curricular structure and financial struggles of each institution. Chapter 5 continues with the Atlanta institutions and explains the GEB's focus on Atlanta as a strategic location to form a center of higher education for blacks, the studies the GEB conducted on the black institutions, and ends with the affiliation of the three institutions. In Chapter 6, I discuss the impact the affiliation had on the nation, each of the three institutions, and the other Atlanta institutions. I also highlight John Hope's leadership acumen and visionary skills in developing Atlanta University, the other black institutions in Atlanta, and the interaction between Hope and philanthropists that led to the creation of the Atlanta University Center. Chapter 7 is the conclusion.

1
Historical Backdrop

To engage in a serious discussion of race in America, one must begin not with the problems of black people but with the flaws of American society—flaws rooted in historic inequalities and long-standing cultural stereotypes.[1] That slave traders and owners brought blacks by force to the United States, used them as slaves, particularly in the South, dehumanized and devalued them, and viewed them as chattel is one axis in the examination of flaws in American society. This group of facts alone marked the essential difference of blacks from any other racial group in the United States. Slavery, however, was just the beginning of the cycle of flaws.

The Industrial Age supplanting the agrarian South was the other axis. Ironically, this second axis of flaws sprang to life in the dismantling of the agrarian South that ended formalized slavery. Decades-long debates between the North and South about new states and territories being declared as free or permitting slavery, coupled with their opposing views on whether the federal government should take precedence over individual states, ultimately led to Civil War. After the war, Reconstruction itself was flawed as evidenced by the opposing radical Republicans and states' rights factions. Both the Congress and the presidents of the Reconstruction Era, in their commitment toward their ideological beliefs, failed to focus on the practical, long-term needs of the newly freed slaves.

One of the most primary and practical need of the newly-freed slaves was basic education. Basic education directly influenced the fulfilling of another equally important need for not only the freed slaves, but also white southerners as well: a means of earning a livelihood. Concomitantly, basic education was needed to lay the foundations for both informed citizenship and higher education, especially for blacks. Perhaps the overarching flaw of Reconstruction was the failure to secure for emancipated slaves the victories of the 13th, 14th, and 15th Amendments, which were effectively nullified by the passage of a series of laws throughout the South referred to as "black codes." The flaw of rampant racism that had fueled slavery was still alive and well.

As Reconstruction ended, the Industrial Age came into its own in America. Industrialism marked a change in economic production and with it a transformation in society. Similar to the mythical phoenix rising from its ashes to recreate itself, so too did America after the ending of the Civil War and Reconstruction. Overlapping the ending of the Reconstruction Era was the beginning of a decade often dubbed the Gilded Age. As the term gilded indicates, the "gold" of this era was a superficial outer covering, not solid gold. This was a time when great aggregations of capital rested in a few hands that in turn created a new social class in the country; simultaneously, the masses of newly-freed slaves and defeated white southerners suffered great poverty.[2] Corruption and scandal lay beneath the gilding of progress. The United States became a world industrial power while the old Confederacy smoldered in ruins. The rise in industrialism marked the final death knell of the agrarian economy of the Old South while, paradoxically, society enacted Jim Crow laws and customs to protect a southern way of life that no longer existed. From the perspective of blacks, emancipation, reconstruction, and industrialism together marked yet another New World in which they needed to stake a claim.

John D. Rockefeller Sr. and John Hope are two men who played a significant role in this Industrial Era and in the affiliation of the Atlanta institutions, and whose distinctive personal histories shared commonalities that positioned them to positively address and correct some educational needs of the black masses. Despite the nearly 30-year difference in age, a difference in race and in geographic regions of birth, Rockefeller Sr. and Hope shared remarkably similar upbringings, strong religious convictions, and life experiences. When their paths ultimately crossed, they were together, along with others, able to redress some of the educational inequities borne of slavery and Reconstruction. Their efforts are evident in the continuing existence and success of the Atlanta institutions, Clark Atlanta University, Morehouse College, and Spelman College, in the twenty-first century.

John D. Rockefeller Sr.

John D. Rockefeller Sr. conducted every aspect of his life methodically in a systematic, business-oriented approach that resulted in eliminating waste and using resources most efficiently. Perhaps one can best understand such an approach given his background, upbringing, and religious convictions that were his foundation and became the framework from which he developed his philanthropic giving.

In 1839, John D. Rockefeller Sr. was born in "a barefoot bedroom measuring eight by ten feet" in Richford, New York, to William Avery and Eliza Davison Rockefeller.[3] Ron Chernow, one of Rockefeller's biographers, describes Rockefeller's father (William) as a philanderer and a "flimflam man" who had several jobs and frequently traveled to several towns. Despite this, Rockefeller showed appreciation for what he had learned from his father, when he wrote, "I owe a great debt in that he himself trained me to practical ways." Because his father was engaged in different enterprises, Rockefeller learned the principles and methods of business from him, but developed his entrepreneurial skills and business tactics early in life on his own. As a young boy, he bought candy and sold it to his siblings for a profit; he stole turkey eggs, raised the chicks, and sold them for a profit. By age 16, he had an apprenticeship as a bookkeeper.

In 1855, Rockefeller and his family moved to Cleveland, Ohio, and rather than attend a regular college, he decided to attend E. G. Folsom Commercial College where he learned "some of the fundamental principles of commercial transactions."[4] Within eight years and during the Civil War, he bought into a refinery venture. Two years later, when the war had ended, he went into business for himself as a partner in a Cleveland oil refinery. Within ten years, he was a dominant figure in the oil industry.[5]

Rockefeller might owe some of his thrifty and industrious nature to his father, but the deeply rooted religious beliefs that heavily influenced his decisions, he owed to his mother. Rockefeller's mother, Eliza Davison, a devout Baptist, was a "good deal of a disciplinarian"[6] who grounded him in his religious beliefs, specifically the Baptist doctrines, and firmly established his philanthropic impulse. As children, she encouraged him and his siblings to put pennies into the collection plate at church. This simple act led him to believe that "God wanted his flock to earn money and then donate money in a never-ending process"—the more you make, the more you give.[7] Later on, he expounded on this belief when he discussed philanthropy and said, "The giver of money, if his contribution is to be valuable, must help attack and improve underlying conditions."[8]

During Rockefeller's upbringing, much as it is today, "religion in its American form contributed to philanthropic habits and institutions through direct gifts to church organizations and, indirectly, by motivating contributions to secular causes and institutions."[9] This was certainly true for Rockefeller in that his strong religious convictions and his philanthropic philosophy intertwined and were evident when he said, "If we can help people to help themselves, then there is a permanent blessing conferred."[10] For him, the best philanthropy was:

> The investment of effort or time, carefully considered with relations to the power of employing people at a remunerative wage, to expand and develop the resources at hand, and to give opportunity for progress and healthful labour where it did not exist before.[11]

Being white and living in a free state afforded Rockefeller the luxury of using the industrial skills he honed to create business opportunities that led him to amass great wealth. This in turn led him to contemplate on how he would give some of it away.

Despite humble beginnings, by the time he was in his early 30s, he had built an oil empire. However, the majority of blacks living in the South did not have such luxuries of using their skills to create business opportunities for themselves.

Life in the South

After the Civil War, there were "five million freed blacks in the United States," 92 percent of all blacks resided in the South until 1900," and the majority of them were illiterate.[12] In Georgia, for example, slaves' taxable value was "$302,694,855 in 1860, far more than the value of all taxable land"; however, when the Civil War ended, the structure collapsed. Banks were "ruined, capital destroyed, property worthless," and the state had a debt "of eighteen million dollars." Amendments to the State Constitution of Georgia in 1865 included provisions for public education of white citizens, but no such provisions for blacks. The idea of educating blacks, during this time, was no different than "attempting to educate a mule,"[13] and in 1870, 80 percent of blacks over the age of ten were illiterate.[14]

Whites could no longer confine blacks in physical bondage and use them as forced labor; therefore, they created Jim Crow laws that maintained the status quo.[15] In *Philanthropy and Jim Crow in American Social Science*, John H. Stanfield noted, Jim Crow was "an ideology and practice in social, economic, legal, and political spheres...a reality construction created and maintained through a mixture of taken for-granted and conscious biological and cultural ideas about race and the normative separation of the races in a rigid caste order."[16]

In essence, this normative separation of the races was the system of segregation, "a social system represented by group relations of dominance and submission, unequal distributions of wealth and means of production, prohibitions on social advancement, and the designation of inferior biological and social status through legal means and power of the community."[17] Whites had dominated southern society for a long time. However, because they were unable "to cope with the ill effects of a rapidly industrialized economy coupled with popular rebellion in society," conservative whites found another contrivance to secure captivity and to maintain the subordination of blacks by a caste system that "resorted to racist appeals."[18]

Economic, social, and political frustration generated aggressiveness among the masses of whites, and blacks became the scapegoat for their aggressions. For C. Vann Woodward, preeminent historian of the American South and race relation, "The doctrine of racism reached a crest of acceptability and popularity among respectable scholarly and intellectual circles," and confirmed the maltreatment of blacks, crystallizing the idea that the "'Anglo-Saxon' or 'Caucasian' was the superior of them all."[19]

As this idea of superiority manifested itself, blacks developed a mental disposition from segregation that W. E. B. Du Bois later termed "double consciousness," of seeing themselves through the eyes of others.[20] Other scholars, such as Frantz Fanon, agreed. In his clinical study, *Black Skin, White Masks*, Fanon, a Martinique-born French-Algerian psychiatrist, used psychoanalysis and psychoanalytic theory to explain blacks' feelings of dependency and inadequacy in a white world. Though his study examined Algerians, his conclusion was nevertheless applicable to southern blacks' plight during segregation:

> The Negro is comparison; that is, he is constantly preoccupied with self-evaluation and with the ego-ideal. Whenever he comes into contact with someone else, the question of value, of merit, arises.[21]

Segregation was a systematic negation of black people and an intense determination of whites to deny blacks all attributes of humanity, which in turn caused blacks to experience self-doubt and feelings of anomie. Directly linked to this negation was mental pathology, a psychosis that was the direct product of oppression. David P. Ausubel, American psychologist, found that in most cases this psychosis started at a young age and carried through to adulthood.[22]

Segregation was also a negation of blacks in their own communities. Blacks' skin tone or hue often determined economic and social opportunities. Gunnar Myrdal made this fact most prevalent through his study of race relations, *An American Dilemma: The Negro Problem and Modern Democracy*, sponsored by the Carnegie Foundation in 1944. He noted, "In slave society there came to be a social stratification within a slave community, as house servants and skilled mechanics acquired a level of living and enjoyed a social prestige different from that of the field slaves. The blood ties of the former group of slaves with the white upper class widened the difference."[23] The cachet that blacks with a lighter or fairer hue had more privileges than blacks with a darker hue extended beyond slavery, and in some cases, caused dissension between the two groups. Such a cachet still exists today.

Though segregation was the norm of the time, there was no basis in law for it; social customs largely and simply enforced it by statute, custom, and the institutional segregation of schools, churches, and private organizations, even the railroad. Although blacks were free to travel from place to place, the railroads adopted the custom of refusing blacks' admission to the first class or ladies' cars. On smaller cars, for example, the railroads "relegated blacks to old cars, freight cars, or open platforms."[24] To this end, segregation was "far from being the result of instinctual or a natural tendency, clearly was the product of an economic system of special oppression, with a complex legal, social, and ideological system" justifying oppression.[25]

Life in the South was a world framed by "white" and "colored" emblems that not only meant to separate, but also to denote superior and inferior status. The expenditure in funds and efforts to maintain segregation was immense. Separate water fountains, rest rooms, eating facilities, schools, and even days to shop were among the more obvious expenses undertaken for the sake of segregation. However, signs were not the only physical reminders of separation and second-class citizen denotations. Unpaved streets and the absence of sewers, running water, and electricity spoke volumes about "place" in the South. Atlanta, Georgia, was no different and enforced the caste system in "city parks, on streetcars, and in shopping districts," just as other cities in the South had done.[26]

This conundrum was never more prominent than during the enforcement of segregated practices that ensued. By the end of

Reconstruction, segregation had crystallized into a comprehensive pattern that remained unaltered until the middle of the twentieth century.[27] As such, Jim Crow laws and segregation marked this second New World for blacks that presented three obstacles: poverty, ignorance, and opportunity. However, not all blacks in the South shared these experiences; some, like John Hope, lived an entirely different set of life experiences.[28] In time, he would rise up and become an agent for resistance that helped blacks stake their place in this New World.

John Hope's Background and Foundation

John Hope was the sixth of eight children, born in 1868 to James Hope and Mary Francis (Fanny) Taylor in Augusta, Georgia. Only three years after the Civil War had ended, Hope's birth placed him in a society that deeply regarded race as a primary source of identification and social status.

Hope's father, James Hope, was white and was born in Langholm, Scotland in 1805. His grandfather, Matthew, was a miller in Dumphreyshire, Scotland. Later in life, John Hope recalled how his grandfather had "lost everything and migrated [with his father, James] in 1817" to the United States.[29] James's fondest memories when he arrived in New York was not just the voyage and excitement of a new country, according to John Hope's biographer Ridgely Torrence, it was:

> [The] people who belonged to that remarkable race, the Negro...there were dark-skinned boys, agile, and strong... brown girls moving like queens as they balanced bundles or brimming pitchers on their erect heads...small dark children at their dancing play.[30]

From his first day in America, James recognized black people were "far more than a race merely equal to other human beings. To him they were figures of romance."[31] As fate would have it, this sentiment would manifest itself years later when he married and became John Hope's father.

Although James Hope, along with his brothers, Thomas and Anthony, had established a successful grocery business in New York by 1831, in this same year, he moved to Augusta, Georgia.[32] Within ten years, James became a successful businessman and was listed in Augusta's city directory as "a director of the Augusta Insurance and Banking Company." He later "served as secretary and general manager of the Augusta Manufacturing Company," and in 1847 "helped organize a steamboat company and other enterprises."[33]

John Hope's mother, Mary Francis "Fanny" Taylor, was a quadroon—having one-fourth black blood,[34] born in 1839 (the same year as Rockefeller) and raised in Augusta, Georgia. Fanny's mother, Althea, was a free black and had her own home where she raised and educated the neighborhood children and her own.[35] However, when Fanny became older, her mother knew she had to continue her education elsewhere. Since Georgia was segregated and had no formal schools for blacks, Althea sent Fanny to a school in Charleston, South Carolina, for quadroons or mulattos, because "it was famous among Negroes as a place where they could get an education, especially if their fathers were white." When Fanny completed her education, she returned to Augusta.[36]

Despite Fanny's education, the segregated society in Augusta limited work opportunities for free blacks outside of those in a domestic capacity; as such, Fanny found work in George Newton's home. Newton was a physician who played a major role in establishing the Medical College of Georgia in the early 1830s. Later, he became chair of physiology, professor of anatomy, and dean of the faculty. Over time, Newton and Fanny developed more than an employee-employer relationship, eventually living as husband and wife. The city's telephone directory supported this spousal relationship and listed Fanny as "Mrs. Dr. George M. Newton at their home address after Newton died."[37] From all indications, Fanny was Newton's only wife.

James Hope was Newton's business associate, had dined often with him, and had grown fond of Fanny. After Newton's death, James was responsible for executing Newton's will. As circumstances would have it, James had to sell Newton's home; however, he bought Fanny another home and made sure of her and her two children's security. As time progressed, James and Fanny's friendship developed into a loving relationship. Despite James Hope being "old enough to be her father," the two married and remained together until James died at the age of 71.

Despite the laws in Georgia prohibiting and refusing recognition of a miscegenous union, John Hope indicated that his parents' union was not exceptional and remembered other white men and black women who lived openly as husband and wife in Augusta.[38] Reminiscing about his parents and how they lived as husband and wife, and even dined with other white businessmen at their family table, Hope wrote:

> I speak reverently of my mother and father as wife and husband, although the laws of Georgia would not recognize such a thing. They lived openly all the days and nights. My father's children walked with him hand-in-hand through the business street of Augusta. They went shopping with him.
>
> As for my home, although white women did not visit, my father had as visitors in a social way in our home some of the foremost business and professional men of Augusta. And when they came they sat with my father's children at the table, my father at one end of the table and my mother at the other.[39]

Hope grew up in a loving Christian home where he learned the values of honesty and responsibility. On Sundays, he accompanied his Aunt Nannie and Uncle James Butts, his mother's sister and brother, to church and Sunday school at Springfield Church, which was the oldest black Baptist church in America. His Aunt Nannie, a "strict and resolute Baptist" and the "most ardently religious member of the family," spiritually guided him and was the one responsible for strengthening Hope's religious beliefs.[40]

Although Hope's family lived a privileged life in many ways, after his father's death in 1876, his family life was "fraught with hardship and struggle."[41] James had left his estate in "the hands of men whom he greatly trusted." Although he expected his family to be taken care of, these individuals "turned out to be shiftless and financially dishonest." However, as John Hope recalled "there was enough even then to keep the household together and up to my mother's death she was still receiving a slight income."[42] Despite the income Fanny received, financial hardship terminated the education of Hope's oldest brother and a sister at Atlanta University, and postponed another sister's completion of studies.[43]

During his formative years, Hope learned that his family status no longer protected him from the harsh reality of racism in the South, and he now had to deal with his blackness in a white world. From age ten to twelve, Hope found employment and worked with two lawyers, cleaning the floors and running errands after school. Then, at age 13 and upon completion of the eighth grade, Hope worked at Lexius Henson's "first-class" restaurant that catered to white patrons, and continued there until he was 18. Working in Lexius Henson's restaurant provided the opportunity for him to interact with several affluent patrons and to gain experience and knowledge in the areas of finance and management. Initially hired as a wine steward and waiter, he soon became a culinary connoisseur of sorts, by learning to pair particular kinds of foods and champagne. Eventually, he was responsible for the restaurant's books and accounts. Within two years, Henson recognized his talents as "a marketer and selector of food" and promoted him into a position of helping him with the details of management.[44]

By 1886, while Rockefeller and other industrial philanthropists had begun formulating and establishing their philanthropic endeavors, Hope, at age 18, attended Worcester Academy in Massachusetts where he rose to become the class historian.[45] Throughout his life, Hope tended to attract "liberal white men with power," which proved to his advantage later in his personal and professional life. While attending Worcester, Hope met a white philanthropist with whom he began a relationship that continued throughout his life. Once again, Hope had financial difficulties and struggled to remain in school. Edward Burr Soloman, a white businessman and philanthropist from Ohio, learned of Hope's circumstances and offered him money to continue his education on the condition that he become a minister. Though he had once contemplated becoming a minister, he instead chose education as his pulpit and refused the money. Since Soloman "admired young John's honesty and determination," he gave him "the money without stipulation, and helped Hope periodically throughout his years at the Academy."[46] This act of generosity made it possible for Hope to complete his education at the academy.

After graduation from Worcester in 1890, Hope attended Brown University and majored in philosophy.[47] Founded in 1764, Brown was the third college in New England, the seventh in America, and the first Ivy League school to accept students from all religious affiliations.[48] At Brown, Hope drew from the curriculum "to support his belief in the efficacy and superiority of a liberal arts education."[49] His journalism skills were highly recognized and, after the establishment of the *Brown Daily Herald* in 1891, he became a member of the editorial board. He was also a correspondent for the *New York Tribune* and worked for the *Providence Journal* and the *Chicago Tribune*. In his junior year, he struggled to pay his debts and went to Chicago to work for a few months. While there, he met Lugenia D. Burns, who a few years later, became his wife. In this same year, John D. Rockefeller Jr. had begun matriculating at Brown. It was Hope's senior year that teaching won its final victory over the ministry as an immediate career choice. In 1894, Hope graduated from Brown with Phi Beta Kappa honors, received a bachelor of arts degree, and his classmates chose him to deliver the class oration.[50]

After graduating from Brown and rejecting an offer from Booker T. Washington to teach at a higher salary at Tuskegee Institute,[51] Hope began his career teaching natural sciences at Roger Williams University. Roger Williams was "a struggling liberal arts institution"[52] for both black men and women, located in Nashville, Tennessee, across from Vanderbilt University and was one of four colleges founded for newly freed slaves. It began in 1864 as Bible classes in the home of Daniel W. Phillips, a white minister from Massachusetts; yet in time, it became one of the largest Baptist colleges in the area for educating blacks.[53] Reflecting back on his career, Hope remarked:

> The day after my graduation from Brown University I was handed my appointment by Professor Charles Phillips, the son

of old Dr. Phillips who founded Roger Williams University. This appointment was from the American Baptist Home Mission Society to teach at $500 a year at Roger Williams University. Now I should say in a very definite way that this was the beginning of the 40 years that I have just finished.[54]

Roger Williams was similar to the other institutions Hope had attended and supported by the American Baptist Home Mission Society (ABHMS). It had a "rigid New England Victorian code of conduct"; all of the faculty and administrators were "staunch Baptists who were expected to concern themselves as much with the students' souls as with their ability to read, write, and do arithmetic."[55] Hope also experienced his first attempt at fundraising while teaching at Roger Williams. As a science teacher, who was aware the school needed a new lab, he successfully raised money to build the facility.[56]

Though Hope was "shy and introspective," he was very charismatic and developed "a considerable power in public speaking"; in that, he "could interest, move, [and] under certain circumstances enchant, an audience." He was "no spellbinder, but the intimate quality of his speeches always made a deep impression on his listeners" to the point that his speaking ability proved to be one of his strongest assets that he used as a tool for advocating equality, equity, and a liberal arts education for blacks.[57]

In his second year of teaching, Hope stopped through Atlanta from one of his trips and heard Booker T. Washington's 1895 Atlanta Compromise speech at the Atlanta Cotton States and International Exposition. Hope opposed segregation, disfranchisement, and Washington's educational philosophy of industrial education, and believed that blacks should not waver on the issue of social equality. After Washington's speech and upon his return home, Hope addressed a black debate society in Nashville, and at the end of the speech, he said:

> If we are not striving for equality, in heaven's name for what are we living? I regard it as cowardly and dishonest for any of our colored men to tell white people or colored people that we are not struggling for equality. If money, education, and honesty will not bring to me as much privilege, as much equality as they

bring to any American citizen, then they are to me a curse, and not a blessing... Yes, my friends, I want equality. Nothing less. I want all that my God-given powers will enable me to get, then why not equality? Now, catch your breath, for I am going to use an adjective: I am going to say we demand social equality. In this republic we shall be less than freedmen, if we have a whit less than that which thrift, education, and honor afford other freedmen. If equality, political, economic, and social, is the boon of other men in this great country of ours, then equality, political, economic, and social, is what we demand.

Let your discontent break mountain high against the wall of prejudice, and swamp it to the very foundation. Then we shall not have to plead for justice nor on bended knee crave mercy; for we shall be men. Then and not until then will liberty in its highest sense be the boast of our Republic.[58]

In the same year, he made another speech, "The Need of a Liberal Education for Us," undoubtedly a rebuttal to Washington's speech in Atlanta. On a public platform in Nashville, Hope argued, "the Negro must enter the higher fields of learning. He must be prepared for advanced and original investigation." When Hope spoke, it was with reasonableness, never wavering in his conviction for equity in education for blacks, and presented this message at different venues throughout his career.[59]

Although he was successful teaching at Roger Williams, Hope always wanted to return to Georgia; however, there were no teaching positions available after he graduated from Brown. Hope was in constant contact with William Holmes, the only black faculty member at Atlanta Baptist Seminary in Atlanta, Georgia. In his fourth year of teaching at Roger Williams, he received word that a position was available at the seminary. In 1898, at age 30, Hope joined the faculty at Atlanta Baptist Seminary because "its history was closely intertwined with his own town of Augusta and his boyhood."[60]

When Hope arrived at Atlanta Baptist, he was the second black faculty member in the institution's 31-year history. His arrival transformed the institution and elevated it to a higher academic status. He brought culture with him and an educational background of "the highest and noblest qualities of a gentleman and scholar." He not only taught the classics (e.g., Greek and Latin) and science, but also received extra money as the institution's bookkeeper. Just as it was in his youth, working at Lexius Henson's restaurant, being the bookkeeper for Atlanta Baptist enabled him to gain knowledge about the inner workings of the ABHMS.[61]

At the time of Hope's teaching appointment, George Sale was the president at Atlanta Baptist. Sale, a Baptist minister of long standing with the ABHMS, was also an "experienced fund-raiser and an able administrator"; and from Sale, he gained immeasurable fund-raising and administrative skills.[62]

Students were "startled by [Hope's] white features and aristocratic bearing." However, his "stern disposition and formal manner" was fitting for the seminary because it had begun to place more emphasis on its "academic program [rather] than its theology department." He was very demanding of students; yet over time, the relationship between them grew into kinship and respect, inside and outside class. So much so, in 1899, Hope introduced football, and by 1900, he had organized "the school's first competitive team." In the years 1908, 1912, and 1916, the team was the "unquestioned champion of the colored South."[63] This relationship with students and his ability to bring together a winning team would prove most important in developing his career, in negotiating with philanthropists that led to the affiliation of the Atlanta institutions, and in helping sustain higher education for blacks.

Higher Education for Blacks

When one thinks about the education of blacks, particularly in the South, the inequity that existed before, during, and after the Civil War comes quickly to mind.[64] Blacks in the South "were kept in a state of deadening illiteracy by laws which deprived them of formal education," and black colleges and universities compensated for the lack of public educational opportunities and provided for elementary through high school levels of learning. One of the most obvious outgrowths of the segregated system of the United States was the black colleges and universities. The history of these institutions was, and still is, a unique chapter in the development of this country's educational system.[65]

Throughout the nineteenth century and into the early twentieth century, white-run society continuously administered public education using race and class biases to prohibit the educational achievement of blacks, and to confine them to a lower-class status.[66] How blacks would survive after slavery became a critical issue; thus was born one of the quandaries of the twentieth century—the "negro problem"—educating the massive number of blacks and helping them to reach self-actualization.[67] No one expressed this state of urgency regarding blacks' circumstance better than Du Bois, when he wrote:

> We must realize that this is an age of tremendous activity; that today no race which is not prepared to put forth the full might of its carefully developed powers can hope to maintain itself as a world power...unless we develop our full capabilities, we cannot survive.[68]

Nevertheless, that was the problem. Blacks were unable to develop to their full capabilities because of the obstacles in front of them; and according to scholars, such as Du Bois, there also existed an "economic quandary" for people who were "in the transition from slavery to freedom."[69]

A report on the 1895 Atlanta Cotton States Exposition stated the exposition "showed that slowly but surely the negro [was] making progress not only in the moral, intellectual, and material condition, but in the esteem of Southern white people." Despite the report indicating the "negro problem" was considered "the darkest cloud hanging over the nation," it also suggested "if the negro problem...[was] solved in a way so just and beneficent, there [was] nothing left for the South to fear."[70] Regardless of whether the solution involved uplifting a race or providing economic stability, education was the vehicle to achieve it. An integral part of blacks' struggle for equality was to gain access to higher education; however, the question was, what form of education would society provide for individuals deemed as second-class citizens.[71]

The need for higher education in the South became more critical than ever after Reconstruction, and some entity had to provide the avenue from which the leaders of the race would come. In time, the plight of blacks became visible to the federal government, denominational missionary societies, and philanthropic societies, and they realized that the only way to uplift blacks was through education.[72] By 1865, at the end of the Civil War and during the Reconstruction Era, Congress created the Freedmen's Bureau to assist blacks' transition into freedom by "furnishing supplies and medical services, establishing schools, supervising contracts between freedmen and their employers, and managing confiscated or abandoned lands by leasing and selling some of them" to free blacks. Headed by Union army general Oliver Otis Howard, the bureau helped blacks secure "political rights, as well as a social structure and economic independence." Six years later, once federal enforcement subsided, "Southern state and local government adopted a policy of segregation and devalued [black] education that supported limited and rudimentary training for black children."[73]

Three separate philanthropic groups emerged and were responsible for the promotion of higher education for blacks and the training of black leadership. Northern white benevolent societies and denominational bodies (missionary philanthropy) and black religious organizations (black philanthropy) were the first two groups to establish higher education for blacks in the South during a "critical time when public secondary schools for southern blacks were almost nonexistent."[74] Although more emphasis herein is on the missionary societies, it is noteworthy to mention that blacks were instrumental in educating their own. By 1870, blacks had spent an estimated $1 million on the education of their children. Unfortunately, economic conditions forced many communities to ask for assistance from missionary organizations and the government; in the end, this resulted in blacks losing control over their circumstances.[75]

Using curricula focused on classical or liberal education, missionary societies believed that this type of educational focus would not only train blacks for leadership positions within their communities, but would also be the best avenue by which blacks would attain racial uplift.[76] Correspondence between Thomas Morgan and Wallace Buttrick, both of whom were members of the American Baptist Home Mission Society (ABHMS), highlighted this sentiment:

> The one all-important function of these institutions, the work to which they must give their strength for many years to come is that of raising up a competent leadership; men and women who can think; who are independent and self-reliant; who can persuade and lead their people; they should be men and women who are themselves models and examples of what their people can and ought to be, especially should they be persons capable of teaching and preaching. No modification of their curriculum or their spirit and purpose should be allowed to interfere in any manner with this as the supreme purpose of their existence.[77]

Since the Southern states did not take responsibility for educating former slaves, most of the black institutions were initially primary and secondary schools that gradually developed into normal schools to train teachers, then evolved later into colleges and universities.[78] Thomas Morgan, corresponding secretary for the ABHMS, provided a glimpse of the conditions in which some of these institutions were established and operated, when he explained:

> [Black colleges and universities] began in the most primitive fashion. Lumpkins [sic] jail in Richmond; a Negro cabin in Raleigh; the damp, dark basement of the Friendship Church in Atlanta, were the best accommodations that could be had for the work in those cities, and are fairly representative of the whole. Few books and less furniture, no blackboards or charts, or apparatus of any kind. Many of the pupils were elderly people, unable to read or write, and the instruction given to them was necessarily of the most elementary kind.[79]

He further explained:

> These [missionary society schools] and similar Christian institutions founded by Northern beneficence afford the only opportunities that the great mass of the Negroes have for securing higher

education. All the white Southern Colleges are shut against them. Very few of them can or will come North to pursue their higher studies.[80]

Atlanta University, Morehouse College, and Spelman College in Atlanta, Georgia, that affiliated and became the Atlanta University System provide examples of missionary societies creating educational opportunities for blacks in the South. With the help of resources from the American Missionary Association (AMA) and the Freedmen's Bureau, former slaves and northern Congregationalist missionaries established Atlanta University while Atlanta was still in ruins after the Civil War.[81] In 1865, the Congregational church "accepted the AMA as its agent for work among the freedmen." Although Atlanta University eventually became independent, its initial leadership was "dominated by Congregationalists."[82]

The assemblage of Atlanta University underwent several changes before situating into what later became Atlanta University. James Tate and Grandison Daniels, former slaves, created the first school in Atlanta for blacks in an "old church building." However, because they possessed "more zeal and desire than competence, these pioneer teachers readily relinquished the responsibility to better trained teachers from the North." Commissioned by the AMA, Frederick Ayer, a minister and missionary with the AMA, came to Atlanta to assist the thousands of blacks who had "flocked to the city from the rural areas in search of the Promised land." In addition to the school first established by Tate and Daniels in one location (Jenkins Street), the AMA acquired a discarded old boxcar and gave it to Ayer to use as a school in another location (Walton Springs). Ayer, along with Frank Quarles, minister of Friendship Baptist Church, placed the boxcar on the church's land. In 1866, these two schools combined to form the Storrs School, with Edmund Asa Ware as its first principal.[83]

Edmund Asa Ware was born in 1837 on a farm in North Wrentham, Massachusetts. By age 15, his family moved to Norwich, Connecticut, where he attended Norwick Free Academy and graduated as the class valedictorian. By age 21, Ware wanted to attend Yale University, but his father had limited resources. Thus, he had to rely on receiving financial assistance from individuals "who had observed his development and agreed to lend him money." One of these individuals was John D. Rockefeller Sr.

Upon graduating from Yale in 1863, Ware taught two years at Norwick Academy and, in 1865, "he began his career in the South as an agent of the AMA." His first position was overseeing the white public schools in Nashville, Tennessee, where he met General Clinton B. Fisk, assistant commissioner of the Freedmen's Bureau for Tennessee. At this time, Fisk and the AMA agents were in the process of establishing Fisk University. While showing interest in the process, Ware also became interested in "providing an adequate education for the former slaves and free Negroes." In 1866, Ware moved to Atlanta as the superintendent of schools for the AMA and worked with Ayer to convert the "old Confederate Commissary into a schoolhouse." Later, the commissary was "transformed into a thirty-two by eight foot chapel" and with additional funds raised by the Congregational Church, they erected a "two-story addition of four rooms, each thirty-two by twenty feet in front of the chapel."[84] With this new addition, they created the Storrs School.

Also in 1866, Ayer and the AMA created the Washburn Memorial Orphan Asylum "to take care of the numerous orphans of freedmen who were left homeless following discontinuance of the contraband camps supported by the Freedman's Bureau and the development of a normal school.[85] When the Storrs School and Washburn Asylum became overcrowded, Ayer and the AMA created a third school, Ayer School, at a different location from the other schools.

The faculty of these schools consisted of white missionaries who were graduates of Yale, Oberlin, Mount Holyoke, and other northern colleges. With students in three different locations, the teachers were taken to and from these locations by a "veteran [Civil War] horse and an old army ambulance."[86] Despite these instructors being taunted and threatened for aiding blacks with their educational endeavors, they nevertheless maintained their persistence and continued with their task.[87]

Although the three schools were efficient in aiding blacks, the AMA had planned something entirely different. Accordingly, Clarence Bacote, Atlanta University's institutional historian, pointed out:

> The AMA had planned to establish in Georgia a central institution of higher education, beginning with normal and academic departments and growing, as there should be a demand, into a college and finally a university.[88]

Because Ware felt blacks had demonstrated their ability in the schools Ayer established, and he knew Atlanta was centrally located for a university, he convinced the AMA to merge its vision and all of the schools with his own. In 1867, the AMA secured land and money to combine and move all of the schools to one location. With the various schools united, Ware, along with members of the AMA, businessmen, and black church ministers "presented a petition to Fulton County Superior court for a charter to incorporate the institution as Atlanta University." The University's motto that grounded it was "I Will Find A Way Or Make One," and Edmund Asa Ware was its first president.[89] This was also "the first step in Georgia to meet the demand for education at a higher level than the normal school designed to prepare leaders for the black race."[90]

Atlanta University's purpose was the establishment and management of an institution for the "liberal and Christian education of youth." The permanent faculty reflected those of the initial schools; instructors were from Yale, Oberlin, Dartmouth, and other northern institutions.[91]

The charter for the institution did not refer to race or creed. Most uniquely, Atlanta University was "the people's university embracing all sexes, all creeds, and all colors" and was the "first educational institution of higher learning in Georgia to open its doors to all people."[92] This was a novel step in the South because there was no other institution created with such liberal views to educate blacks and whites together. John Mercer Langston, an inspector of schools for the Freedmen's Bureau, later acknowledged the institution's significance in an address at Atlanta University:

> It is necessary that white and black be educated together to accustom themselves in childhood to their new relations, to destroy the spirit of servility and fear in the one and arrogance in the other.[93]

Ware was an individual whose goal was to uplift blacks through education. He was convinced that "Negroes had demonstrated their capacity to acquire knowledge," and believed that blacks "could develop to the fullest their potential as citizens only through exposure to the best education." The best education to which Ware referred was a higher education that had the purpose: "to train talented Negro youth, [to] educate teachers, and [to] disseminate civilization among the untaught masses." The latter affirmed the view most of society had of blacks—uncivilized beings who needed paternalistic guidance. However, Ware was more progressive than his counterparts who believed that blacks were incapable of pursuing a liberal education and advancing beyond the elementary level.[94] Despite the importance of such an institution in Atlanta, its liberal stance on race was inevitably a double-edged sword that would haunt Atlanta University at critical times when it needed financial support.

After Atlanta University's creation, profound changes took place in denominational societies. The sectarian competition "began to divide the missionaries into separate camps";[95] no longer was there simply a need for missionary societies "to bring light to the souls of blacks." Now, there was a drive to increase denominational ranks with black members. A missionary society's goal was not only to have "control of churches that were to be," but also to develop "schools which they hoped would become the favorite resorts of ministers and scholars, and the rallying points of religious culture."[96] Subsequent institutions in Atlanta provide examples of the denominational competitiveness philanthropists would later equate to waste and unnecessary duplication of resources.

Historical credit has been given to William J. White, former Baptist minister and cabinetmaker of Augusta, for founding Augusta Institute (later, Morehouse College).[97] But, Richard

Coulter, a former slave and valet, and Edmund Turney, organizer of the National Theological Institute for educating free blacks in Washington, DC, were also instrumental in creating Augusta Institute. In the same year Congregationalist created Atlanta University, the Baptist made decisions that would be the turning point specifically for black male's education. In 1867, White, Coulter, and Turney attended the Baptists' annual meeting where they decided to merge the National Theological Institute with the ABHMS (American Baptist Home Mission Society) and transferred the work of training black ministers to ABHMS. When Coulter returned to his home in Augusta, he carried a letter from Turney granting him the authority to organize a school in Augusta that would be a branch of the institute.[98] However, Coulter had no experience in this area, yet knew someone who had, William J. White. White was a white southerner who had operated clandestine schools for blacks in Augusta, was a member of Springfield Baptist Church, and later the minister of Augusta's black Harmony Baptist Church. Because White was "intensely interested in the intellectual and moral welfare" of blacks, he established the Augusta Institute in Augusta, Georgia, in 1867 and initially housed the 40, mostly adult, students at Springfield Baptist Church.[99]

It took four years for the institute to secure a permanent president and many more years to secure a permanent location. In 1871, Joseph T. Robert, a white southern minister and Brown University graduate, was Augusta Institute's first president. During the era of slavery, Robert realized that the South was no place to raise his children. He considered slavery to be immoral and manumitted his slaves, moved to Ohio, and only returned back to the South to become Augusta Institute's president. Despite the white citizens in Augusta opposing blacks' education and turning against anybody who associated with such causes, Robert nevertheless believed, "that right and morality were on his side, and that ultimately they would triumph." Once Robert became the president, no females were admitted or males under the age of 16, making it an all-male institute.[100]

By 1879, Robert and others realized that Augusta was no longer conducive to effectively meet the growing educational needs of the state, and that the state's capital, Atlanta, was a better location. With the help of Frank Quarles, the "most influential colored minister in the state," minister of Friendship Baptist Church in Atlanta and president of the Missionary Baptist Convention of Georgia, Augusta Institute moved to Atlanta. With the motto of "And There Was Light," the institute incorporated as Atlanta Baptist Seminary and Friendship Baptist Church temporarily housed it in the church's basement (Figure 1.1).[101]

Over the next five years, numerous changes occurred and it was "the dark period in the institution's history." Shortly after incorporating, the seminary moved to another location, "a four-acre lot, located at the junction of Elliott and West Hunter Streets...one block west of the Atlanta Terminal Railroad Station." However, this area was "one of the noisiest and smokiest in the city"; and there were no "provisions for dormitories." Next, the seminary faced financial difficulties; they needed money not only to aid students, but also to purchase furniture

Figure 1.1 Photograph of the basement of Friendship Baptist Church, ca. 1881.

Source: Spelman College Archive Center, Atlanta, Georgia. Courtesy of Spelman College.

for "the recitation rooms." Last, because of instability, the seminary could not maintain a regular faculty.[102]

Atlanta University, though coeducational, had limited facilities and could only handle a certain number of students. Since Robert nullified the coeducation policy once he became president, Atlanta Baptist was now solely male. Despite those in charge of Atlanta Baptist developing an interest in founding a similar school for females, there was an educational void for thousands of freed, black females. While the male-dominated ABHMS and Reverend Quarles contemplated a school for females, two New England women were already en route to implement their own plans to educate black women and girls in Atlanta.[103]

Sophia Packard and Harriet Giles had pious New England backgrounds; both were teachers and had worked at several schools before coming to Atlanta; and both were very active in the Baptist church and the Women's American Baptist Home Mission Society (WABHMS). Neither of the two was married.[104] One of Packard's duties with the WABHMS was to answer the numerous appeals for missionary work among black females, which illustrated that the situation was urgent.

> Among the 5,000,000 freed people, there were 3,000,000 women; one third of the latter were girls under 21. There were thousands of freed slaves among the Indians, a fact not generally known. The need for women missionaries was urgent. Many of the former slaves had no homes, work or wages. None had schools for their children, making this a tremendous task.[105]

Armed with all the information she needed, the WABHMS commissioned a trip for Packard "to study the living conditions among the freedmen of the South." During this trip South, Giles joined her and the two visited several institutions for blacks, such as Fisk University, New Orleans University, and Straight University. Despite leaving the South impressed by the advances made by these institutions, as a whole, they were appalled by the lack of educational opportunities available for black females. Upon their return to Boston, the two were "determined to affect change" and wanted a school of their own.[106]

Struggling with limited to no funds in the treasury, the WABHMS objected to the idea of a school and viewed such an undertaking as an overwhelming responsibility to support a school specifically for "Negro women." Giles and Packard were nevertheless determined and moved forward. The two had observed there was no Baptist school in Georgia for women and girls, and that Georgia had the largest black population, most of whom were Baptist. Deciding to raise the money themselves, Giles and Packard went back to Atlanta and, as Robert had done with Augusta Institute, contacted Reverend Frank Quarles of Friendship Baptist Church for assistance.[107]

In 1881, with $100 provided by "the congregation of the First Baptist Church of Medford, Massachusetts," Packard and Giles began the Atlanta Baptist Female Seminary with 11 female students of all ages and levels of attainment. The Female Seminary was temporarily housed, as Atlanta Baptist had been, in the basement of the Friendship Baptist Church in Atlanta. With the motto, "Our Whole School for Christ," the initial curriculum heavily reflected "the tenets and educational philosophies of its founders" and was structured "to purify and educate newly-freed black women for missionary work, household industry, and racial uplift." Within three months, the enrollment increased to 80; and by the end of the term, it had increased to more than 100.[108]

By the 1880s, Henry L. Morehouse was the corresponding secretary for the ABHMS and John D. Rockefeller Sr. was its chief benefactor. During this year, Rockefeller had turned his attention to charities, benevolence, and higher education. The latter started with the establishment of the University of Chicago. There were two reasons the Baptist created the University of Chicago. First, "the Baptists lacked a first-rate Midwestern college, forcing their children to study at eastern schools."[109] Second, the Methodists had several colleges in the area that were worth millions of dollars in property and a large enrollment of students. In 1882, out of sheer denominational competitiveness with the need for a strong Baptist presence in the Midwest, Rockefeller endowed the University of Chicago, through the ABHMS, with an initial $600,000 of his own money for its creation. This experience was Rockefeller's first effort at organized giving, that is, giving money through a third party.

Also in 1882, Giles and Packard made fund-raising trips to the North soliciting money for their struggling Female Seminary. One of their stops was to Wilson Avenue Baptist Church in Cleveland, Ohio. While there, they appealed to Rockefeller Sr., a member of the church and in the audience, and the other congregation members for funds. Packard and Giles's commitment and appeal moved Rockefeller so much that he not only "emptied his pockets when the [collection] box was passed" and further pledged more money for their "building fund," but also became "unalterably committed to black education." Rockefeller's only condition was that Packard and Giles assure him they were committed to the seminary and would continue this endeavor.[110]

In the following year, enrollment grew quickly; three teachers taught classes in a small cramped space. Giles and Packard had neither the space to educate all the students adequately nor the money for another location. They faced not only the dilemma of conducting classes in small quarters, but also the possibility of losing their institutional identity in a merger with Atlanta Baptist.[111] In such a predicament, Giles and Packard were desperate for funds to expand their program, and sent a request to Henry L. Morehouse.

In 1883, the ABHMS purchased nine acres of land and five buildings formerly used as Union Army barracks and a drill field during the Civil War. At this time, the Female Seminary had 293 students, of whom 30 boarded on the campus. By January 1884, student enrollment was 450 with 100 boarders, and by April, the number of boarders had increased to 120. Morehouse was adamant that the ABHMS could not "afford to pay for two separate properties." On the surface, he believed that the two institutions, Atlanta Baptist and the Female Seminary, had to become one, which meant the Female Seminary would be "The Girls Department of the Atlanta Baptist Seminary." However, Packard and Giles vehemently opposed this merger and wanted the Female Seminary to remain independent. Morehouse and the ABHMS agreed that if Packard and Giles paid the balance of the cost of the land, $15,000, then the new site "would be turned over to them."[112]

Morehouse was one of the "missionary vanguards" in black education. He was the one who interested Rockefeller in major support of Baptist educational endeavors and "stood clearly and unswervingly for black higher education and for the development of advanced technical schools to prepare blacks for executive and administrative posts."[113] Unknown to Packard and Giles, and behind the scene, Morehouse approached Rockefeller with the Seminary's predicament. Rockefeller made a "confidential agreement with Morehouse to give the balance required to pay off the debt of the Atlanta Seminary, some $4,950.00, in addition to [his] former pledge of $2,500." Although Rockefeller was "socially conservative" and, at the time, did not publicly address the issue of blacks' education, he nevertheless privately showed concern for their educational welfare. In a response back to Morehouse, he wrote:

> We have a great problem in their education. I am thankful to have had some little part in it and want to further pursue the study of the question with a view to understand better my responsibility in the case. Kindly assure the colored people of my sympathy for, and interest in them and tell them, I hope they will in addition to securing knowledge from books, strive to learn to do all kinds of work, and better than any other class of men.[114]

Rockefeller's wife, Laura Spelman Rockefeller, her sister (Lucy Spelman), and her mother (Lucy Henry Spelman) also became involved with the Atlanta Baptist Female Seminary.[115] Laura Spelman Rockefeller's family had assisted blacks in gaining their freedom and pursuing educational endeavors. Her parents, Harvey and Lucy Spelman, were strict Congregationalists; and as such, Laura Spelman Rockefeller was "thoroughly indoctrinated with the Puritan virtues of thrift, industry, and piety." The Spelmans "were uncompromising abolitionists and temperance activists." Using their home as a station for the Underground Railroad, the Spelmans sheltered slaves, such as Sojourner Truth, and helped them on the last leg of their journey to freedom.[116]

With Rockefeller's wealth and his wife's family background of aiding former slaves, particularly females, and the nudging of Henry Morehouse, this combination positioned them to make one of the largest impacts on black higher education in Atlanta, particularly for the Female Seminary.

When the Female Seminary celebrated its third anniversary in 1884, they invited the Spelman and Rockefeller families to attend the ceremony. In his address to the audience, Rockefeller said, "It is in your hearts to make the school one that people will believe in. God will take these small beginnings to do a great work. I am thankful to be here." During the same time, the Seminary wanted to honor Rockefeller by renaming the Seminary after him, but he discouraged such an idea. Consequently, the Female Seminary changed its name to Spelman Seminary to honor the interest and substantial help of both the Spelman and Rockefeller families.[117]

Though all three of the Atlanta institutions made advancements, limiting black educational endeavors continued to be the mind-set of society in the late 1890s. Historian David Levering Lewis, Du Bois's biographer, best described this decade, when he wrote:

> The creed of the nineties held that it was a dangerous conceit to expose black people to literature, history, philosophy, and "dead" languages, thereby, "spoiling" them for the natural order of southern society in which their place was as voteless, industrious farmhands, primary schoolteachers, and occasional merchants.[118]

Even though society viewed blacks in this manner, major changes occurred at Atlanta University and Atlanta Baptist, which elevated the curriculum and widened awareness of the institutions. In just a couple of years after the US Supreme Court upheld racial segregation with the *Plessy v. Ferguson* (1896) doctrine of "separate but equal" racial status, W. E. B. Du Bois joined the faculty of Atlanta University; at the same time, John Hope joined the faculty of Atlanta Baptist. Both men believed in full equality for blacks, as well as blacks' training in higher education, and the two would form a friendship that lasted for almost 40 years.[119]

W. E. B. Du Bois came to Atlanta University in 1898 as professor of economics and history, became "the most popular teacher," and conducted "several studies and essays on 'the Negro problem.'" Besides teaching multiple advance courses in economics, history, and sociology, Du Bois also taught "a class in American citizenship and another in civil government in the high school."[120] The addition of Du Bois to the faculty at Atlanta University brought prestige to Atlanta University as he had "established himself as one of the great scholars of the world." Atlanta University was the springboard from which Du Bois's international acclaim and recognition manifested.

Atlanta University "had to get Du Bois for its faculty," because they wanted to create an annual series of "systematic and thorough investigations of the conditions of living among the Negro population of the cities."[121] No one was better suited for this undertaking than Du Bois. He was the first black to receive a PhD from Harvard, had trained at Fisk University and the University of Berlin, had taught at Wilberforce University and the University of Pennsylvania, and was a scholar of blacks in Philadelphia. Du Bois was a man ahead of his time. For example, his study *The Philadelphia Negro* "was remarkable as an example of the new empiricism that was fundamentally transforming the social sciences at the beginning of the 20th Century."[122] This study was a breakthrough in that it was "an important and virtually solitary departure from the hereditarian theorizing of the time."[123]

Fulfilling the university's reasons for adding him on the faculty, Du Bois developed several publications on the living conditions of blacks and established conferences from which he disseminated his findings, and became an international scholar bringing the world to Atlanta University.[124] He wrote his most famous magnum opus, *The Souls of Black Folks* (1903), while on the faculty of Atlanta University. However, his criticism of and attacks on Booker T. Washington brought not only praise from some, but also displeasure from philanthropists.

The impact of Du Bois's studies "pushed the Atlanta University's studies to the frontier of American social science research, to the point that the cost to fund the conferences was a burden." His studies and essays appeared in the *London Spectator*, *Publication of the Southern History Association*, *American Journal of Sociology*, and the *Chicago Tribune*. In 1904, during his American visit, Max Weber, renowned German sociologist, came to Atlanta University and participated in a conference on crime. Afterward, Weber ran reviews of Du Bois's work in *Archiv fur Sozialwissenschaft und Sozialpolitik*. The French version of Weber's reviews appeared as "L'Ouvrier negro en Amerique" in the periodical *La Revue Enconomique Internationale*.[125] Though the notoriety was good for Atlanta University, the conferences were too costly for Atlanta University to maintain; in 1910 Du Bois resigned.[126]

By the 1900s, as a political, economic, and social mechanism to keep blacks from achieving equality on all fronts, whites created an extension to Jim Crow laws and segregation. Cloaked in the guise of protectionism and patriotism, whites induced an intense fear of blacks that was termed "negrophobia." The phobia of blacks and its accompanying social milieu of racial unrest reached a climax and sparked a series of race riots throughout the country.[127] Politicians and white supremacists launched news stories of black men's crimes against white women, miscegenation, and white subservience all across the nation; however, they were more prevalent in the South. Mark Bauerlein, in *Negrophobia: A Race Riot in Atlanta*, explained, "respect for white women [was] a cornerstone of Southern honor and essential to Southern manhood" and that "no Southern man would observe...beastly assaults...without striking back against the villain."[128] The villains, during this time, were blacks.

Whites in the South felt a need to maintain the status quo. Under the old matrix of society, blacks were slaves and had no economic power or political voice; there was no threat to the status quo. However, under the new social structure, blacks were free, had the opportunity to compete with whites in the labor market for jobs, and received a ballot with the potential of disrupting the political arena. Whites saw their position of superiority and dominance crumbling, which forced them to devise a mechanism to maintain their commitment to the status quo and position in society.¹²⁹ Ultimately, this mechanism involved keeping blacks in a static position and the only way to ensure this was by limiting their education. Despite this being the case, philanthropic groups rose to counter these measures and ensure that blacks would receive the education they so desperately and justly deserved.

Early Philanthropic Groups

Black colleges and universities were "deplorable" by the 1900s, as historian John Hope Franklin noted; yet, he also acknowledged that blacks had made advancements and the twentieth century marked a new beginning, when he wrote:

> In 1900 there were 28,560 Negro teachers…more than 1,500,000 Negro children in school. Thirty-four institutions for blacks were reported as giving collegiate training, and a large number of blacks were being permitted to enter the universities in the North. There were four state colleges for Negroes, in Virginia, Arkansas, Georgia, and Delaware. By 1900 more than 2,000 Negroes had graduated from institutions of higher learning, while more than 700 were in colleges at that time.¹³⁰

There was no longer a need for missionary societies to establish institutions for blacks; this process was completed. College enrollment had increased; the cost of maintaining the institutions had increased; and campaigns to secure more funds for the institutions were steadily growing. Most black institutions lacked sufficient endowments necessary to survive, and there was no way for continuance without financial assistance. College presidents found themselves devoting more effort to obtaining a steady flow of income to cover increased expenditures.

World War I produced economic and social changes, the missionary societies had become financially weak and almost bankrupt, and their "campaign to develop black higher education was rapidly diminishing in scope and activity." As a result, the missionary's approach to education coupled with financial inadequacy left the "fate of black education, particularly higher education, to the attitudes and interests of the nation's wealthiest families," those individuals who represented the "political power in the region."[131]

By the end of the nineteenth century and into the twentieth century, a new era arose, the "age of philanthropy." This third philanthropic group, industrial philanthropy, significantly benefitted black education. Individuals interested in uplifting blacks thought it was imperative to elevate blacks to a level of intelligent citizens. Education was the most appropriate avenue to implement plans for self-improvement; philanthropic support would translate the ideals of the intellectual ability of blacks into actuality.[132] As the subsequent chapters discuss, philanthropists and educational foundations emerged as the source that provided financial resources needed to sustain black colleges and universities; they also shed light on how a black college leader, John Hope, emerged and led the charge.

2

Mythical Phoenix and the Ashes It Spreads

American colleges and universities have always been basically dependent upon philanthropy, whether private or public. In the post–Civil War years, the university could not have developed without the Cornells, Hopkinses, and Rockefellers.

—Laurence R. Veysey[1]

From the end of the Civil War through the beginning of World War I, the third group of philanthropists, industrial philanthropists, emerged. More visible than missionary societies, this group was comprised of wealthy individuals, such as Andrew Carnegie (steel), J. P. Morgan (banking, later steel), Jay Gould and Cornelius Vanderbilt (railroad), John D. Rockefeller Sr. (oil), and large philanthropic foundations. The most important of the secular foundations during this time were the Peabody Education Fund, John Slater Fund, Daniel Hand Education Fund for Colored People, Julius Rosenwald Fund, Phelps-Stokes Fund, Carnegie Foundation, and General Education Board.

Initially, philanthropists directed higher education and its curricula to center on industrial education, or training for manual labor, and away from classical education.[2] However, with any transformational process, metamorphosis takes time and situations and circumstances have to align for it to take place. Just as the missionary societies shifted the focus of their philosophy of and curriculum for black education, so too did the industrial philanthropists. Over time, they realized an industrial curriculum would not produce the type of leaders the black community needed, such as teachers, doctors, and lawyers, and that some black institutions had to implement a liberal arts curriculum in order for these leaders to emerge.[3]

During the late 1800s into the 1900s, wealthy philanthropists adopted and used the ideologies of Social Darwinism and the Social Gospel to justify their accumulations of wealth and their business maneuvers. Social Gospel produced and advocated a new noblesse oblige for America's new industrial and corporate giants. Before Charles Darwin's book *Origin of the Species*, Herbert Spencer wrote, "life was lived in a jungle, that it was governed by jungle laws. Only the fittest could survive, and all progress was due to the evolutionary process that removed the unfit."[4] These wealthy men certainly lived by this creed. Social Darwinism not only justified the means by which they acquired their wealth, but it also set in place their modus operandi from which they dealt with all their endeavors whether in the business world or the world of academe. This was particularly true for John D. Rockefeller Sr.

These men juxtaposed, however, the survival of the fittest ideal with the Social Gospel, a religious social-reform movement dedicated "to the betterment of industrialized society through application of the biblical principles of charity and justice."[5] People who followed the principles "accepted the validity of a historical-critical approach to the Bible and [drew] from Darwinism theories of evolution."[6] This movement also implied that God had blessed these individuals with great fortunes by "virtue of their superior business skills and scientific minds to rise above the common population to assume a stewardship that would benefit those plagued by social ills."[7] By the late 1890s, the Progressive Era had emerged and its tenets connected progress, change, and social activism and political reform. Based on these tenets, wealthy men deemed it a necessity to rid society of its faults and defects—removal of the unfit. This era also ushered in philanthropy and brought with it "the expectation of prominently displayed altruistic motives in all lines of endeavors."[8]

Practicing the ideologies of Social Darwinism and the Social Gospel presented a conflicting view of philanthropists and their philanthropic giving, and highlighted the complexity of these men, particularly when one of the resounding "faults and defects" in society related to blacks. The notion of helping "your fellow brethren," those who were less fortunate, was one aspect; yet another was that philanthropists condoned the segregationist practices of the South and the inhuman treatment of blacks. For example, Rockefeller Sr. claimed to have interest in the development of all people and especially in the education of blacks, yet he neither publicly denounced segregation nor addressed the issue of race.

At the turn of the twentieth century, also problematic for philanthropists was the disclosure of their ruthless business tactics and corruption. This disclosure was particularly true and disparaging for John D. Rockefeller Sr., and it meant he would spend the rest of his life trying to clear his reputation and his family name. Ida Tarbell's 1902 exposé on John D. Rockefeller Sr., *The History of Standard Oil*, appeared in *McClure's Magazine* and caused such public interest and following that the series ran "for almost two years and became one of the longest pieces ever published in a national magazine."[9] Based on solid evidence, Tarbell disclosed all the details of how Rockefeller willingly sacrificed "anything and anyone in his pursuit of profits and power," so much so that Rockefeller's image "was permanently damaged in the public mind."[10] Rockefeller tried to justify his actions at Standard Oil by saying he did not "ruthlessly go after the trade of our competitors and attempt to ruin it by cutting prices or institute a spy system." However, by doing just that, he was able to create a monopoly that most felt was based on his desire to "eliminate competition, the same as waste, in the oil industry." Regardless of his rationale, in the end, Tarbell's investigation successfully tied the Rockefeller's name to corporate greed and tarnished it for many years to come.[11]

The US Attorney General later prosecuted Standard Oil under the Sherman Anti-Trust Act (any monopoly in restraint of trade was illegal), and Congress enacted several sanctions over the next few years. Congress passed the Hepburn Act (1906) that regulated and imposed penalties for rebates. The Federal Circuit Court "held that the Standard Oil Company was in violation of the Sherman Anti-Trust Act (1890)" that prohibited business activities that reduced competition. By 1911, the US Supreme Court affirmed the Federal Court's decision that Standard Oil was in violation and therefore "dissolved it into thirty-eight separate and smaller corporations."[12] Today, ExxonMobil, Chevron, and British Petroleum (BP) are among the Standard Oil companies still in existence.

Interestingly, in the early twentieth century, men of great wealth had similarities that went beyond earning great fortunes, and at least three are of interest. Men such as Andrew Carnegie, Jay Gould, J. P. Morgan, and John D. Rockefeller Sr. were born within a five-year period of each other, 1835–1840, most from humble beginnings.[13] They used similar business tactics and acquired domination of specific business industries through various or previous business ventures. Last, the noblesse oblige notion of the Social Gospel was omnipresent. These individuals believed they were superior, intellectually and financially, and specifically chosen to spread their gifts to the masses. Industrial philanthropists made an enormous impact in the business industry; however, one of the greatest influences that secured the continuation of this industrial cycle and ensured their manner of thinking and influence was through the establishment and continuation of higher education in the United States.

In the late nineteenth century into the early twentieth century, "the modern university was beginning to mirror the business world," especially in the case of majority institutions "when philanthropists offered money, most institutions accepted it regardless of the consequences that lay ahead."[14] Despite this being the case and probably true of most institutions, philanthropists would later find out not all institutions or college leaders would be so compliant and accepting of money without negotiating their own terms.

Philanthropy and Higher Education

Andrew Carnegie was perhaps the first industrialist to provide a glimpse into the mind-set of the wealthy and to offer a rationale for his philanthropic philosophy. He wrote two essays in

1889 and explained how he (and possibly other industrialists) viewed his wealth. In "The Gospel of Wealth," he explained having enormous wealth created "an arduous task to administer it to the common good of people." Because this task was so difficult, he believed it "must inevitably flow in the hands of a few exceptional managers of men who know what to do with it." Further, he thought one of the best uses to "which a millionaire can devote his surplus is in the founding of universities."[15]

In his second article, "The Best Fields of Philanthropy," he felt men of his financial status should use their wealth to "promote the permanent good for communities from which they have been gathered." However, he suspected that "public sentiment would soon say of one who died possessed of millions of available wealth which he might have administered [given away]...dies with disgrace." Ultimately, for him, the "Gospel of Wealth but echoes Christ's words," because it called upon the "millionaire to sell all that he hath and give it in the highest and best form to the poor." Millionaires would accomplish this act "by administering his estate himself for the good of his fellows before he is called upon to lie down and rest upon the bosom of Mother Earth."[16] Rockefeller shared the same sentiment when he wrote Carnegie and said he wished:

> More men of wealth were doing as you are doing with your money but, be assured, your example will bear fruits, and the time will come when men of wealth will more generally be willing to use it for the good of others.[17]

A few years later, Rockefeller Sr. also expressed this view of philanthropy in his book, *Random Reminiscences*, when he wrote, "one's ideal should be to use one's means, both in one's investments and in benefactions, for the advancement of civilization."[18]

For these philanthropists, especially Rockefeller Sr., one way to advance civilization was through education and research; yet, another way was by setting examples. In *The Rockefeller Conscience*, authors John Ensor Harr and Peter J. Johnson wrote, "In an open society that allows individuals to amass great wealth, by definition no one can tell wealthy men how to spend their money. One can only set examples."[19] Although it is hard to discern whether wealthy men of that time bequeathed their resources from fear of public disgrace, fall from the grace of God, egoism, or even guilt, industrial philanthropists nevertheless did set examples in more ways than one. They also contributed back to the community from which their great fortunes came and created an avenue by which they and their loved ones could be immortalized.

Beginning in the late nineteenth century, one example industrial philanthropists set was by establishing, supporting, and maintaining higher education institutions. Ezra Cornell and Johns Hopkins were two founders of institutions who "made benefactions to higher education fashionable leading into the twentieth-century." These initial endeavors not only "set standards for other wealthy individuals to follow suit," but also "moved higher education much closer to ways of thinking shared by the practical and the wealthy."[20] The most impressive of the industrialist involved in higher education at the time, however, was Leland Stanford, who financed a complete university, Stanford University, with thirty million dollars of his own money.[21]

The postindustrial era growth of the middle class also made possible the expansion of higher education. In the late nineteenth century, three elements were catalysts for the emergence and transformation of colleges and universities in the United States. First, there was a new concern for practicality and utility in the colleges' curriculum (e.g., vocational, industrial training, and then later liberal arts), which reflected subjects that were useful to the community that surrounded the institution and the business industry.[22] Second, there was a democratic effort to extend the benefits of education to a wider portion of society. However, disparities existed regarding who had access to these schools, particularly since the wider community had its own preconceived notions of who should and should not be educated, and how to teach these individuals.[23] The last catalyst, and probably the most prominent, was a new interest in research, the advancement of knowledge—learning for its own sake. During the nineteenth century, German universities became influential sources of scholarly research and exemplars of academic freedom. Many students from foreign countries, including the United States, studied at these universities.[24]

Through philanthropy, men of wealth played an important role in higher education by contributing substantially either to the establishment, development, or continuation of higher educational institutions. Most of their benefactions initially educated individuals from the white upper and middle classes and did not address the disparities that limited educational access to any other group, particularly blacks. Though the missionary and denominational societies initiated the task of providing educational opportunities for blacks, it took the establishment of educational foundations to sustain black institutions.

Despite higher educational institutions being the vehicle to which wealthy individuals initially bequeathed large sums of money to establish institutions, by the turn of the twentieth century, the focus of giving substantially changed. There was no longer a need to establish institutions; at this time, there was a need to maintain the "stronger, more superior ones." This maintenance came in the "form of foundations, which alleviated the individuals who made a career of giving wealthy people's money to others, collecting information, evaluating applications for aid, and dispensing advice, encouragement, and criticism."[25] Several foundations became highly influential in educating blacks in the South.

A couple of years after the Civil War had ended, George Peabody, a banker from Massachusetts, established the George Peabody Fund with $2 million allotted for both white and black common schools and teacher-training schools in the South through cooperation with state and local officials. The fund "aided in the beginning of city systems of public schools throughout the South," encouraged, and aided the states in developing state normal schools for the training of teachers.[26] It was the "pioneer educational foundation...in the support of Hampton and Tuskegee Institutes, and other private schools for Negroes, and finally contributed the bulk of its capital ($1,500,000) to...George Peabody College for Teachers, affiliated with Vanderbilt University at Nashville."[27] Wickliffe Rose, former president of the fund, noted that the fund "during the forty-seven years of their administration the Trustees contributed...toward the encouragement of public education in the Southern states about three and three-quarter million dollars." However, when it dissolved in 1914, they gave the remaining $350,000 to the John Slater Fund.[28]

John F. Slater, a Connecticut textile manufacturer, established the John Slater Fund in 1882 with a $1 million endowment and specified that the intent of the fund "was to aid in the Christian education of Negroes" and "wished the training of teachers to be encouraged."[29] The Slater Fund was the first philanthropic foundation devoted exclusively to black education,[30] and between 1882 and 1911, "assisted both private and church schools in their teacher-training programs and made donations to public schools...." Slater gave a considerable amount of money to institutions that focused on industrial and vocational training; in 1911, it supported country-training schools.[31] The fund was also of "material aid in developing the Trade Schools at Hampton and Tuskegee, the Hospital and Teacher Training Department at Spelman Seminary, the industrial work at Claflin University, and many other institutions."[32]

In 1888, the American Missionary Association (AMA) received $1,000,894 from Daniel Hand, a native of Connecticut who made a fortune as a merchant in Augusta, Georgia. Although the AMA established and administered the Daniel Hand Education Fund for Colored People, its emphasis and concerns were not directly in higher education. They used money from the fund "for the general promotion of the work of the [AMA] in the field of Negro education."[33] Having this amount available for black education was significant for higher education because it freed the existing colleges to develop "as true institutions for higher learning instead of serving as preparatory schools."[34]

During the early 1900s, several other philanthropists established foundations. The Phelps-Stokes Fund was established in 1911 through a million-dollar bequest of Caroline Phelps-Stokes, a New York philanthropist with "a lifelong concern for the educational needs of the underprivileged." By the second decade of the twentieth century, Anson Phelps Stokes, her nephew, guided the fund toward improving the lives of blacks and supported "out of its income a study of leading Negro schools and colleges, and certain fellowships at the University of Georgia and University of Virginia for the study of the Negro problem." This dedication toward assisting college students resulted in both black and white students studying and improving educational facilities for blacks in the United States and in Africa.[35]

Julius Rosenwald, a Chicago businessman, clothier, and part owner and former president of Sears, Roebuck and Company, was the son of first-generation, German Jewish immigrants. In 1917, he created the Julius Rosenwald Fund. Although Rosenwald initially created the fund for the "well-being of mankind," through his association with Booker T. Washington, his fund promoted rural schools for blacks in the South. The fund gave one-third of the total required for the erection of industrial rural school buildings, established libraries for blacks, and gave black scholars fellowships for research projects.

At the turn of the twentieth century, Andrew Carnegie and John D. Rockefeller Sr. were in the forefront, setting examples for philanthropic giving in higher education. Their philanthropic endeavors transformed, standardized, and professionalized the educational field. Carnegie's aim was to assist the masses "to stimulate the best and most aspiring poor of the community to further efforts for their own improvement."[36] Following the philosophy of survival of the fittest, he wanted to encourage individuals who were striving by personal effort to cultivate their intellect and improve their position in the world. However, in contrast, Carnegie did not view blacks in this same manner—a hypocritical stance for one who upheld the tenets of the Social Gospel. During Reconstruction, the largest population of people who needed assistance was blacks, and Carnegie initially failed to assist them on a large scale.

He gave more than $350 million to various educational, cultural, and peace institutions. Although he lacked a formal education, he developed a love for books, so much so that the greatest portion of money he gave away was for the establishment of free libraries, though initially they were segregated ones.[37] In 1890, he created the nation's first publicly funded library—Carnegie Free Library of Allegheny (now, Carnegie Library of Pittsburgh). Over the next 20 years, he would not only establish libraries throughout the United States, but also educational and research organizations, as well as an endowment.

1896 Carnegie Institute of Pittsburgh, to improve Pittsburgh's cultural and educational institutions
1900 Carnegie Technical School (now Carnegie Mellon University), to deliver distinctive and first-quality education and to foster research
1902 Carnegie Institute of Washington, to encourage pure research in the natural and physical sciences
1905 The Carnegie Foundation for the Advancement of Teaching, to train, teach, and conduct research
1910 The Carnegie Endowment for International Peace, to disseminate information that promoted peace and understanding among nations
1911 The Carnegie Corporation of New York—the largest of Carnegie foundations and the last—to advance and diffuse knowledge and understanding among the people in the United States.[38] The Carnegie Corporation also contributed funds to colleges, universities, and libraries throughout the world, and provided funding to conduct research and training in law, economics, and medicine.

Initially, Carnegie only gave millions of dollars to white institutions and their initiatives rather than black institutions; however, Tuskegee was the exception, with Carnegie giving the institution its first endowment in 1903. Eventually, the Carnegie Corporation gave significant sums of money to black colleges and libraries, black improvement organizations, and research projects related to blacks.[39]

One thrust of philanthropic involvement in higher education, as Rockefeller Sr. believed, stemmed from the idea that through research and the dissemination of knowledge to the masses, an entire society would benefit. Philanthropists and foundations transformed higher education and the circumstances of university research by establishing standards that institutions would follow, as well as provided the financial resources for direct expenses to conduct organized research.[40]

Because society viewed standardization as rationalized behavior back then, as it does now, the line between higher education and secondary education was made more distinct by setting "admission standards in units of work rather than specific levels of knowledge [which] in effect defined the length of secondary education." Institutions had to "adjust to a more bureaucratic system demanded by an urbanizing society." Philanthropy, specifically the Carnegie Foundation, was responsible for this level of standardization. In determining institutions qualified for its faculty pension, it was impossible for the foundation to distinguish between the levels of education colleges offered (e.g., four years of academic studies, high school preparation, or grammar school). As a result, the Carnegie Foundation urged "the abolition of collegiate preparatory departments and the admission of students before high school graduation."[41]

Through the Carnegie Foundation, Carnegie also created the "most startling and epoch-making force for improvement of professional education." The foundation sponsored research, such as Abraham Flexner's *Medical Education in the United States and Canada* (1910), later known as the *Flexner Report*. This report produced a "veritable revolution in medical education" and resulted in the closing of many medical schools that were inferior.[42] Visiting 155 medical colleges, Flexner was "appalled by the experience" and concluded that most colleges still languished "in the dark ages of medicine." Because of his findings, more than one hundred of the inferior schools "either perished...or were absorbed by [other] universities." Those medical schools that survived had to upgrade their standards, readjust their programs, and change their teaching methods, that is, if they expected to receive any future money from philanthropists.[43]

Though Carnegie had amassed great wealth and contributed to the educational process, it was John D. Rockefeller Sr. whom society considered the richest man in the world—America's first billionaire—and who reigned at the top of business industry and the philanthropic arena (Figure 2.1). By the late 1890s, Rockefeller Sr. received numerous charitable requests, realized "he needed organizational help in carrying out his charitable

Figure 2.1 Photograph of John D. Rockefeller Sr.
Source: The Rockefeller Archive Center, Sleepy Hollow, New York.

work," and enlisted assistance from Frederick Gates, the secretary of the American Baptist Education Society. By 1891, Gates began helping him "gain control over the flood of charitable requests and organize his philanthropy to make it more efficient." With Gates's assistance, Rockefeller Sr. devoted himself to philanthropy by creating institutions and organizations that would work, and in true progressive spirit, "to solve the ills that plagued society."[44]

Rockefeller Sr. gave money to create and establish several foundations; however, in 1902, one of the most important foundations was the General Education Board (GEB). Rockefeller Sr. pledged, "to the Board a sum of One Million Dollars ($1,000,000) to be expended at its discretion during a period of ten years, and [made] payments under such pledges from time to time."[45] With guidance from his son, John D. Rockefeller Jr. (Junior), members of the board carried out its mission with a degree of anonymity.[46] Its objective was to "establish or endow elementary or primary schools, industrial schools, normal schools, training schools for teachers, or schools of any grade, or higher institutions of learning; to cooperate with any association engaged in educational work."[47] The entire field of education was open to the GEB, of which it made great progress and development throughout the United States, particularly in the South.

It is not clear whether Rockefeller Sr. devoted himself altruistically to philanthropy for the well-being of humanity, to dispense his fortune as it rapidly increased, or to clean up his public image tarnished by Tarbell's exposé and other journalistic critics. What is clear is that the foundations he created did serve a larger good for humanity. Just as Carnegie had done, Rockefeller Sr. along with his son, Junior, created several major philanthropic institutions over a span of almost 20 years.

1901   The Rockefeller Institute for Medical Research, created for scientific medical research
1902   The GEB to promote education throughout the United States
1909   The Rockefeller Sanitary Commission for Eradication of the Hookworm Disease, established "to cure and prevent the [hookworm] disease, particularly in the southern United States," and considered "a landmark in epidemiology and preventative medicine"
1913   The Rockefeller Foundation, created to "promote the well-being of mankind throughout the world"
1918   Laura Spelman Rockefeller Memorial, Rockefeller Sr.'s last major philanthropic commitment created to promote various causes that his wife championed (Figure 2.2).[48]

Figure 2.2 Photograph of Laura Spelman Rockefeller.
Source: The Rockefeller Archive Center, Sleepy Hollow, New York.

Although other industrialists also created dynasties, Rockefeller Sr.'s creations and dynasty were unmatched and had an enormous impact. Two elements have to exist to have such an impact: "a set of principles to guide succeeding generations and the presence of an heir willing and able to live out those principles."[49] Indeed, Rockefeller had both. His strong religious belief developed his philanthropic philosophy and his moral values were omnipresent in his life and in the upbringing of his son, Junior (Figure 2.3).

Figure 2.3 Photograph of John D. Rockefeller Jr.
Source: The Rockefeller Archive Center, Sleepy Hollow, New York.

Raymond Fosdick, one of Junior's biographers, noted that he "subscribed to the principles that guided his father's giving."[50] Junior acknowledged his philanthropic principles and undying loyalty to his father in a letter he wrote to his father:

> I appreciate more and more each day what your wisdom and intelligence and broad vision in giving has meant to the world. I realize increasingly the tremendous value that attaches to your endorsement of an enterprise, business or philanthropic, and I

need not assure you that it will be my great pride, as well as my solemn duty, to endeavor, while emulating your unparalleled generosity, to live up to the high standards of intelligent giving which you have set.[51]

Junior, in turn, passed these same principles onto his five sons and daughter.[52] Today, his son, David Rockefeller Sr., at age 97, is the patriarch of the Rockefeller family and is his only surviving child.

The General Education Board and Higher Education

Junior's principles and loyalty resonated through his leadership in the establishment of the General Education Board (GEB). Like his father, Junior's belief that home and church were the center of his life was embedded in him, but he also had a "deep and abiding interest in the education and welfare of the Negro race." Knowing his grandparents were abolitionists who championed for blacks' achievement, as a boy, Junior wrote an essay on how blacks escaped to Canada, and how his parents took him on trips to the South to visit black institutions, such as Spelman Seminary and Hampton Institute.[53] Junior's interest in the education of blacks stemmed not only from this family legacy of aiding blacks, but also from being stimulated further by trips to the South as an adult.

Robert C. Ogden, an executive with the Wannamaker Department Stores in New York, organized conferences that discussed and proposed solutions for the improvement of education for blacks in the South. Ogden also arranged a train trip, "The Millionaires' Special," in 1901 that took a cadre of influential men, including Junior, throughout the South to visit black institutions, such as Hampton Institute, North Carolina College for Women, Tuskegee Institute, Spelman Seminary, and Atlanta University, to give them a firsthand look at their future benefactions. Allan Nevin, one of Rockefeller Sr.'s biographers, confirmed that "Rockefeller Jr. went because his father and he were now keenly interested in the possibility of giving to Negro education." Ultimately, this trip lit a fuse in Junior "that would grow for the rest of his life."⁵⁴

Rockefeller Sr. once contemplated establishing "a trust fund for black education," and Junior mentioned to Ogden that he and his father had deliberated the "question of colored education," obviously, more expansive than what Rockefeller Sr. had already pledged and given to Spelman Seminary. Junior had hoped the train trip would create a venue from which his idea for a "Negro Board of education" would emerge.⁵⁵ However, despite Junior's childhood and family experiences motivating his mission in creating such a board, passengers on the trip quickly dismissed his plan as an undesirable approach to educating blacks. To Junior, Henry St. George Tucker, president of Washington and Lee University, expressed his and all the other passengers' sentiment on this subject:

> If it is your idea to educate the Negro you must have the whites of the South with you. If the poor white sees the son of the Negro neighbor enjoying through your munificence benefits denied to his boy, it raises in him a feeling that will render futile all your work. You must lift up the "poor white" and the Negro together if you would ever approach success.⁵⁶

Ironically, Rockefeller Sr. once said his policy was to "hear patiently and discuss frankly until the last shred of evidence [was] on the table, before trying to reach a conclusion and to decide finally upon a course of action."⁵⁷ However, there was neither deliberation on the creation of an education board exclusively for blacks from Rockefeller Sr. nor a strong enough sense of duty for Junior to fulfill his innermost desires on this trip, because he never created a board of education solely for blacks.

In an account regarding the creation of Rockefeller Sr.'s foundations, Edwin Embree, a trustee and president of the GEB, explained that Frederick Gates led Rockefeller into endeavors that were more philanthropic. Gates, a former Baptist minister, trustee of the GEB, and Rockefeller advisor, was concerned that Rockefeller's money was increasing too rapidly and feared the consequences if he did not immediately do something with it.

They both decided it was time for him to give to charities other than those supported by the Baptist Society and reached the conclusion that "education in any large sense could not properly be organized on a purely denominational basis." Gates further wanted "to establish a great foundation which [could] stimulate and promote education of any sort, at any place, and under any auspices throughout the United States."[58]

When they established the GEB in 1902, its general purpose was "the promotion of education within the United States without distinction of race, sex, or creed."[59] However, this "general purpose" was cause for great contention. There were two major criticisms surrounding Rockefeller's foundations, particularly the GEB, that Embree acknowledged. Critics claimed, "One of the purposes of the new board was to control education." Embree affirmed, "in a sense they were probably right."[60] The other criticism related to why the GEB was created:

> [The purpose] could have only a vicious motive and that the intention of Mr. Rockefeller was to control education for the purpose of "training wage slaves" or in other words of catering to the special interests of the wealthy directors of the capitalistic system which Mr. Rockefeller represented.[61]

Concerning this criticism, Embree offered no rebuttal, and this silence led many to conclude that if the first criticism was "probably right," so too was the second. Many believed the education of blacks was an economic policy motivated by capitalistic greed and that philanthropists were mainly interested in implementing and supporting industrial education to produce generations of cheap labor, which would continue the industrial cycle.[62] On the surface and just viewing the GEB's start up and actions, this appeared true; however, when viewing the totality of the board's work, this was not the case.

On January 15, 1902, the GEB began informally with a few individuals who met "for the purpose of discussing the probable scope and methods of an educational organization."[63] At the second meeting, a month later, the members—including

Junior—submitted the articles of association for which the GEB began its preliminary operations. The charter was granted and incorporated by January 1903 with a membership that consisted of nine men: William H. Baldwin Jr.; Jabez L. M. Curry; Frederick T. Gates; Daniel C. Gilman; Morris K. Jesup; Robert C. Ogden; Walter H. Page; George Foster Peabody; and Albert Shaw, who were businessmen, philanthropists, ministers, and intellectuals.[64] The GEB's membership recognized that the

> feasibility of cooperation between private and governmental agencies and the large opportunity open to individual initiative in dealing with social and educational problems are among the distinct advantages of a democratic social order. But the usefulness of any particular effort in these directions must depend on the wisdom with which it is conducted—i.e., on the competency and disinterestedness of those charged with its direction.[65]

The creation of the GEB "marked the coming together and expansion of two distinct lines of interest and activity: higher education and education in the South." It also incorporated the "main principles and practices of the Baptist Society and extended them, dropping the denominational and other limitations." In time, the GEB would serve as a clearinghouse for gifts made from the Rockefellers and other philanthropists, making it a "vehicle through which capitalists of the North who sincerely desired to assist in the great work of southern education may act with assurance that their money will be wisely used."[66]

However, unlike any other contributions made thus far that were to denominational organizations or for the auspices of Baptist causes, Rockefeller knew his contribution to create the GEB would be different. He felt the GEB was an "organization formed for the purpose of working out the problems of helping to stimulate and improve education in all parts of the country."[67] In doing so, the GEB was "built on analysis and investigation," which meant its board members had the latitude to scrutinize organizations or institutions they supported (Figure 2.4). Kenneth W.

Figure 2.4 Photograph of officials of the General Education Board, *Third from left*: Jackson Davis, field agent, *Fifth from left*: Wallace Buttrick, secretary and later president.
Source: The Rockefeller Archive Center, Sleepy Hollow, New York.

Rose, former assistant to the director of the Rockefeller Archives Center, explained this further, when he wrote:

> With more money, a larger staff of professionals, and more clearly defined mission, the General Education Board provided grants to promising institutions deemed worthy of support. The GEB kept in much closer contact with specific institutions and kept particularly close watch on finances. The ability to investigate conditions, analyze problems, and recommend and fund specific solutions set the GEB apart from the ABES [American Baptist Education Society], and distinguished all subsequent philanthropic corporations established by Rockefeller.[68]

With its initial million-dollar gift from Rockefeller Sr., the GEB's immediate task was to determine the greatest need for allocating funds and to devote "itself to studying the needs and aiding to promote the educational interests of the people of the Southern states."[69] The GEB's conception was for a comprehensive system of higher education in the United States that incorporated institutions with and without denominational ties. However, parts of the United States, mainly the South, operated within a segregated system that excluded blacks from receiving educational, economic, political, and social opportunities. Analyzing the situation and perhaps remembering Tucker's remarks during Ogden's train trip, members of the GEB accepted that the only way to educate blacks in the South was to have the support of southern whites, and the only way for that to happen was to extend support to educating whites first, and then blacks.

The board undertook the task of conducting systematic studies in order to learn details about the white colleges and universities that existed. Wallace Buttrick, a former Baptist minister and executive secretary of the GEB, surveyed the white institutions "to ascertain the number of institutions of higher learning in the country, the purposes, agencies through which they had been chartered, their location, their resources, sources of strength, and relations to their respective communities, educationally and otherwise."[70] In doing so, he determined the greatest area of need and the point of departure for the GEB.

In 1902, he explained that 700 institutions "calling themselves colleges and universities" was an absurdly high number and reported that most were not functioning on a collegiate level, when he further reported:

> Many were hardly more than secondary schools...others offered one or two years of college work. Only a minority rightly called college or university. Imitation had led some of the better to cherish unwarranted academic ambitions...no general design had controlled their location or establishment...larger cooperation between all the institutions of a given state had not yet been thought of.[71]

The existence of some colleges and universities, as he concluded, was merely because the community wanted one or a rival denomination already had one.[72] In conformity with the Rockefeller commitment to efficiency, the GEB assumed the responsibility of bringing order out of chaos; in essence, it provided funding for the stronger institutions and consolidated some of the others to eliminate waste.

The GEB credited religious bodies for their "plentifully planting" of "colleges and universities, in order to protect their several denominations and to secure a competently educated ministry,"[73] but they also stated:

> If only some general conception or purpose could from the outset have controlled the planting and development of higher institutions of learning, all might have been well. But no such ideal has at this time dominated or even greatly influenced the course of events... Waste and confusion have been the consequence.[74]

As a result, the GEB appropriated more than $10 million to select white institutions located throughout the United States ensuring financial stability. This action cleared the debt of these favored colleges and universities, increased their teachers' salaries, created new departments, increased the enrollment of students, and increased the communities' responsibility in supporting the institutions.[75] The GEB's actions in building up these institutions were a deliberate measure to force the weaker institutions out of existence.

Turning to the problems of the lower school, the GEB believed no system of education in the South was feasible until better economic conditions existed to provide sufficient financial support from the community. To facilitate economic improvement, the GEB held farm demonstrations to help farmers (black and white) produce more crops, which increased income generated from it and in turn supported a public education system. The GEB "deliberately decided to undertake the agricultural education not of the future farmers, but of the present farmer, on the theory that if he could be substantially helped, he would gladly support better schools in more liberal fashion."[76]

They also appropriated money to its sister organization, the Southern Education Board, which was promoting the idea of tax-supported school systems in the southern states at the elementary level. Founded in 1901, the Southern Education Board, whose president was Robert C. Ogden, functioned as an executive branch of the Conference for Education in the South. The GEB took further steps to create a high school system in the

South by devising a plan that financed the salaries and expenses of secondary education college professors, who were "marshals" in the legislative force to promote the development of high schools in their states. These professors were responsible for traveling throughout the state to determine "a favorable establishment for high schools, help county authorities organize high schools, and try to create enough backing so they would be permanently supported under local leadership." The GEB's financial aid and powerful persuasion were substantial enough to roll out this plan throughout the South.[77]

In 1905, Rockefeller Sr. gave the GEB a permanent endowment of $10 million that was "to be distributed to, or used for the benefit of such institutions of learning, at such times, in such amounts, for such purposes...as the Board may deem best adapted to promote a comprehensive system of higher education in the United States."[78] During this same year, the GEB achieved its original goal of serving as a clearinghouse for other wealthy individuals (and later foundations) to funnel their resources toward educational purposes in general and black education specifically.

Anna T. Jeanes, the daughter of a wealthy merchant from Philadelphia and a Quaker, pledged to assist the GEB with their endeavors to provide education to blacks in the South, particularly industrial institutions. She gave them $200,000 to "improve Negro rural schools in the South." The GEB used these funds to assist southern states by providing salaries for instructors and funds for buildings and equipment at Tuskegee and Hampton Institutes. A few years later, she gave $1 million to expand the program and the GEB-aided black education at the secondary and postsecondary levels. The program educated and trained individuals to teach in industrial, rural schools in the South and paid their salaries. Over the next four years, the GEB received $32 million from Rockefeller Sr. to add to its endowment and for the "specific objects within the corporate purposes of the Board," making this the largest sum "ever given by a man in the history of the race for any social or philanthropic purposes."[79]

In the early 1900s, most states' public education systems ignored the education of blacks and made little effort to provide support for teachers' training. Several black communities raised money and established their own educational facilities with assistance from missionaries and church denominational organizations. Although the GEB considered black institutions "the nucleus of a system of schools for the higher education of Negroes," they were resigned to the fact that "while certain privately managed institutions must be aided, its main purpose required that [the GEB] cooperate with progressive Southern sentiment in creating publicly supported educational systems."[80]

The GEB and other educational foundations initially gave most of their funds to institutions such as Tuskegee and Hampton Institutes, whose curriculum emphasized industrial education, and believed industrial education was the most beneficial educational curriculum for blacks. In the South, most blacks lived in poverty; 80 percent lived in the rural South on farms, had limited prospects, and were governed by prejudices they had to overcome. The GEB deemed the best way to help a black person help himself was "through his private schools, not so much by working upon him as by working with him; not by founding and supporting schools for him, but rather by helping him to found and support schools for himself."[81]

Since white institutions were financially secure and flourishing, the GEB used the same systematic approach and turned its attention to the education of blacks. The board gave grants to state normal schools already in existence for blacks; however, these grants only helped a small portion of blacks who were capable of education beyond elementary and secondary educational levels and did not reach the majority who lived in rural areas. For blacks in rural areas, the GEB set up farm demonstrations and industrial schools, as they had done for whites, which resulted in the black farmer "eagerly taking advantage of his opportunities to attain economic independence in the country." These demonstrations also brought the races somewhat together because black teachers went to white schools and explained their methods of teaching, and whites went to black schools to observe and learn what they were doing.[82]

Since southern whites championed the cause of blacks learning a skill that "fit" them for actual life rather than attain a university education, the GEB believed the "industrial education idea provided an avenue for the wall of opposition to black education in the South to be dismantled." Accordingly, it was more beneficial that the bulk of their donations went to select black private colleges in addition to those institutions that emphasized agricultural and industrial training, such as Hampton and Tuskegee.[83] Observing the situation, the GEB's committee on black education made three recommendations.

1. That to state departments of education desiring such cooperation the General Education Board contribute a sum not to exceed $3,500 to any state to be used in payment of the salary and traveling expenses of a state supervisor of rural schools.
2. That contributions be made from time to time to extend the work of country supervision of rural schools under the general direction of the state supervisor as provided for above.
3. That small contributions be made from time to time toward the industrial equipment of country training schools for the negro race.[84]

Some of the GEB members' mind-set and perception of blacks as inferior cannot be denied. Its involvement with perpetuating industrial education raised questions and scrutiny, and rightfully so. However, the debate over whether blacks received a vocational or industrial education was partly an educational issue. The main conflict stemmed from "the ever present equalitarian American Creed, on the one hand, and the caste interest on the other."[85] Even though "behavior is as always a moral compromise," the American Creed was in contrast to the actions of most white Americans and their treatment of blacks.

The first three decades of the twentieth century witnessed an increasing focus of attention on black colleges and universities. W. E. B. Du Bois, then professor at Atlanta University, was perhaps one of the first to conduct studies on black colleges and universities with his *The College-Bred Negro* (1901).[86] While on the faculty of Atlanta University, Du Bois continued conducting studies on black education and organized conferences to disseminate his findings. In 1905 when the Atlanta Conference celebrated its tenth year, Du Bois sent Wallace Buttrick a letter inviting him to the conference. In it, he mentioned:

> I would especially like to have you and Mr. W. T. B. Williams present. Will you not make an effort to come, and in any case send Mr. Williams? I think that a great cooperative effort to study the Negro problem involving cooperation between the General Education Board, Hampton and Atlanta would lead to great results.[87]

Despite Du Bois's ideal of cooperation and repeated invitations to Buttrick to attend the conferences, Buttrick declined.[88] A few years later, in a letter to Buttrick, Du Bois disclosed the turmoil in Atlanta regarding the type of education proposed for blacks and was forthright when he inquired about the GEB's involvement:

> You perhaps know that the Governor of this State and his followers are making a campaign for reducing the time in the Negro schools so that one half may be given to "Manual Labor" (not even "Manual Labor."). I would like to learn if you know of this campaign, and what the General Education Board or the Southern Educational Board is doing to counteract it, and in what way we can co-operate with you?[89]

In response to Du Bois's letter, Buttrick said he "had not been informed of the campaign," and stated that the "General Education Board does not undertake to direct public sentiment or influence public policy. Our work is for the whole country and is entirely financial in its character."[90] Despite Buttrick's response, the GEB had influenced the southern states to become more active in the education of blacks, particularly with schools in the rural areas. It financed country schools, state superintendents, and teachers' salaries. Unknown to Du Bois, and behind the scene, philanthropists had plans for conducting their own surveys.

In 1912, the Phelps-Stokes Fund, in cooperation with the Federal Bureau of Education, sponsored Thomas Jesse Jones's study, *Negro Education: A Study of the Private and Higher Schools for Colored People in the United States*. While Jones's work received accolades and support from philanthropists, it simultaneously provoked heated debates in the black community because of its defamatory nature and tone.

His study critically "attacked black higher education that questioned the legitimacy of nearly all black institutions of higher learning." In his two-volume work, Jones described most black colleges and universities as "deplorable" and "disclosed that only 33 of the 653 existing private and state schools were teaching any subjects of college grade." For Jones, Howard University, Fisk University, and Meharry Medical College were the only institutions that "had a student body, teaching force, equipment and income sufficient to warrant the characterization of 'college.'" His report also "issued the predictable Progressive educator's warnings against unnecessary duplication, dead languages, and the neglect of 'scientific gardening.'" Jones provoked a "major crisis in black higher education," because "black colleges, however segregated, could not exist apart from the power and control of white standardizing agencies." His report caused the same result as the *Flexner Report (1910)* had with the medical schools: some black colleges closed; there was an immediate desire for cooperation among other colleges, and recommendations ensued to build up a few select institutions. In the end, the Jones report brought about a more scientific approach to the problem of black higher education.[91]

Philanthropists realized there was a need for more qualified black teachers to teach the masses in the South. Perhaps a letter from Rockefeller Jr. to Buttrick in 1914 referencing black education along with the results of Jones's study not only ignited the GEB, but also motivated their commitment to black higher education. Rockefeller Jr. had "felt for some time that possibly the Board was not performing its full duty to the negroes and that [they] should consider the situation fully and seriously."[92] Philanthropists were also cognizant of the need for better-qualified black ministers, lawyers, and doctors and the only way to ensure qualified professionals was by supporting select black colleges and universities.[93] However, before making such a commitment, they once again surveyed the institutions that remained in existence.

Upon surveying southern black institutions in 1914, Buttrick found some of the same inconsistencies he had observed 12 years earlier with the white institutions; chief among them was the lack of a systematic organizational pattern. Several black institutions were located throughout the South; some were competing against one another in the same communities. Various denominations controlled numerous institutions; yet, many of these institutions were financially struggling to survive. Most of the denominations had founded several schools, and almost all of them were "poorly equipped and meanly supported."[94] Ultimately, he believed there was a need for colleges for blacks that would "train those who [would] lead the race in its efforts to educate and improve itself and that there was not a single institution strong enough to perform this function satisfactorily." Further, he reported, "The waste and the duplication are particularly distressing because the resources would be meager enough, even if concentrated." His recommendation for black colleges and universities was the same as white institutions, "under existing conditions only a few efficient colleges for Negroes can or ought to be maintained."[95]

He also reported his findings to Junior and recommended the development of two or three higher education institutions for blacks and that "something should be done to develop two or possibly three of the medical schools for blacks."[96] As they had done with the white institutions, though with much smaller appropriations, in 1914, the GEB approved $140,000 for seven select black institutions in the South:

$8,000—Atlanta University, Atlanta, GA
$13,000—Florida Baptist Academy, Jacksonville, FL
$70,000—Fisk University, Nashville, TN
$7,000—Lane College, Jackson, TN
$12,500—Livingstone College, Salisbury, NC
$18,000—Shaw University, Raleigh, NC
$11,500—Virginia Union University, Richmond, VA[97]

Interestingly, Atlanta University was one of the seven institutions that received funds; however, the official list recorded neither Morehouse nor Spelman on it, when both had received funding.[98]

During this same time, there were a series of correspondence between Edward Ware, president of Atlanta University, and members of the GEB regarding the possibility of some cooperation. However, there were difficulties forming any type of cooperation because all of the institutions, except Atlanta University, had denominational financial support. Although philanthropists did not allow that to halt their plans of moving forward, the issue was in the forefront when they pointed out, "Morehouse College [was] a strong Baptist institution with very strong support from its denomination, any effort at formal federation would be exceedingly difficult."[99]

In 1918, the GEB sponsored W. T. B. Williams to conduct a study of Atlanta University, and he indicated it "deservedly [had] the reputation for doing good work..... It [had] sent the great majority of its graduates into the cities and larger towns of the South, where they have given good account of themselves as teachers and professional men and women.... In fact it is very largely a local institution." Williams mentioned, however, that the college and the college department should be enlarged, strengthened, and increased. He concluded, "the first great need of Atlanta University...[was] assistance in defraying her debt of $50,000."[100]

Armed with the financial means and the collected data that led to evaluations of each black Atlanta institution, the GEB was poised to act on its decision to "develop two or possibly three higher institutions for blacks." Despite this being the case, there were two critical questions they needed to answer before they could accomplish this task. One, how would they bring these institutions in Atlanta together? Two, who would be the leader not only to bring the institutions together, but also to satisfy all constituencies of the three institutions? The GEB would find the answer to both questions in the person of John Hope.

3

John Hope: Hallmark of the Truest Greatness

> *I knew of most of the major principles in their lives for which my parents gave credit to Dr. Hope: absolute equality without delay; staunch support for his close friend W. E. B. Du Bois; the highest and most rigorous standards for our schools and colleges, if their graduates were to compete successfully in the larger world; impeccable public and private morality, if blacks were to eradicate unjust accusations of laxity and licentiousness. There were other principles—some large, some small—that also became a part of the honorable precepts of living my parents recited almost daily and attributed to Dr. Hope.*
>
> —*John Hope Franklin*[1]

Franklin's heartfelt description of John Hope's positive and inspirational influence in the moral, civic, and personal lives of his parents, qualities passed along to Franklin as "honorable precepts of living," affectionately expressed the charismatic power of John Hope. True humility undergirded Hope's notions of "honorable precepts of living." Perhaps this humility, so unlike the flamboyance of Du Bois or the political artfulness of Booker T. Washington, diminished Hope in the public eye as well as in history books. Even the academic world of higher education studies, particularly black higher education, seemed blind to the depth of influence John Hope had as an educational leader of the early twentieth century.

John Hope Franklin is a name most readily recognized, and few realize that the renowned historian was in fact named for the man who was so pivotal in the historical outcomes of black higher education.[2] Franklin himself admits his knowledge of John Hope came primarily from his parents and secondly from the institutional histories of Atlanta University, Morehouse College, and Spelman College. Franklin also professed he truly did not comprehend Hope until he read his biography by Leroy Davis,[3] published 62 years after his death.

Hope shaped the course of higher education for blacks through his educational leadership and vision, as well as his social and racial activism. Power did not motivate Hope, though he had it. His sense of obligation and commitment was his motivation. One the one hand, he was obligated and committed to the development of black higher education, which meant cultivating relationships with whites and white philanthropists to generate financial support. On the other hand, he had the same obligation and commitment to resolve race problems, which meant treading the waters lightly so as not to disrupt the funding stream for his institution. Thus, Hope struggled with two dilemmas all of his life: an "inner turmoil that resulted from attempting to balance John Hope the college president with John Hope the race leader." Accordingly, Hope "epitomized radical black leadership in the South during the age of Booker T. Washington," which would earn him a place within the spectrum somewhere between Washington and Du Bois.[4]

There were several momentous events in Hope's life. Two of them were his becoming the first black president of both Morehouse College and Atlanta University. Undeniably, Morehouse College's ranking with philanthropists at the turn of the twentieth century was not solely because of its rich history or educational achievements; in 1906, Morehouse's president was John Hope, whom Wallace Buttrick and other members of the GEB regarded with affection and respect.[5] During his presidency at Morehouse, Hope earned the reputation of being a great educational leader and was so noted for his acheivements that by 1929, after the affiliation, he became Atlanta University's first black president.

Given Hope's record, it is of little wonder that his associates and colleagues had a high regard for him and considered him an "outstanding educational statesman of his time," as well as a "Maker of Men." Though Hope was of medium stature, five feet seven inches, he had an undeniable presence, "an imposing figure," and was a man with a "dignity of bearing that singled him out of a crowd."[6] However, most descriptions of him in literature pay particular attention to his physical features denoting his ancestry. This was something the GEB and its members took notice of along with his educational commitment to blacks. Raymond Fosdick, GEB member and later the GEB's president, for example, wrote:

> [John's] father was a Scotsman, and he himself, with his blue eyes, was so light-colored that no one would have guessed that he had Negro blood; he was a quiet, shy, self-deprecatory man, with a genius for administration and a passion for bringing education to his own race.[7]

Though clearly recognizing Hope possessed black blood, it is plausible that Fosdick's reference to Hope's physical appearance, his features, and his background made him more acceptable to philanthropists.[8] Edward A. Jones, author of Morehouse's institutional history, *Candle in the Dark*, also provided a visual image of Hope, when he wrote:

> Much of his Scottish ancestry showed in his reddish hair, which when later it became gray, further enhanced his physical appearance. Mr. Hope's blue-gray eyes, with their fixed penetrating stare, often made the timid student and young teacher uncomfortable and nervous in his presence.[9]

Though Hope was "technically a mulatto" and "looked like a white man with no visible traces of African blood," from birth throughout adulthood, he consistently maintained his black identity, along with his family, and refused to take the alternative path to whiteness that his physical appearance afforded him (Figure 3.1). By contrast, one of his sisters, Sissie, and her family not only left the South because of racial disparities, but also

Figure 3.1 Photograph of Hope family; *Seated left*, John Hope; *Standing left*, Edward Swain; *Standing right*, John Hope Jr.; *Seated right*, Lugenia Burns Hope, Atlanta University Photographs—Individuals.
Source: Atlanta University Center Robert W. Woodruff Library, Atlanta, Georgia.

left behind their black identity. As Davis, Hope's biographer, pointed out, Hope was mindful of his features; in that, his complexion embarrassed him, and he "resented the attention his complexion engendered but seemed to relish every opportunity to reinforce his" black identity.[10] Accordingly, he would elevate himself to a stature that compelled philanthropists to enlist his help in building up higher education for blacks in the South, particularly in Atlanta.

Becoming a President

Throughout Hope's life, he continuously played various roles in his jobs; his experience at Atlanta Baptist was no different.

Because Hope had perfected his oratory skills at Worcester, Brown, and Roger Williams, he was, once again, placed in a speaking position, only this time as a fund-raiser. Growing support of Washington's philosophy of industrial education threatened the ABHMS schools. After Washington's book *Up from Slavery* was published, the support for industrial education for blacks became even more widespread. Having Hope travel around the country and speak on behalf of liberal arts education was the ABHMS' plan of attack against industrial education.[11]

Hope's personal convictions were the driving force behind his seeking a better life for himself and individuals within his reach. He was adamant about education being the vehicle that would provide a better life for blacks. His educational ideology for blacks was more akin to Du Bois's classical education rather than to Washington's industrial education; in that, he wanted an education for blacks that emphasized "the education of the whole man—liberal arts education."[12] However, contrary to belief and in spite of having different philosophies and approaches, neither Washington, Du Bois, nor Hope totally opposed eliminating either type of education. Each realized that blacks needed both types of education, industrial and liberal arts, to become fully educated. Du Bois and Hope maintained:

> There was a place in Negro life for both the Tuskegee type of school with its emphasis upon industrial proficiency and the liberal arts college with its emphasis upon training of teachers and leaders of the race.[13]

Du Bois's recognition of a need for both emphases was also evident in the last two principles of the Niagara Movement's platform. The sixth principle indicated recognition of higher education, and the last stated "a belief in the dignity of labor."[14] Hope also clearly believed that blacks needed both types of education when it came to the education of his son, Edward:

> It came to me very personally with reference to my own boy, now fourteen years old. I took him out of the public schools in Atlanta, and put him into our school, when he finished the fifth

grade. I did not want to do it, because I believe in public school education, but he had absolutely no opportunity in Atlanta to learn anything about working with the hands. Negro children in Atlanta have no opportunity for industrial education in the public schools.[15]

Examining Washington's policies, Kelly Miller pointed out that Washington recognized industrial education was not the only means of education for blacks, when she wrote:

> Mr. Washington is provokingly silent as to the claim of higher education, although his personal actions proclaim loudly enough the belief that is in his heart. The subject of industrial and higher education is merely one of ratio and proportion and not one of fundamental controversy.[16]

In the summer of 1898, the same year Hope began at Atlanta Baptist, the ABHMS sent him on several trips throughout the Midwest and East to persuade Baptists to give money to the society's southern colleges for blacks, to "spread the doctrine of a liberal education for Negroes," and to erode Washington's emphasis on vocational education.[17] In one speech to a church group, he stated:

> Baptists of the North, I have in a simple manner tried to show you the place the higher education among my people...A Negro may specialize [doctor, teacher, or minister], but he must know many things first, for he is a leader.
>
> There is a great host of people, lacking any sort of information about the Negro and totally indifferent as to what is going on among us in the South....The question with the best friends, not of the Negro but of the country ought to be: How shall we reach that great mass of people who are totally unacquainted with one of the greatest problems of this country and absolutely indifferent to it?[18]

Hope was a popular speaker known for "the breadth of his knowledge, his uncanny ability to recall facts instantly, and his mounting confrontations with the status quo." His fund-raising skills, persuasive speaking abilities, and dedication to the ABHMS also made him popular among members of the ABHMS, such as Henry L. Morehouse, Thomas J. Morgan, and Malcolm MacVicar, who controlled both Roger Williams University and Atlanta Baptist. He also became a notable figure in the black community and among the educational leaders of black institutions in Atlanta.[19]

In the late 1890s, black Baptist constituents were at odds with the Mission Society and wanted more control of black institutions; consequently, separate groups of black Baptists emerged. In the midst of this controversy, George Sale resigned as president of Atlanta Baptist and became secretary of education for the ABHMS, leaving a presidential vacancy. Although Hope was not the perfect candidate for the position, the ABHMS felt he was the best candidate available. In June 1906, Hope became Atlanta Baptist's first black president. This was especially significant because he was "the first of his race ever appointed president of any ABHMS school in the organization's seventy-four-year history."[20] Because blacks wanted more control of Baptist schools, and more representation on the boards of Atlanta Baptist and of Spelman, appointing Hope as president served to sublimate some of the strife that was occurring. For David Levering Lewis, historian and Du Bois's biographer, Hope's appointment as president "was proof that black-run institutions were no longer ipso facto synonymous with retrogression."[21]

Hope received congratulatory wishes from several people on his appointment to the presidency, with one being from Wallace Buttrick, then secretary of the GEB:

> It was with great pleasure that I learned from Dr. Morehouse a few days ago that you had been appointed Acting President of Atlanta Baptist College. The appointment meets my hearty and most cordial approval...I am confident that you will do a good work in the very best way, and in all you may be sure of my friendship.[22]

However, not all of the ABHMS members shared Buttrick's level of confidence in Hope. He was obviously on trial because of the "acting president" title that Buttrick referenced. Some members, such as Malcolm MacVicar, believed it "would be one hundred years before colored people would have men prepared to be presidents to preside over colleges."[23] Many in black society and some liberal whites also had reservations about Hope in this position.

The ABHMS observed Hope's presidency for a year. The prospect of having more black college presidents in the future was contingent upon his performance. His temporary status gave the ABHMS time to examine his administrative abilities and to prepare for the possibility of future demands of appointing more blacks as presidents to other Baptist colleges.[24]

Despite reservations and a probationary period, Hope participated in several events that demonstrated his activism and his commitment to blacks' equality. Just two months into his probationary presidency, he was "the only college president (black or white) that took part in the deliberations" of the historic Niagara Movement meeting. Convened in August 1906 at historic Storer College in Harper's Ferry, one hundred participants, mostly black with a few white northern whites, came together under the leadership of Du Bois in order to "rededicate themselves to the principles of full equality."[25] Hope recalled this was a bold step for him to take, especially since the movement was "the most radical activity of the race, in direct opposition to the theories best supported by financial supply." Moreover, as a newly elected president of a college, "wholly dependent on outside help," he later admitted that this course of action was a "precarious and even dangerous" one to take.[26] Nevertheless, he joined the movement and became the chairman of the Education Committee. At this meeting, he "prepared the report and led the session that reflected the organization's steps to improve [black] education." In doing so, he made the following recommendations: "Prepare a pamphlet on conditions in southern black schools to be sent to legislatures and the public; increase efforts to secure the cooperation of [black] editors and ministers; and sponsor educational forums."[27]

Hope not only attended this meeting because he believed in the movement's philosophy of equality for blacks, but also because he was close friends with Du Bois. He and Du Bois found each other "companionable" and were "two of a determined group of colored men in Atlanta who constituted the progressives and radicals of their time."[28] Lewis, Du Bois's biographer, described this close relationship as one in which "Hope became not only [Du Bois's] most intimate male friend but one with whom Du Bois always dealt as an equal."[29]

Correspondence between Hope and Du Bois revealed a steady flow of communications throughout Hope's life where they shared their feelings and beliefs regarding blacks' plight in America. Correspondence also shed light on how Hope provided Du Bois with information regarding the situation in the South and facts about blacks, of which some of them Du Bois later incorporated into his editorials at *The Crisis*.[30]

Ironically, while Du Bois, Hope, and others were initiating the Niagara Movement (the foundation of what was to become the National Association for the Advancement of Colored People [NAACP]) in order to have their voices heard and hopefully to inspire political actions that would grant blacks full and equal rights under the law, a wave of "negrophobia" swept over the country. Atlanta in particular experienced the most "sensational riot" of the entire South three months into Hope's probationary presidency and one month after he attended the second Niagara Movement meeting.[31] The riot lasted four days in September of 1906. Gary M. Pomerantz, in *Where Peachtree Meets Sweet Auburn*, detailed how boys delivering the newspapers added to the frenzy when they shouted through the streets of Atlanta:

> *Extra! Third Assault on White Women by a Negro Brute!*
> *Extra! Bold Negro Kisses White Girl's Hand!*
> *Extra! Bright Mulatto Insults White Girls!*[32]

Newspaper articles intensified feelings against blacks, so much so that "one editorial called for the revival of the Ku Klux Klan, and another went so far as to offer a reward for a 'lynching bee' in Atlanta." Several historians, such as John Hope Franklin, provided descriptions of whites' fear when he wrote, whites formed "an outraged, panic-stricken mob" against any black in sight; that "blacks were beaten, killed, and their houses were looted and burned."[33] As the base of organized racist aggression,

Atlanta became the hub of American negrophobia—an attitude that reigned for 40 years. These events combined with Thomas Dixon's controversial novel, *The Clansman: An Historical Romance of the Ku Klux Klan*, the second novel of his Klan trilogy published in 1905, undoubtedly added fuel to the riots. When reviewing Lugenia Hope's notes of the riots, Davis indicated she wrote:

> White men dispersed in all directions looking for [blacks] on whom to vent their anger.... The mob concentrated on unsuspecting [blacks] caught in the downtown area.... The victims were maimed, mutilated, and killed in the most grotesque fashion.[34]

The Atlanta Baptist campus was located not too far from downtown. Fearing the race riots would reach the campus and harm its residence, Hope, armed with a gun, along with other men, patrolled the campus until the governor of the state deployed militia to stand guard. The riots, in the end, did not reach the campus. In the aftermath of the four-day Atlanta riots, most blacks moved away from whites and concentrated their residences and businesses between the downtown area of Atlanta and near the west side of Atlanta University; some blacks moved to sections in east Atlanta.[35]

After the riots, one of the first priorities Hope embraced as president of Atlanta Baptist was expansion of the college, and this meant enormous fund-raising efforts. Hope's initial attempts were futile. He wrote to people in the North describing what he was doing at Atlanta Baptist to no avail. Some of the people in the North were not yet convinced of the idea of teaching liberal arts to blacks, neither were philanthropists.[36]

Before becoming president of Atlanta Baptist, Hope had once criticized Andrew Carnegie as the "man with the pocketful of libraries," disapproved of Carnegie's "publicized doubts as to the Negroes' capacity for full citizenship," and publicly protested against Carnegie providing money for a public library in Atlanta exclusively for whites.[37] Despite these indictments of Carnegie, pragmatism and realism mitigated his personal beliefs. Being cognizant of the numerous obstacles confronting black education, he understood that, "blacks did not yet have the economic resources, administrative skills, or political clout to assume full responsibility for their own educational development." Inevitably, he wrote Carnegie for funds; and not surprisingly, Carnegie denied his request.[38]

He then enlisted help from his friend Major Robert R. Moton of Hampton Institute, and asked Moton to intercede on his behalf.[39] In a letter to Wallace Buttrick, executive secretary of the GEB, Moton asked Buttrick to appeal to the GEB and Andrew Carnegie on Hope's behalf, when he wrote:

> In my opinion, he [Hope] has very good ideas as to what should be done in educational institutions, and I feel very sure that his ideas would coincide with yours. [Hope] is hopeing [sic] this year to raise about $10,000 or $15,000 to put up a new building and I suggested to him that he get a letter from you or Mr. Gates or Mr. Carnegie, or someone who would be willing perhaps to put up such an amount into such a work. If Mr. Hope should write you, I am sure you would give him all the aid and advice you can. I think it is a splendid opportunity to work out an ideal plan of education, and I think Mr. Hope will do it. You know of him and his work as well as I do.[40]

Although Buttrick once claimed he had confidence in and a fondness for Hope when he was elected president, he nevertheless refused to assist him on behalf of the GEB and suggested that he contact the ABHMS:

> I cordially share your high estimate of [Hope's] worth as a man and an educator.
> I wish it were practicable for me to give him a letter to Mr. Carnegie, but my associates do not think it wise for me to give letters of introduction and commendation even to my own personal friends from the fact that it is not possible to dissociate Buttrick the man from Buttrick the secretary of the General Education Board.... My recommendation, therefore, would be

that President Hope shall confer with Dr. Sale, superintendent of education for the Home Mission Society, and have him bring the matter to the attention of Dr. Morehouse, the corresponding secretary.[41]

After Hope's attempt through Buttrick failed, he had a choice either to function without the much-needed funds, or to rely on the one person able to convince philanthropists to give money to a black institution. Again, being the pragmatist that he was, he chose the latter. Booker T. Washington was ironically the person Hope sought aid from in matters of fund-raising, particularly in gaining support from white philanthropists. Though despised by some blacks in the country, during this time, Washington was the one "Negro educator capable of tapping the sources of Northern philanthropy."[42] He had cultivated relationships with white philanthropists unlike any other black at the time such that they not only "gave him money," but also "offered advice because he seemed to be one of them."[43] Illustrating his influence with philanthropists and demonstrating his lack of constraints, Washington wrote to Carnegie on Hope's behalf, and said:

> This is one of the oldest and best established colleges for our people in the South. It is doing real college work and sending out men of the highest type of usefulness. We have several employed as teachers at Tuskegee, and I know what they are accomplishing is useful all through the South. Besides, this institution has the confidence and good will of the leading white people in Atlanta. Several of the leading white people are on its board of trustees.
>
> Professor John Hope, the president is a man of the highest and cleanest character.
>
> I feel that if you can see your way clear to help this school, you will be doing a good thing.[44]

By his action, Washington not only helped Hope receive funds from Andrew Carnegie and the GEB, but also introduced him to these wealthy philanthropists and opened the door for him to develop a lasting relationship with them.[45]

Du Bois and Hope's other friends were displeased, and chastised him for accepting money from Carnegie. However, Hope felt that the only person who warranted an explanation was Du Bois because he had been loyal to Du Bois and his point of view, "not blatantly so," but loyal nonetheless. Hope had followed and believed in Du Bois, even tried "where [Du Bois] was not understood, to interpret him and show that he [was] right."[46] He explained to Du Bois:

> It is also true that through the kindness of Mr. Booker T. Washington I was enabled to secure a conditional offer of ten thousand dollars from Mr. Andrew Carnegie.... Without any effort on my part, a friend of the school first approached Mr. Washington and pointing a way to me which seemed, and still seems, to me perfectly honorable and so generous as to have called for selfishness on my part not to accept on behalf of a school that needed the assistance and ought to be helped rather than hampered by its president.... Then without any persuasion or pressure from any one I went frankly to Mr. Washington, told of what I heard; told him my purpose for the school and that larger facilities would mean better opportunity for carrying on the work of the school as it now is without any change in its educational policy and ideals. After hearing this, he was quite as willing to help and did so.[47]

With the funds he received, Hope erected Sale Hall, a three-story building of red brick and sober architectural design. This structure contained the administrative offices on the first floor, classrooms on all floors, and a spacious auditorium with seating capacity for seven hundred. In the basement, they used additional space for the Manual Training Department, and in later years used it for classrooms.[48] The Manual Training facility was essentially a printing office that produced the institution's paper, *The Advance*.[49]

During Hope's first ten years as president, Atlanta Baptist flourished. His chief interest was "the education of men and boys"; in that, he gave of himself "to his work in such whole-hearted fashion largely accounts for the rapid advance that Morehouse College has made." In 1913, the institution changed its name from Atlanta Baptist College to Morehouse College in honor of Henry L. Morehouse, secretary of the ABHMS. The college's academy was four times larger in 1915–1916 than it had been in 1905–1906, with 178 students in comparison to 41, respectively.⁵⁰

However, in the midst of Morehouse's flourishing, flames rose from race riots and violence against blacks erupted throughout the country. In 1909, Hope was the only college president to attend a protest meeting in New York that addressed the race riot in Springfield, Illinois. The NAACP was founded at this meeting. By 1915, the NAACP appointed Hope to the Advisory Board. Although he served on the Board, he declined to "accept the position of national organizer because of his allegiance to Morehouse."⁵¹ Ironically, this was the same year philanthropists started focusing more heavily on race matters, particularly as it pertained to education.

Interracial Conference on Negro Education

At various times, correspondences between Hope, philanthropists, and members of the GEB provided terms for discussing racial issues separately from the cultural norms and allowed giver and receiver to transcend historic inequalities and long-standing cultural stereotypes current in the mainstream. One such time was the GEB's first annually sponsored Interracial Conference on Negro Education in November 1915, the same month of Booker T. Washington's death.⁵² For two decades, 1895–1915, Washington was the liaison between white philanthropists and blacks and the most influential spokesperson for blacks. Upon his death, a void prompted the philanthropists' search for a new black educational leader. There is little doubt John Hope's appearance, demeanor, business and leadership acumen, and rapport with individuals fostered his appeal to the GEB, as they regarded him as "a new generation of leadership among the Negroes, new in a sense that was more dynamic and more sharply defined."⁵³ Hope therefore became the black leader the GEB collaborated with and relied on in building up higher education for blacks, particularly in Atlanta.

Hope attended the 1915 conference and was very straightforward expressing the concerns blacks had regarding the type of education they would receive, as well as the negative consequences of eliminating or combining denominational institutions. The minutes from this conference are almost two-hundred pages, of which a large portion involved Hope. The attendees included individuals such as Abraham Flexner, Bruce Payne, E. C. Sage, James H. Dillard, Thomas Jesse Jones, Fayette McKenzie, Jackson Davis, Wickliffe Rose, W. T. B. Williams, Robert R. Moton, and Sidney Frissell. From all indications, this conference outlined the first steps in developing policies that built up higher education for blacks. It also indicated that the GEB had begun to give considerably more thought to the education of blacks, particularly in the area of higher education.[54]

The purpose of the conference was the GEB's desire to "develop a general program of principles and policies that would guide in determining the specific things to be done in each state." The five topics on the agenda for discussion were as follows.

1. What might the Board do to cooperate with public school authorities in developing state school systems for Negroes, adequate in extent and adjusted in content to local need?
2. What is sound policy in reference to private secondary and industrial schools supported by:
   (a) Negro organizations
   (b) Northern boards
   (c) Independent boards?
3. How can such schools be controlled and supervised?
4. What contributions can be made by the large and strong institutions, such as Tuskegee, Hampton, etc.? For example, how can these larger institutions train teachers who will adapt themselves to small and modest surroundings?
5. What is sound policy in respect to the number, scope, support, and development of higher education institutions for Negroes?[55]

Soon after the conference had begun, Hope spoke out on every issue, such as low teacher salaries, the inadequacy of job opportunities for his graduates because of the low salaries, the school system for blacks, and the higher academic institutions for blacks.[56] Early into the conference, Hope questioned the board's use of terms, when he inquired of Hollis Frissell, the chairman of the conference, "I thought I would like to get this clear, Doctor, just what we mean by 'adequate in extent and adjusted in content.' I would like to know about that."[57] Abraham Flexner answered, which led to further deliberation for the committee members to ponder, and explained:

> What can we do in the way of cooperating with State and municipal authorities that will bend in the direction of developing as adequate a school system for Negro children as now exists for whites. Of course, that is a long look ahead, and it is the direction that we are, for the moment, concerned in, rather than the expectation of any easy or immediate attainment, but that is what we are working toward.[58]

Though Flexner reinforced the GEB's position of working within a segregated society, Hope was not completely satisfied with Flexner's response. He further explained blacks' concerns with the type of education they would receive, while he simultaneously tried to get clarification of the terminology used, when he responded back to Flexner and stated:

> I had just come from a meeting of Negro teachers of the South, and they are more concerned than they would tell you what the various superintendents of education intend to do for Negro schools in the country and in the city. I heard one man, last Friday, raise this question, whether you are going to give actually a different kind of education for negroes [sic], and one place they have stopped giving the colored teachers the same examinations they give the white teachers, and the question is arising whether there is to be a public school education for white children in the South and another education for colored children in the South, and I was just wondering whether this "adequate in extent and adjusted in content" had any reference to that at all.[59]

Although Hope clearly presented his concerns, it was obvious that blacks would not immediately receive the same educational opportunities as whites, but not without a good reason. Flexner affirmed this when he said, "blacks should not want the same education as whites received," especially when the education for whites was not as adequate as they had once thought.[60] Neither the type of education expected to be provided nor an explanation of what was meant by "adequate in extent and adjusted in content" was decided at the time, only deliberated.

As mentioned in Chapter 2, the GEB conducted surveys on black colleges and universities and found them too numerous and the curriculum too varied and not effective. The discussion had begun at the conference surrounding the possibility of supporting a few select black institutions. When the discussion later turned to the "sound policy in respect to the number, scope, support, and development of higher academic institutions for Negroes," Chairman Frissell opened the floor for discussion and asked Hope to lead the discussion. However, seemingly surprised by this request, Hope responded, "When you get to talking about colleges, you are talking about denominational schools almost altogether, and I was coming up to find out what was the policy of the General Education Board." To this end, Flexner responded to Hope and stated, "We are asking you to make it."[61] The following is the exchange regarding this matter.

> *Dr. Hope*: The first thing I thought of was the word "number," and then of course I thought about Georgia. Georgia is a very big state, and it is not nearly so full of people as it is going to be, and I do not believe there are going to be many more colleges for Negroes established very soon, and I had in mind a criticism of the schools in Atlanta, that there are so many of them there together, when they ought to be separated, and as I thought that over, I have wondered why in the world the white people have not seen that thing and profited by it, but they are doing exactly the same thing. They are increasing the number of institutions of higher education in Atlanta. In the last two years, they have put in two more, and I am beginning to wonder whether after all it is a bad thing to have all those schools in that great center, such as Atlanta is going to be.
>
> I believe it is possible to have the same kind of relationship between the schools so that they won't be under such heavy expense as they are now, and might increase the efficiency, but it is going to be a pretty hard job to talk about dismantling any of them. You take our own school, for instance. It is

a Baptist school; Spelman Seminary is a Baptist school, and the denominational challenge that the North is getting rid of is growing strong in the South. It is among the white schools as well as the colored schools. Instance the starting of that great Methodist school at Atlanta because they thought that Vanderbilt was not quite as Methodist as it ought to be. It seems to me we have to reckon with those schools as we have them, and help them as far as we can. The number of Negro college students is increasing every year. There are more than twice as many Negro college students in our school than there were when I became President nine years ago, and I think Fisk University will be even more than that, and I really think when we come to realize how big a population we are going to have, and we looked to the future of it today, it is a serious question in my mind whether we ought to think about getting rid of those schools. I believe that is one thing that we have in our mind, how to get rid of them.

It might be a good thing to get rid of some of them, but where they are as efficient, or as I said this morning have a backing, that is, a Negro constituency, it's a serious question whether we ought to get rid of them.

Take in Atlanta, I think perhaps Mr. Jones might perhaps criticize Morris Brown College as not being up to standard. Morris Brown College has a great big Negro constituency back of it, and with all its faults is an example of Negro self-help, which you have got to reckon with. You take our school; You say Lane University is doing the same work we are doing. You may say that Spelman Seminary and Lane University do the same work, but what is happening? Here come along 300,000 Negro Baptists who say, "We will do more for education this year than we have ever done," and they mention a lot of their schools—two schools which White people are supporting, namely Spelman Seminary and Morehouse College. You have to think a long while before you get rid of these schools because if you did, you would be getting rid of a certain amount of incentive of Negroes to pay for their own education. I do not know that I have touched the topic at all, so I would rather you would ask me some questions, but I know that Atlanta has been under fire for years as having too many colleges, and about fifteen years ago I wrote an article myself, to say how we might handle that situation. I thought I knew it very finely then, but I do not know so much about it now as I did then. (Laughter)

Chairman Frissell: What proportion should you say we ought to allow, President Hope? That is what proportion of College men should you say we ought to get from the Negro race at present time?

Dr. Hope: Doctor, I have never thought that out, but I do think this, that the race is suffering greatly for lack of good, strong leadership which we ought to expect from the colleges, and if the colleges are not furnishing that kind of leadership, then we ought to fix the colleges up so that they will give it, because it is to be expected that the colleges would furnish that kind of leadership; not necessarily the kind of men that would make the harness or do the farming or build a railroad, not necessarily that, but a man who can think and guide the harness or farm or railroad. I remember hearing a gentleman from Japan say that when Japan merged from its old self to its Western self, that the men who led Japan out of its ancient self into its modern self were men who had been taught philosophy and the use of the sword.

Chairman Frissell: The what?

Dr. Hope: The use of the sword, but he said that that vehicle, that means of education, had been so thoroughly worked, that the men were educated, and I believe that is really what we are to look out for, whether Hampton or at Fisk. We have got to look for certain number of educated men who, and it does not matter what their vocation is, will have a sufficient breadth of vision to guide the Negroes. For instance, I told my boys last year that Negro firemen on the railroad would be in far better shape to make demands if a certain number of educated Negros became railroad firemen, and I believe that.

I used to wonder about sleeping car porters, and a great deal has been said about the college men going into the work of Pullman porters, but I am beginning to see that a sprinkling of college men among the Pullman porters might do a great deal towards organizing those five thousand or seven thousand men, so that as a group of Negroes they would really be felt in the nation. There are about seven thousand of them. It seems a pity that seven thousand hard working Negro men should not have some kind of understanding among themselves so that they could be felt, and we have to prepare a certain number of Negros—I could not answer the question how many, but we do need down-right broad Negro leadership.

Dr. Sage: May I ask a few questions?
Chairman Frissell: Certainly.
Dr. Sage: I would like to ask Dr. Hope how many colleges the Negro people need. Now, when I speak of "colleges," I mean colleges. I mean institutions whose work is above that of high school. I am speaking of distinct work, college work. I do not mean institutions that have elementary and secondary grades, and the whole lot. I am not speaking of institutions which now call themselves colleges, but I mean colleges. How many colleges do the Negroes need?
Dr. Hope: Doctor, I have learned so much here today, I could not answer that as I could have this morning (laughter). I will have said the little State of Massachusetts has ever so many colleges, and every one is needed, and certainly when Georgia has as big a population as Massachusetts, she would need more colleges than Massachusetts needs now, but I would not quite answer it that way now, because Dr. Flexner has said that that does not make any difference, about what these other schools have done; we have got to think about educational questions anew, the one that you did keep or the two that you did keep would have to be pretty big institutions of learning. We have in our school now college classes with over thirty.
Dr. Sage: Freshmen; what are they, freshmen?
Dr. Hope: I say classes. They are mixed.
Dr. Sage: This is the point. I am speaking now about a college. I am not speaking about mixed classes. I am not speaking about an institution [,] which is now called a college.

After much debate over how many students were in the classes, of which Hope indicated they only had 60, and the fact that it was a relatively low number to make a college, the attention returned to Georgia and the South.

Dr. Sage: Then if all the college students were all together, they would not quite make one good college at the present time, one small college? They would not make one small college at the present time?
Dr. Hope: Yes.
Dr. Sage: Of course Georgia is very far ahead many of the other States in the matter of number of college students. Now the

question comes back to this, how many colleges for the South, for your Southern people, do you need?

Dr. Hope: We said a while ago we were going to take conditions. One Negro college boy means the sifting out of hundreds of fellows from the grades and the academy, and they have to have that incentive to bring them up. Now, the denominational element is very strong. A lot of those people would not send their boys and girls to a school if it were not of their denomination, and it is the denominations that are fostering this college idea to a very large extent, so it would not be so easy to have one college without reference to its denomination. There is the difficulty.

Referring to the institutions in Georgia, Hope admitted there were too many colleges in Georgia doing the same work and that he could see the colleges possibly forming some kind of relationship in order to eliminate heavy expenses. Yet, Hope warned:

But here is the thing I fear, and this very question came up last summer in Cincinnati. If we should do away with these denominational schools that are run very largely by the Northern societies and are giving the best sort of education that is being given, what would happen? The Negroes would say, "We are going to educate our children in our own schools," and they would start up another college, and we would be worse off than we are now. That is exactly what would happen in Georgia, if we should do away with Morehouse College and Spelman Seminary. That is exactly what would happen. The Negro Baptists of Georgia would start a Baptist College of their own.[62]

The discussion continued to focus on the Atlanta institutions and duplication of effort. At this point, they yielded the floor to Dr. Jones and his study of the institutions:[63]

Dr. Jones: The duplication is not as great, as frequent, as one would think at first. I have been looking over the field. We have been talking of Atlanta, the duplication is apparently more there than anywhere else in the South. Dr. Dillard has told us of the change that has taken place in New Orleans where it was second in duplication. We have in Marshall,

Texas, a good Baptist school and a good Methodist School that are trying to do the same work. In Austin, Texas, we have a Methodist school and another school trying to do the same work. In Columbia, South Carolina we have two schools, and A. & V. (?) and a Baptist, and so on. There are a number of cases, but when you examine carefully the duplication is not as great as at first appears.

Dr. Flexner: Dr. Jones, if you look at it, however, from the standpoint of trained eligible students, not locally, not how many duplication is there in Atlanta, but how many competent college students are there in these southern states, and then how many colleges are there? Is there any great superfluity, even if you do not call it "duplication"?

Dr. Jones: There is no doubt if you think of these schools, according to their names, that there is a superfluity as well as duplication.

Dr. Flexner: Don't they all spend money according to their names, more or less?

Dr. Jones: Oh no, they differ tremendously. Morris Brown, for instance, which is in Atlanta, has only ten college students. It has but five hundred students altogether. A lot of them elementary.

Dr. Flexner: Who teaches the ten college students?

Dr. Jones: The teachers who are in the secondary grades give part of their time, and there is where a great deal of loss takes place. I gave you the extreme example, Holly Springs for instance. There is a danger there within the schools of sacrificing secondary pupils for the sake of a few college students, and there again the land-grant comes in, the agricultural mechanical school.

Dr. Flexner: Just say "land-grant" and then practice it after you get home. (Laughter)

Dr. Jones: They are much more eager to do college work than they are to do secondary or industrial work. If you care, I do not know whether you would like to have me spend the time in analyzing this situation in Atlanta as an illustration. You have there Spelman and Morehouse, both of them Baptist institutions within about two blocks of each other as you know. They represent a denominational affiliation of 340,000 people. Out of 500,000 church members in Georgia, 340,000 are Baptists, and the Baptists are now more and more looking to those institutions.

The other split has practically gone out of existence as Dr. Hope has said. Over the other hill, a mile or so away, is Clark, which is the head of the large system of Methodist school; theoretically at the head. Actually in the school grade, it is not very much in advance if at all in advance of the number of the other schools, who are working in that direction, and the Methodists of the South, that particular branch represents about 300,000, not in Georgia alone, but in the whole South that want to make Clark University the head of the whole system, and Atlanta is well suited for that. They have there a big plan. The Theological Seminary has an endowment of $500,000 or more. They have a certain claim therefore to existence, because they do plan and are working very definitively towards that centralization of their system at Clark.

Now the Morris Brown is the head of the system. That has, as its membership, about 500,000, speaking of the whole South. They are trying to make it the strong school. There is not as much centralization there, however, as there in the M.E. I am very hopeful—well, somewhat hopeful, not very hopeful, that they will move from Atlanta to Macon. They have land in Macon, and they have talked of it, and I am inclined to think, with encouragement from the outside, if we bring any influence, that they would agree to go.

Now, the problem that naturally occurs to our mind is Atlanta. Atlanta University has not now and never had a denominational backing. The Congregationalists are very few, but the first school was in Atlanta, and it went with each of these denominations, as they came in, that they do not come in without reason, and they came and there was a good reason for their coming. Now Atlanta in the years it has worked there has turned out and has supplied a larger number of teachers, I think I am safe in saying this President Hope, a larger number of teachers especially for the schools than any other college in Georgia. Would you agree to that statement?

Dr. Hope: I doubt that. Than any other one you mean?
Dr. Jones: Than any other one, certainly. That is what I mean; not all of them.
Dr. Hope: I was thinking this. One reason why you see the University teachers so permanent is that many of them are principals of the city schools. When you think of the country school work, Spelman Seminary has done a tremendous work there.

Dr. Jones: Of course they have contributed largely. I have not made, and it is not possible to make the analysis statistically, but the Atlanta graduates have a wonderful record all through Georgia and all through the South. Its support, while not denominational, is a very real support from the North. It calls on a group of people who would not be as much interested in any other school. It calls on a cultural group, an educational group that has a real contribution to make to the South, and it seems to me that in view of the contribution that Atlanta has made itself to Georgia and to the neighboring states, and because also of the group in the North that will give it aid, that it has a claim, even though it seems to be as much duplicated by other institutions, and so I have rather come to the conclusion that our hope of variation here or of avoiding duplication is by urging these schools to accept a different sphere of activity and that Atlanta University would make itself what is really has been in actual fact, a teachers' college. There is no school in the South that claims to be a teachers' college. Let it take any name, as well as any plan, still more any plan than it is now in the place of teachers' college, and each of the other schools would then be justified, either by denominational affiliation that is large and extensive,—and Atlanta University would get its justification from the type of work that it is doing, and the support it will get for some time to come from the North.

Accommodating the opposing poles of sound business planning in contrast to strong denominational, emotional ties was thus the crux of working out an acceptable plan to all for continuing higher education for blacks in Atlanta. As the next chapters further discuss, working together, John Hope and the GEB in the forefront, with the Rockefellers behind the scene, found the solution.

4

Layers of Complexity

Academics versus vocationalism. Racism versus progressivism. Growth versus regression or stagnation. Irony, paradox, and ambiguity were the mélange of social constructs and life perspectives that collectively capture the complexity of the reality faced by Hope, the GEB, and the Rockefellers, as they worked to create true higher education institutions for blacks. In practical terms, this mélange took form as two broad overlapping layers. Unique insight was required to reconcile the confusing array. Rockefeller Sr.'s systematic methodology honed in his business enterprises, along with the GEB's analysis and investigative approach, had to combine with John Hope's inspirational leadership to solve the problems faced by Atlanta's three nascent black institutions providing higher education.

Two broad layers of complexity challenged the early years of the establishment of collegiate level education for blacks from the outset of emancipation. Northern missionary societies, from the beginning of emancipation, recognized the need for college-educated black leaders and thus were the first to commit to creating educational institutions for newly-freed slaves. The missionaries' goals were to duplicate in the South the curricula of their New England collegiate schools; they envisioned a curriculum consisting of Greek, Latin, and mathematics. These subject matters, however, went well beyond the educational "readiness" of the willing, but unprepared students. Ironically, the condition of slavery had by law prohibited slaves from even rudimentary education, so that initiating collegiate level work could only be accomplished after providing elementary and then college preparatory instruction. Thus, despite using "college" as a designation for these schools, the missionary schools, in fact, functioned as elementary schools, which in time transitioned into high schools, normal schools, theological schools, and ultimately colleges and universities. The ambiguity of calling a school a college or a university, when in reality it functioned as an elementary school, was one broad layer in the array of complexity surrounding the establishment of black colleges.

A need for black teachers, especially for elementary level instruction, was also a part of this layer of complexity. To meet this need, missionary schools eventually created Normal Departments for the purpose of training teachers for primary (elementary) and secondary (high school) instruction. Missionary societies and philanthropic agencies were also concerned with educating black ministers and other missionaries. Additionally, the missionary societies were as concerned with increasing their denominational numbers as much as they were concerned with educating the freed slaves.

Together, these various needs and concerns created among the three Atlanta institutions duplication at each level of instruction and at great expense, particularly when one takes into consideration the relatively small enrollment numbers. Expense and duplication of instruction together formed the connection from the first layer of complexity to the second broad layer of complexity.

The second broad layer involved financing this education. These institutions' financial backing came from benevolent donations of their particular denominations and blacks in the communities. This benevolence, paradoxically, was both beneficial and detrimental. It was beneficial in that it provided a never-before given elementary education, but was also detrimental because it was in many ways disorganized and therefore not effective overall. It was beneficial for southern blacks because southern states' legislators increasingly refused to finance public education for blacks. It was detrimental because industrialists who were willing to use philanthropic agencies to aid these schools were unwilling to finance the duplication in all three Atlanta institutions. Table 4.1 outlines the duplication of

Table 4.1 Overlapping curricular structure

Year	Atlanta University	Atlanta Baptist Seminary (Morehouse College)	Atlanta Female Baptist Seminary (Spelman College)
1865	Established schools on Jenkins Street and Walton Springs Primary/Grammar School 64 students 40 registers in spelling 12 for reading 3 for arithmetic 2 for geography 1 for writing in paper Daily *Bible* used as regular reading Used *McGuffey's Reader* as text[1]		
1866	Storrs Schools—*two former schools combined* Created Washburn Memorial Orphan Asylum AMA erected Ayer School		
1867	Established Atlanta University *(combined Storrs, Washburn, and Ayer schools)*	Founded as Augusta Institute in Augusta, GA *(main focus on the ministry)*	
1869	Opened Higher Normal/Normal Department to train teachers[2]		
1870	University enrollment increased from 89 to 170 students; 124 boarders and 46 day students Opened Preparatory School		

continued

Table 4.1—Continued

Year	Atlanta University	Atlanta Baptist Seminary (Morehouse College)	Atlanta Female Baptist Seminary (Spelman College)
	65 students; 3 years—junior (38), middle (26), and senior prep (1); *(junior prep equal to the first year of high school; curriculum—higher arithmetic, algebra, geometry, ancient history, ancient geography, Latin and Greek)* Opened Theology Department—critical studies of the Bible, lecture on mental and moral philosophy, church history and natural theology, management of minister's duties, etc.; 3 students	52 students Curriculum designed to train ministers and teachers[3]	
1871	Preparatory Department (*high school*); 65 students (38% of the student body); three classes (senior, middle and junior)—*higher arithmetic, algebra, geometry, ancient history, ancient geography, Latin and Greek*	245 students 150 were ministerial students Most students were on the primary and high school levels[4] Primary branches extended to more advanced areas of algebra, botany, geometry, Greek, Latin, "natural philosophy," physiology, and rhetoric	
1872	Split the Normal Department Higher Normal Department—42 students—*four years-grammar and high school curriculum* Lower Normal—trained primary teachers and prepared students for Preparatory and Normal Courses—*primary, grammar school* Opened College Department[5]		

1873	Lower Normal changed to Normal Course—ordinary grammar school and first two years of Higher Normal Courses
	Opened Scientific Preparatory Department—two years; prepared students to pursue college scientific subjects that led to Bachelor of Science degree
	Graduates first students from Higher Normal School; 4 female students
	Graduated recipients of BA degrees
1874	Preparatory Department redesigned as the College Preparatory Department
	Agricultural Department—same as Scientific course, plus, agricultural chemistry, entomology, and zoology
1876	Closed Theology Department[6]
	13 graduates this year; College Department's first graduating class with Bachelor of Arts degree (6); Normal Department (4); and Bible Course (3)
1879	Department of Industrial Training—farming and gardening; household science for females; metal and woodwork for males	Relocated from Augusta, Georgia, to Atlanta, Georgia
1880	Extended Preparatory Department course of study to four years	Normal Course—*three years of grammar school*
	Higher Normal Department changed to Normal Department—four years that consisted of grammar and high school curriculum, arithmetic, algebra, geometry, and geology	Academy Course—*secondary program, high school* Theological Course—*two years*

continued

Table 4.1—Continued

Year	Atlanta University	Atlanta Baptist Seminary (Morehouse College)	Atlanta Female Baptist Seminary (Spelman College)
1881	Changed Normal Course to Grammar School—*five grades consisting of reading, spelling, grammar, geography with maps, US history, elementary geometry, botany, and physiology, writing, vocal music and gymnastics* Transferred work in Agricultural Department to Department of Industrial Training	Normal Course—*three years of grammar school; 41 students* Academy Course—*high school* Theological Course—*two years*	Founded as Atlanta Baptist Female Seminary Curriculum centered around missionary work; household industry and racial uplift
1882	Grammar Department—*extended to eight grades, a five-year course; 61% of student body* Preparatory courses reduced to three years—*junior class (freshmen) transferred to Normal course* Created Postgraduate Course—*two years for graduates of the Normal Department—special training in nursing, household affairs, and organization of mission work*[7]	Dropped Theological Course Normal Course *(two years of grammar school, two years of high school)* Opened Collegiate Department *(included a Scientific Course of four years duration)* Classical Course (six years course—*four years of Latin; three years of Greek, plus chemistry, geology, zoology, logic, trigonometry, astronomy, and political science)*	

1883	154 students Normal Course—*first three years prerequisite for Scientific Course; plus, two years taken from Classical was added to Normal Course* Classical Course (reduced to four years)[8]	293 students	30 boarders Model School opened—*four classes that provided opportunity for observation and practice teaching* Model School Infirmary—*courses in nurse training*
1884	Normal Course— 9 graduates Theological Department— 4 graduates[9]	450 students	100 boarders Elementary Normal School Nursing Department[10] Academic Course—*mathematics, English, grammar and literature, geography and natural philosophy* Industrial Department—*cooking, sewing, general housework, and laundry work*
1885	First Commencement Exercise held jointly with Female Seminary	200 boarding students First Commencement Exercise held jointly with Atlanta Baptist
1886–1887		First Class completed the Higher Normal and Scientific Course 6 students received diplomas and worked as teachers and missionaries
1888		Changed name to Spelman Seminary[11]

continued

Table 4.1—Continued

Year	Atlanta University	Atlanta Baptist Seminary (Morehouse College)	Atlanta Female Baptist Seminary (Spelman College)
1891			464 boarding students Restructured curriculum: Collegiate Department Academic Department—*a thorough English course for prospective teachers or missionaries* College Preparatory course *with foreign languages* Training School Department— Normal Course, Missionary Training Course, Nurse Training Course, and Industrial Course, *including sewing, dressmaking, and type-setting*[12]
1892			Missionary Training Course— *summer months in the field; Bible bands, temperance bands, home visits, assisted ministers of churches*

instruction and chronological changes in early curricular development among the three Atlanta institutions.

Throughout the 1890s and into the 1900s, major shifts occurred as all of the institutions' goals of providing higher education for blacks were realized. Atlanta University made steps to become a full-fledged institution of higher education. As the academic standing of the student body advanced, Atlanta University separated from the preparatory levels of education, and in 1894, it separated the elementary school from the university.[13]

In 1897, Atlanta Baptist Seminary filed an application to the Superior Court of Fulton County to amend the charter granted in 1879 and included "an amendment to change the name of the institution by substituting the word 'College' for 'Seminary.'"[14] The state granted the amendment to the charter, and Atlanta Baptist Seminary changed its name to Atlanta Baptist College, which gave it full college powers under the laws of the state.[15] In 1912, the college changed its name for the last time to Morehouse College, in honor of Henry L. Morehouse, secretary of the ABHMS, longtime advocate of blacks, and "'field marshal' of the Baptist denomination."[16]

In 1879, though not yet a college in name, the Female Seminary opened its College Department with two students. Five years later, in 1884, the seminary changed its name to Spelman Seminary, "in honor of the Spelman family, longtime activists in the Anti-Slavery Movements"[17] and in appreciation of the Rockefeller and Spelman families' interest and substantial financial help that put the seminary on a firm financial basis.[18] By 1924, the seminary changed its name for the last time to Spelman College to reflect the objectives of the institution.[19]

Funding Sources

Defining the curricular structure was not the only challenge black institutions faced; the greatest challenge stemmed from lack of resources and funds. "Fund-raising, difficult enough in even the most auspicious epoch was, at that time, a most formidable task."[20] Black institutions did not have the luxury of endowments and presidents of these intuitions continuously had to generate alternative revenues from which the funds would come.[21] Student tuition generated some income; but with most blacks living in poverty and competing with poor whites for jobs, tuition was severely a restricted source of funding. Black communities and missionary societies generated some donations from speeches in churches in the North, but black institutions desperately needed a constant flow of money to ensure their survival; the Atlanta institutions were no exception. Table 4.2 provides an overview of all three institutions' funding streams and illustrates how funding from philanthropists overlapped.

Atlanta University's financial situation was more precarious than that of Morehouse or Spelman's situation; in large part, Congregationalists established Atlanta University and secured money from the AMA and Freedmen's Bureau. However, it was Edmund Ware's intention to have an institution free of denominational control. In the first two years of existence, Atlanta University received $89,798, of which the Freedmen's Bureau contributed $52,410 and the AMA contributed $19,199. From 1869 to 1874, the AMA "gave the institution $56,589.57, of which $45,059.78 represented direct contributions, and the remainder donations collected under its auspices."[22] Ware also secured funds from the state government, which allowed the institution to free itself from denominational ties, and pushed the institution into the national spotlight.

In 1870, the University of Georgia prohibited blacks from matriculating at the institution, and black members of the Georgia Legislature displeased with this policy pushed for a state institution for blacks. With the need for black teachers increasing, and blacks unable to attend the University of Georgia, Atlanta University provided the only training for black teachers. Simultaneously, Ware tried to secure an annual appropriation from funds the state had from the Morrill Act of 1862, which granted land to States to create state institutions that provided agriculture, mechanical arts, and other areas of practicality. As the only state institution in Georgia with an agricultural department, the University of Georgia was the only recipient of the Morrill Act funds. Ware demanded that the state legislature

Table 4.2 Summary of funding sources

Year	Atlanta University	Atlanta Baptist Seminary (Morehouse College)	Atlanta Female Baptist Seminary (Spelman College)
1867–1869	$89,798 ($52,589–Federal Bureau; $19,199–AMA)		
1869–1874	$56,589.57 ($45,059.78 direct contributions; donations collected under its auspices)		
1874	$8,000 (State of Georgia)		
1877–1878		$200 (individual donations)	
1881			$250 (Rockefeller Sr.)
1884–1885			$13,000 (Rockefeller Sr., Rockefeller Hall)
1887			$7,500 (Rockefeller, 11 acres of land; trees and shrubbery)
			$3,000 (Rockefeller, Packard Hall, dormitories)
			$3,000 (Rockefeller, laundry)
1888			$2,700 (Rockefeller, heating)
			$3,000 (Rockefeller, Packard Hall)
1890			$6,500 (Rockefeller, steam heating plant for three brick buildings)
1892			$50,000 (Rockefeller pledge for new building, Giles Hall)
1990			The Rockefellers authorized improvements of: Resident for the president; erection of a hospital; two dormitories for 75 people each; large dining hall, a kitchen to accommodate 400 people; new power house; laying of brick sidewalk; completion of the iron fence around the entire campus; make all walks

continued

Table 4.2—Continued

Year	Atlanta University	Atlanta Baptist Seminary (Morehouse College)	Atlanta Female Baptist Seminary (Spelman College)
1901			and drive, grading of the campuses; improvements to old buildings including a new stairway to the chapel, bathrooms and toilets in Rockefeller and Packard Halls; repair to the roofs and flooring; sinking and equipment of an artesian well $6,500 (Rockefeller, house for the engineer or superintendent of buildings and grounds)
1902	$5,000 (GEB for practice school) $1,000 (GEB for expenses)		$6,000 (GEB, current operations)
1903	$1,000 (GEB)		$6,000 (GEB, current operations) Housing for nursing students $25,000 (Rockefeller) $1,506.71 (GEB)
1904	$1,000 (GEB)		
1906		Sale Hall ($40,000) $10,000 (Andrew Carnegie) $20,000 (ABHMS) $5,000 (GEB) $5,000 (Blacks in the community)	$250,000 (Rockefeller Sr. to the GEB unrestricted)
1913	Requested funds from GEB (Endowment-$300,000 to maintain the work at the university; proposed to raise $250,000)		

1916	Fiftieth Anniversary (Campaign to raise $500,000 to mark its 50th anniversary)	Robert Hall ($30,000) $15,000 (GEB) $5,000 (ABHMS) $10,000 (constituency, friends and students of the college)
1917	$5,000 (GEB)	
1919	$52,993 Year-end deficit $5,000 (request to GEB for expenses) $100,000 (request to GEB to pay debt and improve equipment)	
1920	$76,000 (received from an estate) Surplus, first time in 30 years	Science Bldg, Hope Hall $165,000 (GEB); $5,000 (Blacks in community) Endowment—$600,000 [with a conditional grant of: $300,000 (GEB); $100,000 (Julius Rosenwald Fund); $50,000 from ABHMS; and $51,771 (blacks and other contributions)]
1921	$10,000 (GEB); $5,000 (Andrew Carnegie)	
1922	$7,000 (GEB)	
1923	$7,000 (GEB)	

either force University of Georgia to accept blacks or create the same opportunity for blacks. The state denied both demands.

As an appeasement to Ware, the state made an annual appropriation of $8,000 to Atlanta University, beginning in 1874, and with this annual appropriation, Atlanta University paid its debts to the AMA and severed all ties.[23] The state appropriation was a continuous flow of money and was a victory for blacks and Atlanta University; however, it was temporary. Racism and segregation, again, attempted to thwart blacks' educational attainment.

Two acts of legislation, the Glen Bill and the Calvin Resolution, eventually repealed the annual appropriation given to Atlanta University.[24] Simply put, the principle of social equality Atlanta University practiced between the teachers and students, and between the black and white students, was the vehicle used by opponents to thwart blacks' educational opportunities. The Glenn Bill made it illegal for any institution in the state to practice social equality between the races, an act devised to force Atlanta University to discontinue its practice of social equality in order to continue receiving state funds. Ware and the institution were unwilling to sacrifice this principle.[25]

As a measure to "restore [the State's] former alliance with the University," the House Committee on Education proposed the Calvin Resolution, which proposed to continue the annual appropriation, if Atlanta University discontinued its admittance of white students, satisfying separation of the races. Again, Ware provided a lengthy argument stating why agreement with the resolution was inconceivable, just as it had been with the Glenn Bill. In the interim, Ware secured funds from educational foundations, such as the Slater Fund and Peabody Fund. Although Atlanta University stood its ground on principle and refused to compromise, in the end, it lost state funding. By 1889, negative publicity forced the state to enact a bill that eventually established a state institution of higher education for blacks—Savannah College of Industry for Coloreds Youth (now, Savannah State University).[26]

When Atlanta University discontinued its primary and grammar school in 1894, it developed the Oglethorpe Practice School, which gave student teachers needed practice for teaching. In 1902, the GEB "contributed $5,000 for a practice school on condition that the College raise $10,000."[27] Additionally, the GEB gave $1,000 a year for three years toward meeting expenses, if the institution secured matching funds. Despite this action by the GEB, there were numerous other requests from Atlanta University that the GEB denied.

In 1913, Atlanta University made an appeal to the GEB for assistance in "raising an adequate endowment for [the institution's] work among the Negroes." Continuing in his father's footsteps, Edward Ware, now president of Atlanta University, wrote the appeal and indicated that in this year, he estimated the institution's property value was $300,000. In order to maintain the work at the institution, he proposed to raise "$250,000 to liquidate the debt and capitalize the expected annual deficiency."[28] Despite Ware's effective case for Atlanta University, the GEB denied the request and felt that "further cooperation and coordination among the institutions for higher negro education in Atlanta, Georgia" was a more important priority. Thus, the GEB "did not find it practicable to grant the request."[29]

Three years later, Atlanta University campaigned "to raise half a million dollars to mark its 50th anniversary," which sparked a flurry of correspondence between the members of the GEB. Because the institution again had requested a contribution from the GEB, the GEB first informed Ware that "the Board did not find it practicable to take action...at this time" and deferred the final decision until their next meeting. The GEB undertook such actions to force Atlanta University into some form of cooperation with the other institutions in the vicinity.[30] Unknown to Ware, the GEB had decided to withhold funds until they conducted a thorough investigation of the institution.

The GEB relied on observations and information on Atlanta University from Thomas Jesse Jones's study on black colleges and universities. In a letter to E. C. Sage, Anson Phelps Stokes wrote, "Thomas Jesse Jones...referred in the highest terms to the remarkably good work being done by the graduates of Atlanta University as teachers in negro schools throughout the South." Although Stokes felt that the GEB did not "appreciate fully the work that Atlanta University [was] doing," he did not recommend an appropriation from the GEB toward an endowment. Rather, he insisted, "Atlanta University's situation was thoroughly studied."[31]

In 1917, the following year, Ware wrote to the GEB and thanked it for a $5,000 grant given to Atlanta University, because it enabled the institution to "close the year without a deficit." At the same time, he appealed for another grant to cover the 1918 expenses.[32] The GEB carefully noted this request.[33] Seemingly desperate, Ware wrote an additional request that year, and asked the GEB for a contribution "to construct barracks for soldiers who are to receive training at Atlanta University." The GEB responded and stated that such a request was unwise, and therefore denied.[34] In the interim, W. T. B. Williams had completed his study of Atlanta University and had given the institution high marks. He affirmed that Atlanta University needed $50,000 to defray existing debts.[35]

By 1918, GEB members gave considerable deliberation "regarding active participation by the Board in the further development of Morehouse College." In a lengthy letter to Wallace Buttrick, Abraham Flexner noted what could have been a turning point in the direction of the GEB. Flexner stated that World War I, "suddenly made clear what had been gradually becoming clear anyhow—namely—that the Negro knows that he does not enjoy a fair and untrammeled opportunity in this world which he has helped to make fit for democracy." He also noted that Hampton and Tuskegee already provided opportunities for industrial education, but that "nothing comparable in equipment or quality exists for the benefit of the smaller number of those capable of and ambitious for, intellectual advancement. Among these men capable of intellectual development, the Negro will find his leaders."[36]

At this time, Flexner felt Morehouse College was the most efficient institution in Atlanta because it was run entirely by blacks and had a black president, John Hope. Morehouse impressed him because the faculty "in point of ability compare favorably with white college teachers." He concluded it was necessary for the GEB to adopt "a generous policy towards Morehouse College," and that this assistance would "represent a fundamental contribution to the solution of a grave and pressing problem."[37] In reply, Buttrick mentioned that he would read Flexner's letter to the members of the GEB and stated that before any "formal action" took place, they needed to discuss and to confer the matter with John Hope.[38]

Atlanta University had a deficit of $52,993 by the early 1900s, and by the end of the decade, the deficit remained.[39] In 1919, Ware wrote a three-page letter to Wallace Buttrick, president of the GEB, where he explained the success and achievement of Atlanta University, and described the much-needed financial assistance. The institution had fallen behind "nine thousand dollars on current accounts."[40] Though Ware had sent a separate request of $5,000 on the very same day for expenses,[41] in this request, he pleaded for assistance in "raising the one hundred thousand dollar fund to pay the debt and improve the equipment [buildings and grounds]."[42]

In 1919, the GEB appropriated conditional grants to black colleges and universities, meaning funds also had to come from the black citizens in the community, and that institutions had to organize their schools, in large measures, according to philanthropists' specifications.[43] Rockefeller Sr. once explained the need of conditional grants when he wrote, "It is easy to do harm in giving money. To give to institutions which should be supported by others is not the best philanthropy. Such giving only serves to dry up the natural springs of charity."[44] He further explained:

> We frequently make our gifts conditional on the giving of others, not because we wish to force people to do their duty, but because we wish in this way to root the institution in the affections of as many people as possible who, as contributors, become personally concerned, and thereafter may be counted on to give to the institution their watchful interest and cooperation.[45]

By 1920, Atlanta University received $76,000 from an estate and was able to liquidate the institution's indebtedness, and ended the year with a surplus of $5,695. In the following year, additional funds came from the institution's students' pageants and the Alumni Association, a gift of $10,000 from the GEB, and a

$5,000 gift from Andrew Carnegie.[46] Ware wrote to the GEB and indicated that this was the "first time in over thirty years the audit of [its] accounts [showed them] free from a deficit." Obviously thinking ahead, Ware requested that the GEB renew its grant.[47] During this same time, Ware became ill and Myron Adams, the dean at Atlanta University, became acting president.

Because the GEB had granted increased annual appropriations of $7,000, the institution was debt free for four years.[48] However, starting in 1923, the financial assistance from the GEB changed. In a letter to Myron Adams, now president of Atlanta University, Trevor Arnett warned:

> Income available for the purpose of annual grants [had] been considerably diminished, due to a reduction in dividends on securities in some instances and to the passing of them in others, so that the Board [had] found it necessary to cut down both the number and the amount of grants.[49]

Unlike Atlanta University, Atlanta Baptist had denominational ties and strong support from the ABHMS. However, these funds were not enough to sustain the institution, in that, "the buildings were dilapidated and in need of repairs everywhere." Atlanta Baptist survived on funds generated from blacks in the community, black churches, and bequests from individuals.[50]

Hope secured money from Andrew Carnegie and the GEB starting in the early 1900s, and Atlanta Baptist received appropriations from the GEB after John Hope became president in 1906. Starting in 1919, the GEB focused its attention on select institutions because it realized the "significant place of the liberal arts college in the education of the Negro or at least a clear idea of how the problem...could be approached." As previously mentioned, one way to build up black institutions was by appropriating conditional grants, and members of the GEB felt "it was natural that Morehouse College in Atlanta should loom on such a list, for its president was John Hope."[51]

Hope remained in good standing with the GEB and continued receiving funds for Morehouse College. In 1920, Morehouse received $165,000 from the GEB and $5,000 from Andrew

Carnegie. Hope spent most of the funds on Hope Hall, a three-story, science building exclusively for biology—the first of its kind at a black college or university—devoted entirely to science. In 1922, he built Robert Hall in response to the increased demand for additional dormitories. These accomplishments and funds solicited helped put the college on a firm financial foundation. By the late 1920s, Morehouse's endowment had grown to $600,000, with a conditional grant of $300,000 from the GEB, $100,000 pledged from the Julius Rosenwald Fund, $50,000 from the ABHMS, and $51,771 from blacks and other contributors. In addition to financial health, by the end of the decade, all aspects of the college—academic life, cultural events, student activities, and faculty growth—had successfully progressed. The institution and its liberal arts curriculum were "winning the fight" against industrial education and recognized for "its leadership and the enviable records of its graduates."[52]

Unlike Atlanta University and Morehouse, Spelman not only secured funds from philanthropists soon after its establishment, but also secured a lifelong benefactor—John D. Rockefeller Sr., making him the "godfather of Spelman Seminary." Although when it began as a seminary and taught "nursing, teaching, printing, and other useful trades, the focal point was training young black women for a good Christian life." The latter purpose attracted Rockefeller's philanthropy more than the former.[53]

Rockefeller's gift to the seminary, in 1882, was his "first gift to Negro education," and with this act, he became committed to black education, though not announcing it too publicly, and continued to aid the seminary during its struggle for survival.[54] Though interested in black education, Rockefeller's commitment to black education did not ensure an endowment for Spelman as it did for the University of Chicago. Presumably, being a black institution made Spelman a different caliber than Chicago, and therefore would not receive an endowment, as is clear from Rockefeller Jr.'s (Junior) letter to the GEB, when he wrote:

> Application has been made to my father for an endowment for Spelman Seminary at Atlanta, Ga.... My father does not feel disposed to create an endowment for any institution of this class.

He does, however, feel a special interest in this institution, to whose material equipment he has made large contributions, and desires to extend to it assistance in meeting its current expenses.[55]

Instead, Rockefeller Sr. gave $250,000 in 1906 as an unrestricted gift to the GEB's general endowment, and the income was to be "available for any of the corporate purposes of the Board." However, Rockefeller hoped that the board would use part of the income for the $10,000 annual appropriations the board had agreed to give Spelman for its current expenses, but made it clear the funds were not an endowment. As Junior further noted, it was his father's express desire that

> this fund shall not constitute an endowment for Spelman Seminary, and that the Seminary shall have no claim, legal or equitable, upon the principal of this fund nor upon the income thereof, except as the Board shall from year to year make an appropriation from it for Spelman Seminary.

It was also his father's desire that the gift "be absolutely confidential to the members of [GEB], and that neither the representatives of Spelman Seminary nor any other persons outside of the Board shall know that such a fund has been created." As he further explained:

> My father's reason for making the gift in this way is his desire that it shall not have the effect of causing other contributors to withdraw their support under the impression that the Seminary has been provided for by permanent endowment. He realizes that the income from this fund will yield only a small portion of the amount of the current expenses of the Seminary, and that considerably larger sums will, in all possibility be needed to meet the increasing opportunities of the institution. It is his hope that, not withstanding [sic] the placing of this fund in your hands, the Board may still continue to make from its other resources such appropriations for the Seminary as it shall consider the circumstances to warrant.[56]

Paying the debt on the mortgage weighed heavily on Packard and Giles's mind and the pressure to "keep the property for an exclusive girl's school was hitting the Home Mission Board from many directions."[57] Packard and Giles sent a request to Henry Morehouse who, in turn, solicited the funds from Rockefeller Sr. The funds from Rockefeller, along with $4,000 from the black community, $3,000 from the black Baptists of Georgia, and $1,300 from other individual contributors enabled the seminary to keep the new location and erect its first brick building.[58] From this point onward, Rockefeller Sr. continuously gave Spelman financial assistance, was an original member of the board of trustees, and became the institution's greatest benefactor.[59]

In the school year 1884-1885, Rockefeller gave $13,000 to help erect Spelman's first brick building, Rockefeller Hall, which included dormitories and a chapel. The following year, he provided 11 acres, and gave money for additional dormitories, a laundry, a dining hall, and numerous other buildings. In the 1890s, Rockefeller selected the trees and shrubbery and sent his own landscape architects to redesign Spelman's campus. By 1900, the Rockefellers had "virtually made over the Spelman campus, paying for a new hospital, two dormitories, a dining room and kitchen, a power plant, and a residence for the school president."[60] In 1906, Spelman received $250,000 from Rockefeller Sr. through the GEB. Though the funds did not constitute an endowment, they did receive substantial funds for expenses.[61]

The Atlanta institutions had come a long way from their humble beginnings in the late 1800s; nevertheless, all of the institutions were vulnerable, and survival throughout the 1900s was questionable. Just as it had taken decades for the institutions to stabilize their curriculum and organization, as the following chapters discuss, so would it take additional decades to solidify the institutions' continuing existence.

5
Creating the Atlanta University System

By the 1920s, there were almost one hundred institutions of higher education for blacks throughout the country; most served elementary and secondary students; most had fewer than one hundred college level students.[1] It was not logical financially to sustain them all; thus, some black institutions would either close or consolidate. The GEB was at a point where it "could either support existing structures of black education or seek to create something more worthy of support."[2] The GEB chose the latter course and gave money to specific black colleges and universities strategically located in the South (e.g., Nashville, Washington, D.C., New Orleans, and Atlanta), which it deemed as most efficient for blacks' higher education,[3] with Atlanta, Georgia, being a major focal point (Appendix A).

There were five black institutions in Atlanta during this time. Three were in close proximity to one another (e.g., Atlanta University, Morehouse College, and Spelman College); two were apart, within the city (e.g., Clark College and Morris Brown College); four had denominational support, and one was solely independent (e.g., Atlanta University). All five, however, were relying on philanthropists for financial support.[4] The GEB studied the Atlanta institutions in the first decade of the twentieth century and reported:

> This multiplication of educational institutions in one city [had] been due to the great importance of Atlanta as a strategic center for educational work for negroes, that city being the railroad and commercial center of the old slave states and the capital city of the state having the largest negro population.[5]

The GEB's observation was unchanged by the second and third decades of the twentieth century. Atlanta was a popular location for business enterprises and for a black education center, for several reasons. First, in the years 1920 and 1930, Georgia's black population was larger than in any other state in the South (1.2 and 1.0 million people, respectively).[6] Atlanta provided an opportune location because of its large populace of blacks and its strategic geographic location in the South. Second, in the late 1920s, the Atlanta Chamber of Commerce launched the first "Forward Atlanta" campaign. Advertising the city in national publications brought hundreds of successful companies to the city, such as Coca-Cola and other corporate giants. Atlanta's economy was "booming." This prosperity was noticeable in the white sections of the city as well as in the black. The black business and financial districts of the world were located in Atlanta on Auburn Avenue. By 1920, "there were 72 black-owned businesses and 20 professionals located on Auburn," and within ten years, it almost doubled. Additionally, in the late 1920s, William Hartsfield, mayor of Atlanta, led efforts and was successful in getting the new southern airmail route through Atlanta, making the city the southern terminus and air center of the region.[7] These combined efforts made Atlanta a dominant commercial and financial center.

Third, as mentioned in previous chapters, the Rockefeller family had a long affinity in Atlanta with Spelman College that dated back to the early 1880s. Last, Morehouse College was located in Atlanta, which for some time had the interest of the GEB. When the GEB contemplated ways to develop liberal arts colleges for blacks, one tactic was to extend conditional grants to a carefully selected group of the most promising black colleges and institutions. Morehouse College with its president, John Hope, ranked at the top.[8]

Atlanta Institutions Moving toward Cooperation

Beginning in the early 1900s, philanthropists and the institutions' presidents discussed the cooperation of black institutions in the South, particularly between the institutions in Atlanta.[9] In 1914,

Edward Ware, then president of Atlanta University, wrote to E. C. Sage, secretary of the GEB, regarding the push for cooperation between the institutions in Atlanta. In doing so, Ware asked about the GEB's notion of cooperation, when he wrote:

> I am much interested in the vote that was taken and would like to know if I may what the General Education Board had in mind when they suggested "cooperation and coordination" among the institutions for higher negro education in Atlanta, Georgia. This suggestion seems to me so much more practicable than the combination of schools now existing in Nashville and Atlanta that I would like to follow up. There are only two schools for higher education in Atlanta now with which I should feel that we could combine profitably, but if the way were opened do not see why this could not be done.[10]

As a measure toward cooperation, in 1915, Atlanta University had begun cooperative measures with Morehouse College in a joint lecture series on Business Law, sponsored by the Phelps-Stokes Fund, that included elements of business law and business ethics.[11] Keeping the GEB abreast of the institutions' steps toward cooperation, Anson Phelps Stokes wrote to Wallace Buttrick and provided the rationale for the joint lecture series. This correspondence also showed philanthropists' determination to have cooperation among these institutions in Atlanta, even if that meant initially starting on a smaller scale, and it was further disclosed that the lecture series was a move on the philanthropists' part to establish future cooperation:

> These lectures are working out successfully. In connection with starting them, I had several points in mind.
>
> 1st The bringing of a prominent white citizen into close touch with the teaching at two of the negro colleges.
>
> 2nd Co-operation between institutions of negro education in Atlanta laying a small foundation from which perhaps larger co-operation between Morehouse College and Atlanta University can be brought about.
>
> 3rd The actual advantage of the instruction provided.[12]

The idea of cooperation was not only on the philanthropists' minds, but also on the minds of Edward Ware and John Hope, presidents of Atlanta University and Morehouse College, respectively. Regarding the lecture series, Ware wrote to Phelps Stokes and suggested that the close proximity of the institutions afforded continuance of the joint law course. He initially focused on the joint business lectures; he then quickly suggested if the course continued and a building was erected, as the enrollment of students on the college level increased at both institutions, they could use the building for future joint work:[13]

> The Atlanta University property extends almost, if not quite, half way to Morehouse College. If this plan of joint work develops, it might be natural and wise, provided all the conditions were favorable, to put up a building on our property nearest Morehouse to accommodate such classes and lectures as could be conducted jointly.[14]

Ware professed his idea was a "pipe dream." However, his acquiescence to "surrender any material consideration or any personal office to see such a plan carried to success, maintaining and strengthening the principles of justice and opportunity for the Southern Negroes" showed he subscribed to the same principle as Edmund Ware, Atlanta University's first president and his father: sacrifice whatever was necessary for the institution's survival and continuance.[15]

Correspondence continued throughout the first two decades of the 1900s with discussions centered primarily on cooperation between the Atlanta institutions.[16] By the late 1920s, presidents of the institutions developed more cooperation, apparently the beginnings of the affiliation. However, in the interim and beginning in the academic year of 1925–1926, the financial stability of Atlanta University was once again in question. For several years, the GEB gave money; however, in 1924–25 it gave $9,000 and stipulated, "no further contributions to Atlanta University for current expenses would be made."[17] At this time, the GEB changed its policy and discontinued the grant.[18] In a letter to Ware, Phelps Stokes noted that the GEB discontinued "its policy of spending a considerable portion of its income in making gifts to General Endowment Campaigns of colleges." Phelps Stokes further explained, "The Board felt that it wished most of its money free for a few major undertakings"; yet, he expressed how strongly he "felt the future of Atlanta University was tied up in bringing [Atlanta University] into closer cooperation with the other Negro colleges of the city."[19] It is quite possible the GEB's "changed policy" forced cooperation between the Atlanta institutions, or the institutions needed to find financial assistance elsewhere. At this point, the institutions considered the virtues of cooperation.[20]

It was also during this time research revealed how members of the GEB and Rockefeller Jr. had respect for and some even developed a friendship with Hope, in that, they played a pivotal role in providing Hope with money after he had surgery and was having personal, financial difficulties. Unknown to Hope, Buttrick spearheaded a drive to raise money and sent letters to Hope's friends and classmates.[21] News of Hope's circumstances traveled around and eventually reached the GEB and Rockefeller Jr. Upon hearing the news, Rockefeller Jr. sent $1,000 through his personal aide, W. S. Richardson, who was also Hope's classmate, and asked Richardson to remit the money so no one would know that the money had actually come from him. This anonymity was confirmed in a letter to Buttrick, when Richardson wrote:

> Dear Dr. Buttrick-
>
> Mr. Fosdick presented your communication of May 20th with reference to John Hope who happened to be one of my college classmates at Brown and for whom I have a great admiration, and the Advisory Committee decided that Mr. Rockefeller might wisely contribute the sum of $1,000, if it could be done anonymously by my sending a check drawn to your order and suggesting that you might think it wise to say to President Hope that friends of yours had provided this amount.[22]

When Hope became president of Atlanta Baptist College, he had difficulty obtaining money from philanthropists; yet, later he received money from them for personal use. Though Buttrick previously stated he could not separate himself from "Buttrick the man" and "Buttrick the secretary of the GEB," it is apparent that his personal relationship with Hope changed over time. He had no such restrictions in assisting in the amelioration of Hope's personal, financial circumstances.

When Buttrick received the money, he was instructed to keep it anonymous; no one was to know it came from Rockefeller Jr. This action, as well as others of similar nature, makes one question Rockefeller Jr.'s true beliefs about aiding blacks. Was this need for secrecy to ward off other personal requests? Was the anonymity a way to keep the relationship with Hope out of the public's gaze and scrutiny? Or was it simply that Rockefeller Jr. was uncomfortable with social relations with blacks?

Over the years, many scholars questioned Rockefeller Jr.'s motives for his philanthropy. Peter Collier and David Horowitz maintained that there was always an undercurrent with Rockefeller Jr.'s philanthropies: "redemption of the family name, power, and control."[23] Others, like Marybeth Gasman, contended that social equality and relations were too radical for Rockefeller Jr.[24] Whatever his motives and beliefs, Junior gave the money; and as instructed, Buttrick wrote Hope and expressed:

> My dear Friend:
>
> I am enclosing [to] you a check for a thousand dollars for your personal use. Mr. Thorkelson called my attention to the fact that you had gone into the hospital and that you were a little short on funds. A personal friend of mine wishes me to send you this check which has nothing to do with the College, but is for your own personal use under existing circumstances.[25]

Buttrick also wrote to Richardson, expressed his extreme gratitude for the money, and explained what he had done with it. He made it a point to mention that Hope "and his wife are my very dear friends," and noted all of the positive work Lugenia Hope had done in Atlanta without compensation.[26] This may have implied the money was justified in not only showing compassion for a friend who was in need, but also for acknowledging the work Hope and his wife had done over the years without ever being compensated or asking for compensation.

By 1926, the presidents of the Atlanta institutions drew up collaborative plans to eliminate the overlapping and duplication of courses. Myron Adams, president of Atlanta University, arranged a meeting among the college presidents regarding "cooperation and exchange of class work among classes of Morehouse College, Spelman College, and Atlanta University."[27] In a letter to Hope, and without going into too many details, Adams explained:

> Some classes are apt to be quite small, as for instance in advanced mathematics. It is also possible that one of the three institutions might have occasionally a subject not duplicated by another and yet of general interest. Might it not be practicable to offer some such courses one to the other, by way of exchange?[28]

The close proximity of the institutions made the exchange possible. Adams noted that the distance between Morehouse and Atlanta University, on foot, was "about eleven to thirteen minutes." The distance between Spelman and Atlanta University was "about fifteen to eighteen minutes."[29] Apparently, this type of initiative had been on the minds of the presidents for some time, as Hope replied:

> I accept your invitation to confer with you and President Tapley [president of Spelman] about the possibilities of cooperation among the schools. With you and me the question is by no means new, and I think for years we have both looked upon it with much favor.[30]

At the same time, another major event took place at Spelman College. Lucy Tapley, president of Spelman, resigned. Tapley had been president of Spelman for almost 40 years. By 1925, a new medical condition compounded her previous physical problem of cataract; she was nearly 70 years old. In a confidential letter to Trevor Arnett, president of Spelman's Board of Trustees, she told him of her plan to resign. She suggested that he and the trustees search for a new president to start in the fall of 1927.[31] Spelman was also in transition from a secondary school to a college; therefore, they had a lot to do. The GEB had been "the principal factor in the development and support of the institution and [was], at present time, its most generous supporter," besides, of course, the Rockefellers. For example, in 1926, Rockefeller Jr. appropriated $175,000 to erect Sisters Chapel in honor of his mother and aunt.[32] Arnett and members of the GEB immediately planned for Spelman's development, which now included finding a president.[33]

Members of the GEB were an "interlocking directorate";[34] as such, they appointed one of their own as Spelman's next president. Florence M. Read, a New York native, was the executive secretary of the International Health Board of the Rockefeller Foundation, under the direction of Wickliffe Rose, GEB's president. She received her A. B. degree from Mount Holyoke and was a member of Phi Beta Kappa. Previously, Read had served as alumnae secretary of Mount Holyoke, secretary to the president and to the faculty, and had been on the administrative committee at Reed College in Portland, Oregon. Though both institutions were white liberal arts institutions and Reed College was a coeducational institution, Mount Holyoke gave Read experience at an exclusively female institution. Arnett and the GEB members felt she was the most appropriate selection for the presidency.[35]

Prior to making a final decision on selecting Read, the GEB conducted another survey of black colleges. In 1927, Jackson Davis, a field agent for the GEB, conducted a study, *Recent Developments in Negro Schools and Colleges*. His findings were very similar to Jones's 1912 study and Buttrick's findings in 1914. At the time of Davis's study, there were 99 institutions for blacks with a total enrollment of 13,197 college-level students; of the 99 institutions, only 21 had enrollments of 200 or more students; 14 different denominations controlled 71 institutions, and states controlled 28 institutions.[36] Although these numbers, according to Davis, indicated "a testimony of the ambitions of the colored people, of their desire for higher education, and of their capacity to receive it," the institutions were "mainly high schools and elementary schools with small college departments." Additionally, there were too many institutions, and they were too scattered to succeed, especially in Atlanta where there were five institutions with a total of 1,057 students. Davis noted only four institutions of "national significance"—Hampton, Howard, Fisk, and Tuskegee—that stood "in a class by themselves." There were also eight important centers with college enrollment of more than two hundred students: Washington, D.C. (1,611), Nashville, Tennessee (1,350), Atlanta, Georgia (1,057), Marshall, Texas (654), Prairie View, Texas (513), Richmond, Virginia (456), Wilberforce, Ohio (430), and New Orleans, Louisiana (360).[37]

Davis acknowledged that "Atlanta [was] undoubtedly a center of first importance," yet he reiterated, "The schools [were] scattered and there [were] too many." Although there had been discussion of cooperation between Morehouse and Spelman because they represented the same Baptist denomination and "were closer in proximity to one another than to any of the others," there was no evidence at the time of the study that indicated cooperation had happened. The other institutions in Atlanta (e.g., Morris Brown College, Clark University, and Atlanta University) were "widely separated"; two had denominational support and one did not. Morris Brown had support from the African Methodist Episcopal Church and Clark had financial support from its association with Gammon Theological Seminary that was Northern Methodist. This left only Atlanta University without denominational support.[38]

The conclusion drawn from this study regarding Atlanta University might have been the catalyst for things to come. Davis strongly recognized Atlanta University's importance, while he cast doubt on the institution's continued existence:

> Atlanta University, the first in the field and with a superb record of usefulness, has outlived the period to which it belonged. In neatness, tone and general atmosphere of culture it is more of a college than any of the others in Atlanta, but the others have the backing of growing denominations, while Atlanta, independent and with inadequate endowment is running behind in its current expenses. The alumni are responding with amazing loyalty but they are not strong enough to shoulder the burden.[39]

It was impossible to bring all the institutions in Atlanta together, because the colleges were made up of "interlapping groups of people scattered over the whole country," and "each domination [had] its own policy." Though he doubted whether these institutions would merge, he mentioned, if it were possible, then "Atlanta [might] become a university center." Much deliberation took place over the next two years about this possibility.[40]

During the same time, from 1926 to 1928, another survey was conducted on black colleges on the federal level. John T. Tigert, United States Commissioner of Education, explained in a letter to the Secretary of the Interior:

> It is generally acknowledged that a report on negro education in the United States published by the Bureau of Education in 1917 has contributed greatly to the tremendous reconstruction of schools for negroes which has taken place during the past 10 years.
>
> In view of the progress made since the appearance of that report, State departments of education, nationally known educators, both white and colored, the officials of universities in the North and South, and the representatives of church and other educational boards and foundations have for a long time urged upon my consideration the need for a resurvey of negro colleges and universities.[41]

In the fall of 1927, Florence M. Read was Spelman's president and an ally for the GEB in the affiliation. It is noteworthy to mention, Read herself stated she refused to accept the presidency at Spelman until "annual grants were capitalized." Charged by Arnett and the Trustees to develop Spelman into a strong liberal arts college, Read immediately joined in the plans for an affiliation.[42]

A couple of decades before Read's appointment, John Hope had prophesied his vision of the institutions in Atlanta developing into a great center; and in 1927, he once again shared his vision for the Atlanta institutions in a lengthy letter to Wickliffe Rose, GEB's president:

> The Atlanta situation had been under consideration for more than twenty-five years, with little accomplished in the way of

elimination, absorption or cooperation thus far. This week I have had conversations with Mr. Jackson Davis and President Read of Spelman College, and have given them my opinion on the Atlanta situation for whatever it is worth.

My impression is that Atlanta, so far as the educational side is concerned, is in effect farther from Nashville than mere mileage might indicate. Its position is strategic from the point of view of geography and Negro population. To my mind, Atlanta is unquestionably well situated to become a great, if not the great, educational center for Negroes.... All this could be done without the purchase of a foot of land. Spelman College, Morehouse College, and Clark University, with their laboratories could do excellent work in the preparation of undergraduates for the field of medicine. Atlanta University, with its sixty acres of land and several buildings, might become the site and the institution for a great medical school for Negroes where men and women could be trained for service among Negroes, not only in this country, but in other countries as well.[43]

Hope's vision along with the presidents' correspondence disclosed how they seriously pondered, more so now than in the past, the idea of cooperation between the institutions. They also discussed ways in which to accomplish such a task with members of the GEB.

By November 1927, the GEB had decided it could not "enter into a general program of aiding all these private [denominational] institutions." At this time, the GEB definitively implemented a policy to "stimulate improvement through selecting a few well-located institutions and centering major efforts at these points."[44] Correspondence between GEB members also disclosed that the institutions in Atlanta were "willing to work together and [an affiliation seemed] to be growing particularly with reference to Morehouse, Spelman, and Atlanta University."[45]

The most urgent consideration stemmed from Myron Adams at Atlanta University. In December 1927, Adams wrote a letter to GEB members, provided a rationale for moving Morehouse and Spelman into a cooperation with Atlanta University, and elaborated how such a move would financially benefit all the institutions. Explaining that the advanced work at the Atlanta institutions was unsatisfactory compared to the elementary work, Adams suggested that the GEB "write to each of the Atlanta colleges," explain the results of recent surveys, and "ask if it would be agreeable to have a conference between the different institutions." Adams believed that a meeting was necessary to "see whether any arrangement [could] be made which [would] help the present situation." Adams ended his letter saying any arrangement would justify and encourage the GEB's appropriations. He felt that his rationale was "a worthy ideal that of getting nearer together would be actually fostered."[46]

Unknown to any of the institutions' presidents and further behind the scenes, by January 1928, plans were already underway "laying the foundations of an unusual center for Negro education in Atlanta, Georgia." The GEB believed that "a library with books, equipment, and endowment for accessions designed to be available for all college students in Atlanta" was the necessary foundation to assure cooperation.[47] The plans of a joint library, if provided, also generated discussions of the other institutions in Atlanta (e.g., Clark and Morris Brown) joining into cooperation in the future. H. J. Thorkelson wrote to Thomas Appleget and explained that the best location for the library was

> on land not now belonging to any of the institutions—that is, on "neutral territory." There are possibilities for a future development of coordinated colleges with the ultimate establishment of a real university on a plan somewhat similar to that at Toronto University if the land between Spelman College and Atlanta University adjacent to Morehouse College can be acquired.[48]

Though Thorkelson expressed the GEB's interest in building up higher education for blacks in Atlanta and creating an avenue for strengthening the institutions, the purchase of the land was kept out of public gaze. Raymond Fosdick, a GEB member and later president, called the transaction a "benevolent conspiracy" between the GEB and Rockefeller Jr.[49]

Thorkelson insisted it was "apparently not practical" for the GEB to purchase the land. However, he stated "if the land [was] acquired from other sources and held until further college developments [were] ready a very real service [would] be rendered to higher education for Negroes."[50] This was no haphazard notion. The GEB was determined the institutions would affiliate, one way or another. The GEB's resolve was noted in that Thorkelson's letter to Appleget included a map of the city highlighting the "sites of the three institutions and their acreage...also an outline that this larger project may ultimately be developed," and an estimated cost between $300,000 and $500,000 for the purchase of the land.[51] The GEB selected the best location for the library and later secured the money for the land, well before informing the college presidents.

The idea of affiliation paired with a joint library centered discussion on creating a graduate school at Atlanta University (because of the city's central location), eliminating the high school work, and building up the college work at the other institutions leading to bachelor degrees.[52] Simultaneously and behind the scene, numerous correspondences between a few select GEB officials discussed the purchase of the land for the library. It was the GEB's plan to purchase the land "anonymously"; even the institutional histories indicated the money was received anonymously. However, a letter from Rockefeller Jr. to Wickliffe Rose revealed he provided the money for the land:[53]

> In answer to my question as to why the General Education Board or the International Education Board could not buy this land, you replied that the land would have to be picked up quietly and slowly and that the whole purpose might be defeated if any publicity were given to the operation. You also stated that since action of the Trustees of the General Education Board would be necessary to authorize its officers to proceed with the purchase of this land, there would be grave danger of the matter becoming known prematurely.[54]

Though Rockefeller Jr. was clear on the officials' rationale, he nevertheless proceeded under conditions and gave immediate directives. He agreed to act "in the capacity of an intermediary," if Rose assured him that either the GEB or the International Education Board purchased the land later.[55] In another letter to Trevor Arnett, Rockefeller Jr. acknowledged his agreement with the purchase of the land "up to but not exceeding a total of $500, 000," only if Rockefeller Jr.'s representatives and Arnett worked out a method "whereby in passing the money [the transaction could not be] traced" to him. Rockefeller Jr. stated that it was "vital that I should not be known as in any way connected with the transaction."[56]

In 1928, Arthur Klein conducted a *Survey of Negro Colleges and Universities,* sponsored by the Phelps-Stokes Foundation.[57] His conclusions were in line with Davis's study. Klein studied 79 black institutions in 19 southern states, and found that the "immediate need [for blacks was] education, better education, and higher education." The lack of teachers was serious, and the solution was "largely centered in higher education. If more teachers adequately trained and prepared for the overwhelming undertaking of educating 5,000,000 boys and girls [were] to be provided, the task must be done in the institutions of higher learning."[58]

Regarding the institutions in Georgia, particularly those in Atlanta, Klein found, "the geographical distribution of the institutions [was] disadvantageous to the higher education of the negro population within the city limits of Atlanta."[59] Since only 10 out of every 10,000 blacks attended college, some institutions' enrollment was too small in comparison to their physical plants. In the year 1926–27, some institutions had as few as 35 college students, while others had 300 students. The report indicated that the total number of college students would be much higher if provisions were made for high schools in the state.

Although Morehouse College and Spelman College received an encouraging report, Atlanta University did not. During the 1926–27 academic year, Morehouse had 300 students enrolled in the college department and significant financial support from the American Baptist Home Mission Society and large educational foundations. Though they acquired most of the funds from church appropriations, Morehouse received an annual income of $112,440 for the academic year. The main recommendation Klein gave for Morehouse was to raise the scholastic standards of the faculty.[60]

Spelman College had only 92 students enrolled in the college department, the lowest number of the three institutions, and its annual income was $86,616. Klein thought that the initial aim of Spelman establishing "a high-grade college for negro women" was only "partially realized" for two reasons. One, the number of students in the college program was too small for the physical plant. Two, the college needed "adequate and assured annual income to guarantee future stability." To rectify part of this problem, he recommended improved library facilities with resources to assist with a bachelor's degree, and an increased enrollment in the college student population. However, he cautioned that Spelman not make a decision in "undue haste in the elimination of its secondary school," because it was the "source for a well-prepared freshman class."[61]

Regarding Atlanta University, the focus was more on the institution's income. Unlike the other institutions, Atlanta University was independent, with no denominational ties, and solely financially dependent on the board of trustees. During the academic year of 1926–27, Atlanta University had 260 college students and an annual income of $61,950. The report indicated that Atlanta University immediately needed "an increase in the permanent income ... as will assure stability of the work it is now carrying on and also provide for the necessary progress that must be made in order to maintain instruction of a standard collegiate character."[62]

Although the report did not recommend that the Atlanta institutions join in any kind of cooperative venture, all of the evidence he provided, along with Davis's and Williams's study, indicated such an action would eventually take place. Philanthropic giving had been drastically diminished to Atlanta University, and the institution was financially struggling. While Morehouse and Spelman had denominational ties and financial backing, all three institutions were receiving funds from philanthropists, yet duplicating courses. Members of the GEB felt it unwise to dispense funds to different institutions, in the same city, that provided the same service and refused to dispense any more funds until the institutions devised a plan of effectiveness.[63] Two things were apparent: one, coming together in some manner would solidify the institutions' survival, particularly Atlanta University's survival; and two, the timing was right—the stage was set and cooperation was the only practical answer.

After the GEB had solidified the means to purchase the land, and before it presented the situation to the presidents of the Atlanta institutions, problems arose. "Rumor and speculation and the magic word 'Rockefeller' spread like wildfire." The GEB's fear had become a reality: the real estate value of the land they wanted to purchase increased. Additionally, people "were afraid that it was a trap by which white people could get possession of property on which they might want to put up a factory or some other undesirable building."[64]

To resolve this matter, they called upon John Hope "in a characteristic role as mediator between the alarmed community and the real estate agents."[65] Trevor Arnett wrote to Hope in August 1928, informed him of the proposed library, and asked for his assistance with securing "the most reasonable terms for the purchase of the land." Thorkelson met with Hope and Read a month later.[66] Then, in October 1928, Arnett wrote to Read and reminded her that "the officers of the General Education Board," had considered "for some time the possibilities of cooperation between the institutions of higher learning for Negroes in Atlanta." Additionally, he asked her, "Whether any plan might be evolved which might promote it." Knowing they had secured the money for the land and each institution had inadequate library facilities, he used the library as the bait for an affiliation. He stating there was a "strong possibility that funds [would] be provided for a central library and for its maintenance." In closing, he suggested that she invite the presidents of the other Atlanta institutions to discuss "a feasible scheme for [the library's] cooperative use."[67]

Read organized a meeting with the other presidents and discussed Arnett's concerns. Relaying the conclusions of the meeting back to Arnett, she stated that all the presidents welcomed "most heartily" his suggestions, that each felt "adequate library facilities" was a necessity, and that each was "delighted to know that there [was] a possibility that funds would be provided for a central library." She also informed him that "President Hope, the ranking member of the group in point of service, was named

Chairman to arrange future conferences and discussions" regarding the library and any other forms of cooperation between the institutions.[68]

As a move forward, auditors balanced the institutions' accounts, presidents sent records of expenses to the GEB, correspondence exchanged documenting discussions of cooperation, Morehouse and Spelman sponsored a joint summer school program, and philanthropists visited the institutions in Atlanta. Morehouse had initially organized a summer school program, in 1921, primarily to enable public school teachers to continue their studies and to qualify for higher state certificates. Each year thereafter, the enrollment increased. In 1928, the program reorganized as "the Morehouse-Spelman Summer School conducted jointly by Morehouse College and Spelman College with the resources and facilities of both institutions at its disposal."[69]

James Dillard also visited Morehouse in 1928, and upon his return drafted a letter to Hope. Dillard expressed how "distinctly pleased" he was with everything he saw at Morehouse, and conversations he had with Hope and Read.[70] In response, Hope stated how he was trying to "make Morehouse College a better school than it [was], on the campus and off the campus."[71] Given his relationship with philanthropists, Hope had indeed made Morehouse a better school. By 1928, Morehouse, under his leadership, had increased "its endowment by $600,000 on the strength of a conditional offer of $300,000 made…by the GEB."[72] Expressing his gratitude and appreciation for this gift, Hope wrote to W. S. Richardson, John D. Rockefeller Jr.'s personal aide, and stated:

> The offer of $300,000 from the General Education Board is one of the biggest things that has ever come to the College, and is an inspiration to me at a time when I must confess that I was needing inspiration. When I raise the $300,000 that must be raised by the College it will mean that the institution in which I have worked now for thirty years will have a guarantee of existence and further growth.[73]

With these accomplishments, John Hope proved he was capable of handling the administrative responsibilities of a president and was prepared for the next step of his career.

Morehouse had 12 acres of land, a strong administrator in Hope, a $600,000 endowment campaign ($300,000 from the GEB), and a strong academic curriculum ensured by vigorous faculty. Spelman's relationship with philanthropists was even better with its 20 acres of land and a power plant. Spelman had the best financial prospect with a $3 million endowment campaign and pledges from both the Laura Spelman Rockefeller Foundation and the GEB ($1 million and $1.5 million, respectively).[74] Additionally, under new leadership, Read moved the college into having a strong curricular focus on liberal arts.

While Morehouse and Spelman prospered, Atlanta University was in desperate need of funds.[75] Atlanta University had 55 acres of land, an honorable history, and loyal alumni. However, the institution had "fewer younger college teachers because of its budget stresses and strains"; and Adams, its president, was about to retire. Historian Clarence Bacote best explained Atlanta University's predicament, when he wrote:

> Atlanta University, the pioneer in Negro higher education, the defender of racial equality and academic freedom, and the symbol of academic excellence, was on the verge of dissolution unless it could devise a unique program that would appeal to the foundations. Success in this hinged upon the selection of an able administrator to succeed President Adams.[76]

Throughout the first two decades of the twentieth century, correspondence between philanthropists and college presidents changed the focus of discussion from whether Atlanta University, Morehouse College, and Spelman College would join in a cooperative plan to how the affiliation would form and take place. It is evident Atlanta University would be the lead institution, but who would be the leader of Atlanta University?

The Affiliation of the Atlanta Institutions

All three institutions needed to devise a plan. However, Atlanta University desperately needed "a plan and a president."[77] The success of the plan, however, depended heavily on the next president of Atlanta University. This was serious contemplation because Atlanta University and Morehouse College were rivals, and the search committee was unsure if the Atlanta University alumni would approve.[78] "In order to attract a qualified man," as Read noted, "the Atlanta University Board of Trustees recognized the urgency of finding a field of service, wholly or in part unique; and both a program and a president were prerequisite to raising funds."[79]

The presidents and respective members of the board of trustees convened and mapped out the plans for an affiliation. On February 25 and 26, 1929, Adams arranged a meeting with the committees representing Atlanta University, Morehouse College, and Spelman College.[80] Opening the meeting, Adams gave a brief overview of what had previously occurred regarding "cooperation between the colleges." Afterwards, he stated that he hoped the meeting produced "a series of questions or resolutions [that] might be prepared to be submitted to the three Boards of Trustees." Then, he provided an outline for the possible structure for a "University Foundation," and opened the floor for discussion.[81]

George Hovey, trustee for both Morehouse and Spelman and secretary of the American Baptist Education Society, said there was a "general agreement that Atlanta should be the great center for Negro education, that Atlanta, with Washington, Nashville, and New Orleans, [had] long been considered as of first importance." Hope agreed with Hovey's statement, and added the meeting was of momentous importance in black higher education. Hope drew "a picture of a great university center for Negroes, with graduate schools and professional schools of law, medicine, and business." He further added that the "number of students desiring to do graduate work would be increased perceptibly by the greater accessibility and lower cost in Atlanta."[82]

During the late 1920s, there seemed no reason "to maintain two Negro colleges in the same city anywhere in the country unless their combined college enrollment of college students exceeds 750."[83] The three Atlanta institutions had a combined total college student population of 802, and Hope believed additional students would enroll and increase the number of college students. Because college enrollment at the three institutions exceeded 750 college students, all who attended the meeting agreed an affiliation would preserve each institution's separate identity and existence. Despite this, representatives of Atlanta University provided a more concrete rationale for the affiliation: securing funding and resources.[84]

> Money could be got [from] the General Education Board because it had interest in a cooperative scheme.
> —Willis Weatherford

> It would be easier to get money for a joint scheme than for three separate colleges.
> —Will Alexander

> The idea would appeal to individual givers.
> —James Weldon Johnson

Regardless of this confidence, "no promise had been made to Atlanta University, Morehouse College, or Spelman College," according to Hope, "as to additional funds, if this affiliation" took place. However, Hope felt that common sense and faith seemed "to indicate that the affiliation would be a success."[85] The committee discussed several other factors and outlined the following at this meeting:

1. That a start ought to be made toward a real university in Atlanta, centering on Atlanta University the graduate and professional department.
2. That it seems wise to conserve the name Atlanta University as the name of the University foundation or system.
3. That a University board should be constituted, consisting of representatives in equal numbers from the three institutions, these representatives to elect several members at large (Suggestion is that the board have not more than 15 members—3 from each institution, 3 to 5 at large); this new board to be in charge of the administration of the educational program of the University but if necessary to meet the legal requirements, the

present Board of Atlanta University to continue as a holding corporation to have charge of the present property of Atlanta University.
4. That there should be two undergraduate colleges, Morehouse and Spelman, in the University system, which would not offer graduate or professional instruction; which may retain complete control of the moral and religious teaching each might choose to do as part of its undergraduate work. (Concerning the term professional, it was stated that any course that might be called pre-professional and that would be acceptable toward the bachelor's degree in either of the undergraduate colleges would be permissible.)
5. That hereafter Atlanta University should not accept freshmen and that at the end of three years or less the undergraduate work at Atlanta University be discontinued.
6. That graduate courses be offered as soon as they can be offered on a high plane; that it would be desirable to have at least one professor appointed to the graduate faculty next year; that the graduate courses offered by the exclusively graduate faculty may be supplemented by graduate courses offered by present members of the undergraduate faculties.
7. That the President of the University be elected by the newly organized Board of the University Foundation.
8. That the University President be ex-officio a member of the University Board and of the Boards of Trustees of the undergraduate colleges and that the presidents of the undergraduate colleges be ex-officio members of the University Board.
9. That hereafter the Presidents of the undergraduate colleges should be elected by their Boards of Trustees after consultation with the President of the University.
10. In light of the expectation that graduate teacher training will be given in the graduate school of the University, the Knowles High School and Oglethrope Practice School should for the present be continued.
11. That the plan be submitted to the several boards at the earliest moment legally practicable, action from the Atlanta Board being a necessary first step.[86]

Close to the end of the meeting, the committee agreed that the "term consolidation be avoided" and preferred either the terms "association, affiliation, federation, or co-ordination." They decided on the term "affiliation," so that each institution's identity remained intact.[87]

In April 1929, higher education for blacks rose to a new level, one never before seen in the nation. The efforts of the GEB, representatives of the institutions, the presidents, and Hope's efforts and visions came to fruition. On April 1, 1929, Myron W. Adams, John Hope, and Florence M. Read, signed an agreement and formed "a co-operative educational arrangement in the nature of a University Foundation" (Figure 5.1).[88] In doing so, the purpose of the affiliation was:

> To co-operate in the advancement of college education and university training, both under-graduate and graduate, for colored people and also...to readjust the scope of their individual activities so as to increase the efficiency of all in the work they are doing and desire hereafter to do.[89]

Although each institution remained autonomous, Atlanta University served as the University Board and as the graduate institution for the undergraduate males at Morehouse College and the undergraduate females at Spelman College. The charter so outlined:

> From the date of the execution of this contract Atlanta University shall not accept freshmen, and at the end of three years from this date, or at such time before as the University Board may determine, under-graduate work of said University shall be discontinued.
>
> Morehouse College and Spelman College shall be colleges and shall not offer graduate or professional instruction but each may retain entire control of the moral and religious teaching each may choose to do as a part of its under-graduate work. Each of said two colleges may also maintain a course or courses in pre-professional work, which may be acceptable towards a bachelor's degree in either of said two colleges.[90]

Receiving a charter from the State of Georgia for the affiliation in a university plan, the bylaws were drafted. Everything was now in place, except a president for Atlanta University.[91]

Creating the Atlanta University System 145

Figure 5.1 Photograph of John Hope, Florence Read, and Myron Adams, presidents of Morehouse College, Spelman College, and Atlanta University signing Atlanta University System affiliation agreement, 1929, Atlanta University Photographs—Individuals.
Source: Atlanta University Center Robert W. Woodruff Library, Atlanta, Georgia.

Hope "was the leading candidate because of his stature as an educational statesman and the respect he was accorded" as a black leader in the South.[92] The trustees had no other choice but to select the one person who filled the criteria for the position. When Atlanta University, Morehouse College, and Spelman College joined in an affiliation, the trustees unanimously named John Hope president of the new Atlanta University.[93] However, Hope agreed to accept the presidency of Atlanta University on one condition. Demonstrating commitment and dedication to his endeavors, Hope would only accept the presidency of Atlanta University, if he were allowed to remain Morehouse's president until its endowment campaign was completed.

Hope did not take his new office officially until July 1929, after the retirement of Atlanta University's president Myron Adams, and was simultaneously president of both Atlanta University and Morehouse College until 1931.[94] Despite this, he once debated becoming president of Atlanta University. Recalling his decision he later wrote:

> I do not, as I look back at it, consider that this request on my part was perfunctory. I had to think it out from as many points of view as I could, and I had also to consider it with my wife.... The fact that I was sixty years of age raised considerable doubt in my mind as to whether I should undertake such a job.... I decided to accept the presidency of Atlanta University, with the understanding that I would be allowed to keep the presidency of Morehouse College until the endowment was raised for Morehouse and it was put on a good basis.[95]

Many have credited other people for bringing the affiliation into existence.[96] However, the Trustees of Morehouse College and Atlanta University explained the significance of Hope's appointment:

> When [Hope] assumed the presidency of the Atlanta University system, he undertook a task that called for balance and patience, perseverance and tact, faith and courage, wisdom and high statesmanship, and for the ability to work with black and white, North and South. All of these qualities he brought to that task.[97]

From the philanthropists' perspective, Fosdick made it clear that without Hope's "persuasive leadership," it was "doubtful if the plan could ever had succeeded."[98]

Responding to the affiliation, the change in regime and curriculum, Myron Adams, outgoing Atlanta University president, wrote to the students, parents, and faculty of Atlanta University. Elaborating on the effects of the affiliation and introducing his successor, Adams wrote:

> [The affiliation] proposes that there shall be in Atlanta a strong school for graduate work, equal to what can be found in any

section of the country. This work is to begin at once, in the fall of 1929, on a high plane, with graduate courses to be announced.

For my successor in the presidency, Dr. John Hope, I bespeak your hearty and unstinted cooperation. He is widely and favorably known as both educator and citizen, and is admirably equipped for the carrying out of this forward move.[99]

The affiliation was a forward move and "another chapter in the history of Negro education."[100] News of the affiliation and ensuing accolades resonated nationally and internationally. Stories of the affiliation appeared in several newspapers across the country and explained how this event made "Atlanta the United States['] center of Negro higher education."[101] Sam Small captured the event and possibly solidified the institutions' acceptance in society, when he editorialized in the *Atlanta Constitution*:

> That was a wise action by the Trustees of Atlanta University, Spelman and Morehouse College [sic], all of them educational establishments for the colored race, by which their activities are to be co-ordinated.... These three institutions have thoroughly justified their establishment by the consistent and excellent work which they have done in raising notably the niveau of intelligence among the colored people of this Southeastern area of the Union.[102]

The creation of the Atlanta University System was a monumental event and, if philanthropists, John Hope, and others had not pooled their resources and energies together, it would not have materialized. The next chapter further discusses the GEB's continued support of the Atlanta institutions, as well as John Hope's leadership acumen and vision by means of further developments at the Atlanta University System.

6
Germinating a Black Intelligentsia

> *Happily the time is far passed since the Negro has been considered a people who had best be left ignorant, to be used as truck horses or as machines made to do only the work. Virtually at the end of the "War Between the States" there was no slavery; the Negro was free and had the rights of a free man. But in reality emancipation was a slow process—struggle which was long and hard; one which is still going on. Now the long sought for goal of true emancipation seems to be in sight. The whole country is interested in the education of the Negro and the period of illiteracy seems to be swiftly passing.*
>
> —John Hope[1]

As John Hope's above remark conveys, it took 64 years after the Civil War for blacks in Atlanta to reach this milestone in higher education. Newspapers and magazine articles reported news of the affiliation nationally and internationally. The coverage not only explained the affiliation and John Hope as its leader, but also explained the affiliation's effect on black higher education, the nation, and even race relations.[2] H. S. Murphy editorialized in *The Independent*:

> There is that in him which reminds us of the scholars of the older days; the men who dignified and even mystified their learning in such a manner that their students felt that when they crossed the threshold of that teacher's sanctorum, they were treading on holy ground.

> John Hope's respect for sound scholarship and its outer accompaniments with out laying undue stress on empty honor or appearance has raised him high in the estimation of these who enjoy a democracy of brotherhood.
>
> The consolidation of Morehouse and Spelman Colleges with Atlanta University means more people, more business for our merchants, more traffic for the railroads and street cars, and more work for labor. It means that the money now being spent in the North for professional, university, and higher technical education by the Negro will be spent at the home in the graduate department of the big university system.[3]

The Landmark reported that the affiliation was "the most vigorous development in the field of Negro education going on anywhere at the present time was the development in Atlanta centering on Atlanta University."[4] *The New Chronicle* stated, "The future of the Negro race brightens when they can have such men as John Hope as their leaders."[5] Hope also received correspondence from numerous individuals who expressed their elation about his appointment. Du Bois best captured the synthesis of the affiliation and of the growth of Atlanta University, when he editorialized in *The Crisis*:

> At last the way is open for Atlanta University to come into its own. No institution in the world has the opportunity, which this old and deserving institution has lately been offered. Atlanta University had long been a pioneer, and a pioneer in causes that cost. It stood for higher education when higher education of Negroes was a matter of criticism and ridicule. It stood for the social equality of teachers and students, when both threats and inducements were offered it to make it draw the color line in its own dining room and in its public meetings. In the day when Hampton and Tuskegee, and many leading schools bowed to that prejudice, Atlanta held its unwavering ideal. Atlanta began the scientific study of the American Negro before a single other institution of learning in America offered a course of lectures on the Negro problem or made any attempt to measure or study the black man.[6]

Externally, people heralded the affiliation as "a unique achievement" and considered it a milestone in black higher education;

however, internally, the fervor was not as pleasant. News of the affiliation affected the climate of the campuses of all three institutions, particularly between rivals, Morehouse College and Atlanta University. Graduates from Morehouse were "either doubtful or vociferously opposed" to the idea of an affiliation and "resented the new status of their alma mater as an undergraduate college in an affiliation with Atlanta University." Having John Hope as president of both institutions, however, reconciled the situation.[7]

Under the charter of the affiliation, each institution remained autonomous, with its own finances, board of trustees, president, administrative offices, faculty, and student body.[8] Of all the institutions, the affiliation affected Atlanta University the most and presented a dilemma for the faculty and the students already enrolled at the institution. The alumni at Atlanta University were not as easily appeased and viewed the affiliation as the dismantling of their institution; and, in many ways, it was. The alumni "were violent in their antagonism and, with a sense of dispossession, made fantastic proposals such as to move the stained glass from the chapel, the pictures from the walls, the clock from the tower...even talked about moving Edmund Asa Ware's grave" interred on the campus.[9]

Since Atlanta University was now the graduate institution, they admitted no freshmen after the affiliation; and the following year, all undergraduate courses were discontinued. The students already enrolled had a choice either to complete their undergraduate work at Morehouse or Spelman and receive a bachelor's degree from Atlanta University, or to transfer to another institution, such as Fisk University in Tennessee or Talladega College in Alabama and complete their undergraduate work there. As for the alumni, they resented they would not receive any more "accretion from graduates with the bachelor's degree." The only conciliation for the Atlanta University graduates was that "the name of their institution had been retained."[10]

The faculty members were equally concerned as the students and alumni, but their focus was on their employment and pension. Like most black institutions at the time, most of the faculty at Atlanta University only had a bachelor's degree and were expected to teach any subject they had in college. However, times had changed and the new standards of accreditation in the late 1920s had "shifted the academic tide in a new direction, even for undergraduate education, and specialization was certainly the rule for graduate schools." As a result, specialists who had earned a master's degree and those with PhD degrees replaced most of the faculty.[11]

Despite the graduates' reactions, the affiliation was an onward march of events for the sake of progress. Atlanta University's commencement exercise in 1929 celebrated its sixtieth-year as an undergraduate institution. This was "a memorable event" because it marked "the passing of an old regime with its old loyalties," in exchange for "the beginning of a new regime faced with the task of establishing new loyalties."[12]

In 1931, Atlanta University awarded its first master's degree to Joseph A. Bailey (A. B. Morehouse) for his work in the department of history. For juniors and seniors already at Atlanta University, there was an agreement they could complete their undergraduate work at either Spelman or Morehouse and receive their degree from Atlanta University. In 1931, 16 females from Spelman received bachelor's degrees from Atlanta University; the following year, there were only 12 females, and these bachelor's degrees were the last undergraduate degrees awarded by Atlanta University.[13] Also in 1931, as Spelman celebrated its fiftieth anniversary, Rockefeller Sr. congratulated Spelman and wrote, "Of all the investments which we have made as a family, Spelman stands among the best."[14]

The higher education of blacks and the intellectual aspect of the Atlanta University System were not the only areas of significance. US President Herbert Hoover even wrote to John Hope in 1931, commending his work, and further acknowledging the national importance of the system in improving race relationships between blacks and whites, when he wrote:

> The plan to build up Atlanta University and its affiliated colleges into an institution capable of offering education of the highest type to adequately qualified Negroes so as to prepare them for such leadership of their people will add more strength

to the forces already set in motion by institutions. It should bear fruit in the furtherance of better understanding and improved relations between the races for generations to come.¹⁵

Race relations were one aspect of the Atlanta University System's significance. The System was also to serve as a model for other American institutions in the nation to follow. Hope received several correspondences from individuals, who inquired about different aspects of the affiliation.¹⁶

The affiliation was "novel among negro institutions" and considered a "trail-blazer" for cooperative arrangements among American colleges. According to newspaper reports, the affiliation in Atlanta was the same "plan contemplated by Johns Hopkins University in Baltimore." The only places in the United States that had put into operation similar ideas were in California with the Claremont Colleges and "the one carried on for many years by Clark University in Massachusetts." Although it was not a merger, *The Dallas Express* reported that the affiliation was a "single one of many such mergers to come.... There is little reason for the existence of many institutions in the same city which compete with each other in the same line of work at double the expense or nearly so."¹⁷ This line of thinking was also in the forefront of the members of the GEB's mind as it related to the white institutions in Georgia.

Jackson Davis, GEB field agent, realized the only way for educational standards and opportunities for whites in the South to equal those of the North was through cooperation among white southern institutions. His contention was that "young southern men and women go North for training and often remain there for the opportunities that opened, and in this way the South has lost some of its most brilliant young minds." For this reason, the GEB wanted to use the Atlanta University System as a model in Georgia and attempted to establish the University Center of Georgia that would consist of the University of Georgia, Emory University, Georgia Institute of Technology, and Agnes Scott College.¹⁸

In 1938, the GEB voted and approved $2.5 million toward $75 million to create this center.¹⁹ However, by 1941, education in Georgia had received a setback due to the interference of then Governor Eugene Talmadge. The State Board of Regents, its members chosen by the governor, dismissed three professors who favored racial equality, which resulted in removing both the University of Georgia and Georgia Institute of Technology from the accrediting lists of several university associations. The continued growth of the center was consequently encumbered, and this incident along with the distance between the schools eliminated further efforts of cooperation.[20]

Creation of the Atlanta University Center

News of the affiliation also caused discontent among the other black institutions in Atlanta (e.g., Clark University, its original name, and Morris Brown College). Although the presidents from each institution were present at the discussions previously held with Florence Read and John Hope regarding the joint library, each felt left out, ignored in the affiliation process, and worried about their futures after the affiliation took place.[21] "It was difficult for their constituents to realize that the affiliation was a course so fraught with perils that those who piloted it had no room in their minds at the moment for the inclusion of the other Atlanta institutions."[22] However, this was not the case; consideration was given to these institutions.[23] James P. Brawley, author of *The Clark College Legacy*, indicated this consideration when he wrote:

> While the General Education Board sponsored the early developments of the affiliation, it was no less interested in Clark University and Morris Brown College, and desired that these two institutions be related to the affiliation arrangement, and eventually to become equal partners in this new development.[24]

When Hope accepted the presidency of Atlanta University, it was during one of the worst economic eras in the United State's history. Six months after the affiliation, the stock market crashed and the country was in the midst of the Great Depression and, at the time, the worst in history. Banks failed, prosperous businesses went into bankruptcy, and money was a rare commodity. The Great Depression hurt education all over the country, but it was a hardship, as John Hope Franklin later explained, "especially on the blacks schools in the South,"[25] when he wrote:

> Construction of new school buildings stopped almost immediately, the teaching staff was curtailed to the point that the effective teaching was practically impossible, and miserably low salaries were further reduced. Southern states curtailed expenditures for Negro schools in the same or greater proportion that they were curtailed in white schools. While no Southern community could afford to cut its educational expenditures without seriously impairing the effectiveness of its program, the slightest cut in Negro education often had the effect of taking away the barest essentials in the educational program, including the teacher.[26]

While Hope directed his attention to developing a distinctive graduate program for the first year after the affiliation, the nation's crisis and the Depression's effect on black schools were in the forefront of his mind. Rather than stretch his resources too thinly, he concentrated on only a few discipline areas he thought were the most important for blacks at the time. He believed they needed to train businessmen who would, in turn, lead blacks out of their "economic wilderness." For the 1930–31 academic year, he decided the departments of education, economics and business, history, and English were the priorities.[27] However, in order to develop the departments, he needed to find funding for them.

Despite support from philanthropists and the GEB for the first year for the affiliation, philanthropists, such as Edwin Embree, president of the Rosenwald Fund, were uncertain about the affiliation's future success and hesitant about any future funding. When Atlanta University requested funds from the Rosenwald Fund the year after the affiliation, Embree refused appropriations of any funds until the institution gave him specific programs of study. In a letter to Dean Sage, member of Atlanta University's board of trustees and chairman of the finance committee, Embree wrote:

> I am sure I need not assure you of my interest and that of my associates in the work of the Atlanta group of colleges. But I

have a good many reservations about making another guarantee of any percentage of the budget of Atlanta University for its second year.[28]

Embree further explained the Rosenwald Fund helped the first year because they knew plans would not begin without emergency funds. Before Sage could submit another application to him, he demanded to know "in a good deal more detail the aspects in which [Atlanta University] proposes to make its program *unique*"; Embree also stated:

> I believe Atlanta has an opportunity now which almost never comes to an institution to plan its own work without having to take into account current activities and the momentum of past history. The only justification for building up a new private institution in the Negro field would seem to be a desire to do a very few things superbly well.[29]

Embree's statement sparked a flurry of correspondence, particularly between members of the GEB, Sage, and Hope.[30] Atlanta University had to justify needing funds for the following year, and the responsibility quite naturally fell on Hope. Because the United States was in the midst of a depression, it was impossible for Hope not to consider "current activities" as Embree mentioned. Hope combined "his idealism, his high academic standards, and the practical conditions that faced blacks in the 1930s."[31] Based on these conditions, Hope designed not only a program that applied to the academic year of 1930–31, but also one that applied to the future.

In a lengthy response, Hope answered Embree's inquiry with a "Six-Year Plan" that detailed projected graduate schools of arts and science, education, economics and business administration, music and fine arts, social work, and a library school (Appendix B). In the sixth year, Hope planned to add professional schools of law, medicine, dentistry, theology, and physical education.[32] Hope estimated he needed $6.4 million within the next five years for an endowment, buildings, and equipment in addition to funds for the joint library.[33] Hope's Six-Year Plan, requiring $6.4 million, was an incredible sum of money for blacks, and an even greater task because the United States was in the midst of the Great Depression.[34] After finalizing his plan, Hope sent the matter back to Embree, and said:

> A University plan requires money. There is no getting around that fact. When the three institutions went into the combined enterprise, they took the venture on faith, to be sure, but they expected that the Boards interested in Negro education and Negro welfare generally would give liberally.[35]

Hope firmly held his ground and further criticized Embree for not spending more time at the institutions to better acquaint himself with the work being done. Convinced he had argued his case well, Hope concluded:

> When you look into all this, I believe your faith in the building of Atlanta University will be so great as to prevent further misgiving and hesitation on your part to give it your support. We will guard against mistakes. But if there is danger of making them, to me that is all the more reason why you should come definitely to our support at this time, assisting by your counsel and by a grant of funds from your Board.[36]

Embree agreed and suggested that Hope move slowly with his appointment of faculty and staff, and further suggested that these individuals be "only men of real ability."[37]

Through Hope's vision and leadership, Atlanta University evolved into an oasis in Georgia for germinating a black intelligentsia. Hope hired individuals "who were both capable of assisting him in the development of Atlanta University and willing to play active roles" as black leaders.[38] In doing so, Hope brought outstanding scholars to the faculty, who were at the top of their fields and who conducted studies on black life in America, unlike any other institution for higher education.

In September 1930, Hope hired Clarence A. Bacote, the first professor hired to the graduate faculty in the department of history, who would later write Atlanta University's institutional history. Bacote was one of the leading historians in the country, who had degrees from University of Kansas and the University of Chicago, including a PhD from the latter.[39] Though Bacote was hired at Atlanta University, in an exchange program, he also taught, "required sophomore courses in American history to hundreds of Spelman students through an exchange agreement with Atlanta University."[40] Between the years 1930 and 1935, Hope also brought other scholars to Atlanta University such as Rayford Logan in history, Winfred Nathan and John Whittaker in education, Lorimer Milton and Jesse B. Blayton in economics and business, William Stanley Braithwaite and Luella F. Norwood in English, Hale Woodruff in fine arts, and Ira De A. Reid in sociology.[41] Hope even brought his old friend, Du Bois, back to Atlanta University.[42] Initially, Du Bois was to serve as a guest professor and to assist Hope with a "scientific survey of the economic condition of the American Negro." However, Du Bois eventually became a full-professor in the economics and sociology departments.[43]

Of the $6.4 million estimated requirements for Hope's Six-Year university program, for the years 1930–1936, Atlanta University applied for a $3.2 million grant, $1.0 million for buildings and the balance for the endowment, from the GEB. In turn, the GEB authorized the grant with the first $1.5 million contingent on the University raising the same amount from outside sources before July 1, 1933.[44]

During Atlanta University's endowment campaign, discussions of a different matter ensued, probably unknown to most. When the three Atlanta institutions signed an agreement creating the affiliation, the GEB believed this move was the first step toward a full merger of all three institutions. In a letter to Hope, Trevor Arnett, GEB president, mentioned, "It is an unusual situation in that the affiliation agreement between Atlanta, Spelman, and Morehouse is really a try out and its result in an actual merger...is the end greatly desired and expected."[45] Although much of the attention was on the joint library, at the time, in a letter to Hope, Arnett nevertheless stated:

> It is our confident expectation that the affiliation agreement will lead in due time to an actual merger, and the suggestion of a reverter [of the library] to Spelman College is to provide for a remote contingency.[46]

In a lengthy response back to Arnett, Hope chronicled all that had occurred within the institutions in the year since the affiliation—teachers and students exchanged for undergraduate courses, graduate courses were offered by members of the faculties of the three institutions, and all three libraries were opened to students of the three institutions.[47] In the event of unforeseen circumstances dissolving the affiliation, Hope was very candid regarding the ownership of the library and responded:

> When we consider what has already been accomplished, anything like severing of relations on the part of any one of the institutions seems so remote as hardly to be thought of. Yet we do know that such an outcome is possible.... For we have reason to believe that the broader purpose of the library is that all college and university students in Atlanta, without reference to whether they are the students of the institutions in the affiliation, should have the generous use of the library. It seems to us, then, that it is not so much a question as to what institution owns and controls the library as that whatever institution owns and controls it should honorably and liberally carry out the purpose of its donors.... We think furthermore that it would be well not to limit its use to colored students as we believe that the library ought to be open to all students without reference to race or creed. It is quite conceivable that this library in the future, even in the near future, will be of great advantage to white students.[48]

Though Hope expressed his opinion regarding ownership of the library, he made no mention of a full merger. Hope and Florence Read moved forward and drew up a statement indicating the grant for the library would:

> Be made through Spelman College to Atlanta University on condition that Atlanta University maintain and operate the library for its benefits and for that of the affiliated and other Negro colleges in Atlanta; but that on reversion Spelman College should undertake to operate the library not for its own benefit alone but for that of the other colleges.[49]

Discussions also ensued regarding the other black institutions in Atlanta (e.g., Morris Brown College and Clark University) coming into the affiliation. After the paper reported the news of the joint library, the presidents of both institutions felt that Hope and others had ignored them and left them out of the plan.[50] However, before the GEB would give Morris Brown or Clark any consideration of joining the affiliation, they conducted a survey to determine if such a move was feasible.

In July 1930, Jackson Davis, agent for the GEB, conducted another survey of the institutions in Atlanta. Though he commented, "thus far President Hope and Miss Read [had] more than measured up to our best expectations," he stated that "a University based solely upon Morehouse and Spelman [was not] possible, because it would leave out other institutions." He continued, "Being left out would be human enough to work against it with rivalry, duplication, and waste." For Davis, if Clark and Morris Brown did not come into the affiliation, the same problems that existed prior to the affiliation with duplication and waste would continue.[51]

Like the other institutions, Clark and Morris Brown had strong denominational ties. The Northern Methodist Church established Clark University in 1869 and financially supported the institution. Bishop D. W. Clark, of the Northern Methodist Church, had christened the school Clark University. Davis felt that Clark was an institution of "good standards and assured support." However, because it was located on the South side of Atlanta and affiliated with Gammon Theological Seminary, cooperation was difficult.[52]

The African Methodist Episcopal Church established Morris Brown in 1881 to "meet the needs of the church for an educated ministry and also to provide higher educational opportunities in academic and practical subjects" for black males and females. Morris Brown, located in East Atlanta, "was a different situation," particularly, because "of previous bad management and desperate financial difficulties."[53] While Davis suggested some time was "required to establish the institution upon a firm and assured basis," he acknowledged how Morris Brown's joining the affiliation was favorable. Apparently, he was impressed that Morris Brown represented "a self-reliant group of colored people"; all they had done represented blacks "own efforts, unaided by white people, North or South, except small contributions from the Slater Fund and the General Education Board toward the paying of one or more teachers." Furthermore, President W. A. Fountain had studied the situation and was trying to correct the "deficiencies in organization and financial accounting."[54]

Davis also noted that several individuals supported the idea of Clark, Morris Brown, and even Gammon, joining in the affiliation. However, he was not as optimistic about Gammon Theological Seminary, affiliated with Clark, joining at this time because he felt that "the various denominational groups would not consent to have their ministers trained in a union theological seminary." Despite this, Davis recommended, "something might be done to make Gammon the center for certain general subjects common to all the theological seminaries, then each denomination could give separately its own doctrinal courses."[55] Hope later agreed with Davis's observation and felt Gammon Seminary had rich traditions and good financial resources. Because Gammon was connected to the Methodist church, Hope suggested that it was better for Gammon to join "without denominational ties," which meant "drastic changes" were needed.[56]

In August 1930, Hope met with Arnett and discussed the plans of the library and plans for incorporating the other institutions. With the statement drawn between Spelman and Atlanta University, Arnett informed Hope that he would present the matter of the library to the GEB and suggested Hope make every effort "to promote cooperation and close working arrangements with the other institutions." Arnett advised Hope that Atlanta University needed a definite plan that would garner public buy-in of the University's work, and stated that the GEB "could not consider making annual appropriations indefinitely pending the adoption of a definite financial and educational program." Similar to Davis's earlier conclusion, Arnett also felt that by leaving Clark and Morris Brown out of the affiliation, duplication of courses and wasted resources would continue. But he more so feared that having these two institutions unaffiliated might jeopardize the newly established affiliation by competing against Morehouse and Spelman.

Hope strengthened his plans at Atlanta University, hired other distinguished scholars, created more courses on the graduate level (e.g., English, Latin, French, chemistry, mathematics, and sociology), and dropped home economics from the curriculum. In the interim of hiring the graduate faculty, Morehouse and Spelman's faculty members taught courses in an exchange program.[57] In the academic year of 1931–1932, Atlanta University had 69 graduate students with bachelor degrees from 18 colleges enrolled. By 1932–1933, the enrollment increased to 85 graduate students.[58]

Hope immediately made plans for cooperation with Clark and Morris Brown, met with Dr. Holmes, secretary of the Educational Work among Negroes of the Northern Methodist Church, and assured him Clark and Gammon were welcomed. He also met with President Fountain and made plans to visit Morris Brown to familiarize himself with the plant and the difficulties the institution faced.[59] While Hope met with the presidents of the colleges in the foreground, others held informal meetings and discussions behind the scene.

In the 1930s, the city of Atlanta had a large black population of 84,000 people and represented the largest black center of business in the South.[60] One wonders if this was one of the factors for bringing the other institutions into the affiliation, as it had been with the initial three institutions. In an informal three-day conference, members of the GEB and several white educators discussed the city of Atlanta and the possibility of expanding the affiliation. This meeting consisted of college presidents, such as M. L. Brittain, Georgia Institute of Technology, J. R. McCain, Agnes Scott College, and T. H. Jack, vice president of Emory University, Dean Oppenheimer, Emory Medical School, Mr. Kendall Weisiger, trustee of Morehouse and Atlanta University, and Mr. Clark Foreman, associate for studies with the Rosenwald Fund.[61] Recounting this informal meeting, Davis stated:

> All of these persons are conscious of the opportunity for the development in Atlanta of a center of first importance in the higher education of Negroes. They all expressed an active interest

and their readiness to help, in any possible way, to make the most of the opportunity. The impression prevails that Atlanta University should represent the coordination and affiliation of all of the Negro Institutions including Gammon Theological Seminary and the Atlanta School of Social Work.[62]

When the discussion turned to the possible fields of graduate and professional work, "there seemed general agreement upon the arts, sciences, education, and theology to train high school and college teachers, ministers, and others desiring work of this type. Additionally, there was a general agreement that the field of business should be given particular attention." They discussed the field of engineering; however, since this field was closed to blacks, individuals in attendance felt there was no practicality for this type of department. They also decided there was no need for another medical school for blacks in the South because Howard University in Washington, D.C., Meharry Medical College in Nashville, Tennessee, and the developments at University of Chicago provided adequate service for individuals who were ready for such endeavors. Considering the other institutions and the library, Davis noted Morris Brown's situation, suggested that Atlanta University temporarily rent its old buildings to Morris Brown, and that they place the location of the library between Morehouse and Spelman.[63] After the meeting, the group met with Hope and reviewed the tentative sketches of campus developments Hope had drawn, as Davis so outlined:

> It seems assured that the development of Atlanta University will be in the neighborhood of Morehouse and Spelman. The lot which has been purchased for the library contains two and three-tenths acres.... If this could be acquired, Morehouse College might be willing to let Atlanta University have the front part of its campus this shaping out a quadrangle in between Morehouse and Spelman. The property on Chestnut Street fronting the library lot and Morehouse College should also be acquired.[64]

With these technicalities resolved, Hope favored Morris Brown's development "on the twenty acre tract" and was willing to rent the old Atlanta University buildings to Morris Brown temporarily. Davis concluded that one pressing concern was Hope's dual position as president of both Atlanta University and Morehouse because he was "not free to give even his whole time to Atlanta University." Davis suggested that Hope "be relieved of the Morehouse campaign," and that they give assistance "in every possible way."[65]

Hope received word that the GEB resolved $450,000 in appropriations to Atlanta University for the library in November 1930.[66] Following completion of construction, the GEB appropriated an endowment of $600,000 to provide an income for the maintenance for the building and for the annual appropriations for books and periodicals.[67] Showing gratitude and his amazement of the changing times in philanthropic giving and in society, Hope wrote to Arnett and stated:

> As a man who has spent most of his life in the South, this gift appeals to me as amazing. I do not believe I can quite tell it to you in a letter. I have known Atlanta University in a way ever since I was about four years of age, when I was brought from Augusta, Georgia, to Atlanta by my aunt to visit my brother and sister who were then students in this institution. It seems strange to me that after a lapse of so many years I, as president, should be accepting this gift for Atlanta University. How beautiful and practical philanthropy had been![68]

Hope's letter put the institutions' growth into perspective by illustrating the institutions had been "so broadly conceived" after 50 years that "a great library becomes a necessity."[69] However, the GEB had planned this all along; using the library, though an asset to the institutions, as a mechanism to force cooperation among the three institutions.

Also in 1930, Morehouse and Spelman Colleges were elected into the membership of the Association of American Colleges. At this time, only six black institutions were among the 400 members elected: Howard, Lincoln, Fisk, and Wilberforce Universities, and Morehouse and Spelman Colleges.[70] During the same time, the Southern Association of Colleges and Secondary Schools (SACS) added seven black institutions to the approved list. Fisk University was the only black institution that received a "Class A" rating, which signified meeting all standards including salaries. Morehouse and Spelman Colleges received "Class B," along with Johnson C. Smith, Talladega and Virginia State Colleges, and Virginia Union University.[71]

Arnett, Embree, and Sage exchanged letters discussing their individual visits to the Atlanta institutions' campuses, noting that financial challenges were again eminent.[72] The GEB had granted $3.2 million toward the $6.4 million endowment required for Hope's Six-Year Plan for Atlanta University. However, funds that they initially secured to meet the GEB's $1.5 million condition were contingent upon the Rosenwald Fund upholding its $500,000 pledge. When the pledge was due, however, the Rosenwald Fund failed to comply. Most of the institutional histories merely state that Atlanta University received $500,000 from an "anonymous friend,"[73] but reviewing correspondence between philanthropists and members of the GEB, it was revealed that the "anonymous friend" was not so anonymous after all.[74]

Atlanta University secured $1.0 million from Edward Harkness, a philanthropist and Sage's Yale classmate, on condition the institution secured another $500,000 before April 1, 1931. Additionally, Atlanta University had to secure another $500,000 to receive $1.5 million from the GEB. Sage was notified that the Rosenwald Fund denied the $500,000 pledge and believed that Embree, director of the Rosenwald Fund, had "virtually closed the door on a capital contribution." In a letter to Arnett, Sage pleaded for assistance and asked Arnett to bring the matter to Rockefeller Jr.'s attention.[75]

Complying with Sage's wishes, Arnett wrote to Rockefeller Jr., gave an update of the institutions in Atlanta, and stated that the Atlanta institutions offered "the greatest opportunity in America for an outstanding achievement in Negro education."[76] Arnett also explained that Atlanta University was desperate, "virtually without funds," and that the institution "must secure funds to enable it to begin its work at a reasonable level." Though

Arnett admitted that both he and Sage knew neither the GEB nor Rockefeller Jr. was obligated to provide aid under such an emergency, he argued that if Rockefeller Jr. assisted in "putting Atlanta University in a position to function permanently on a modest level," his involvement was justified.[77]

Initially, Rockefeller Jr. felt it was not advisable for him to "make contributions toward supplemental sums to be raised to meet conditional appropriations made by any of the Rockefeller boards."[78] Despite these feelings, just as he had done with purchasing the land for the library and assisting Hope personally, he underwrote the $500,000 and gave Arnett permission to pledge this amount on his behalf; but, he wanted it made in the same manner as his contributions in the past. He gave the money on condition it remained "anonymous and no mention should be of [his] name, except as may be necessary to Mr. Harkness and the General Education Board."[79]

Several other events in the early 1930s had an impact on the Atlanta institutions. By January 1932, Hope received a request from President Fountain for a three- or five-year lease of the old Atlanta University buildings. Morris Brown joined in the affiliation and moved to this location. Additionally in this year, Morehouse completed its endowment campaign, and Hope relinquished his reign of control at Morehouse and was "now able to devote his energies on developing Atlanta University."[80] They also completed the construction of the library (Figure 6.1).

Building the new Trevor Arnett Library provided employment for 275 men who desperately needed work. The structure of the library was of "Georgian style and was designed by James Rogers, who also designed the Harkness Quadrangle at Yale University and the Medical Center in New York City." The space provided for 175,000 volumes of books and had a seating capacity for approximately 600 students; Atlanta University, Morehouse, and Spelman transferred their books to the new library. Before the official dedication took place, a new paved road to "Greensferry Avenue was built." The engineer for the project was Edward Swain Hope, John Hope's eldest son, who had graduated from the Massachusetts Institute of Technology. Official dedication for the library was April 30, 1932.[81]

Germinating a Black Intelligentsia   167

Figure 6.1 Photograph of Trevor Arnett Library, undated, Atlanta University Photographs—Buildings/Grounds.
Source: Atlanta University Center Robert W. Woodruff Library, Atlanta, Georgia

By the end of 1932, Atlanta University, Morehouse College, and Spelman College received a "Class A" rating from SACS, which was "the highest rating of the Southern Association to the bachelor's degree conferred by Morehouse College and Spelman College and to the master's degree conferred by Atlanta University."[82] While it took half a century for this to happen, SACS now recognized all three institutions as fully fledged, accredited institutions of higher education.

Due to dwindling missionary funds, caused by the Depression, the American Baptist Home Mission Society (ABHMS) decided to sever ties with many of its institutions, including Morehouse. By 1935, the ABHMS deeded "two and a fraction of [Morehouse's] land" to Atlanta University.[83] During this same year, President Davage, Clark University, Hope and members of the GEB continued to discuss steps they would take to bring Clark into the affiliation and discussed methods for securing funds for Morris Brown.[84]

It was also during this time that Hope expressed his thoughts of all the institutions joining into a federation (Figure 6.2).[85] In a letter to Leo Favrot, GEB member, Hope mentioned it was necessary for all four undergraduate institutions to be on the same-leveled field (e.g., the same fees for tuition and for room and board) and to have all the colleges' faculties of "equal value" for exchange "in any of the colleges," particularly for the freshmen and sophomore courses. These changes ensured students' preparation so when students met in their junior and senior year, there was "no disparity in preparation." In closing, Hope mentioned that planning was necessary for a "real federation," and that "sooner or later" everyone had to "face all the factors

Figure 6.2 Photograph of John Hope, ca. 1935, photographer—Blackstone Studios.

Source: Atlanta University Photographs—Individuals, Atlanta University Center Robert W. Woodruff Library, Atlanta, Georgia.

involved." Last, Hope believed in the endless opportunities of the Atlanta institutions, when he wrote:

> There is a wonderful opportunity in Atlanta for fine federation among these Negro institutions. To delay this federation much longer might mean the loss of great educational advantages to an institution that could be of nationwide and perhaps worldwide service and influence.[86]

Whether Hope meant a full merger of the undergraduate institutions when he used the term "federation" one will never know. He neither lived to see these plans materialize nor witnessed the other institutions join in the affiliation. Hope worked valiantly to complete his tasks as president of Atlanta University and as a black activist around the nation.

Unforeseeably, three months after he shared his thoughts about a federation, he succumbed to pneumonia. His abrupt death, on February 20, 1936, left everyone who knew him in shock and disbelief. A few days after his death, Hope's funeral services were held at Morehouse's Sale Hall Chapel. For five hours preceding the funeral services, his body lay in state and more people paid their respects than the chapel could hold. The funeral service was "brief and simple," as he had requested. The students and congregation sang several hymns; the Morehouse College Quartet sang spirituals; Samuel Archer, president of Morehouse, gave remarks; and W. W. Alexander provided a prayer. Eight of Hope's students carried his body to "a simple grave" on the campus of Atlanta University, where it remains today[87] (Figure 6.3).

Numerous letters, telegrams, expressions of appreciation were sent to the institution's officials and Florence Read, and editorials highlighted his significance to black higher education and to the nation. The day after Hope's death, John D. Rockefeller, III, sent Florence Read a telegram stating his distress upon hearing news of Hope's death:

> Distressed to hear sad news[.] It is hard to think of the University without the Doctor[.] His passing will be a great loss[.] May I join with his many friends in extending deepest sympathy to his family and his associates[.][88]

Figure 6.3 Photograph of John Hope memorial services, 1936, Atlanta University Photographs—Individuals.
Source: Atlanta University Center Robert W. Woodruff Library, Atlanta, Georgia.

John D. Rockefeller Jr. also stated the same sentiment as his son's telegram, when he wrote, "the death of John Hope [was] a great blow. How sadly he will be missed and how difficult it will be to find someone to take his place!"[89]

However, the most revealing sentiments of Hope were reflected in the July 1936 issue of *The Atlanta University Bulletin*, which was solely dedicated to him. Numerous expressions of appreciation filled the bulletin for him as a president and leader, and for him as a great man:

> I greatly lament the passing of your honored president, John Hope, and send on behalf of his old class at Brown our deepest sympathy in your loss. His regard among the members of our class was very high and ever heightened with the lapse of years. The colored race in America has lost a great educator, friend and guide.
> —Henry D. Sharpe
> *Class of 1894, Brown University*

> I am sad at the death of President Hope, whom I counted a personal friend. The nation has lost a distinguished educator and the race a great leader.
> —Edwin R. Embree
> *President, Julius Rosenwald Fund*

> The country has lost one of its ablest educators and I have lost a dear personal friend.
> —Abraham Flexner
> *Institute for Advanced Study,*
> *Princeton, N.J.*

> The faculty and students of Bethune-Cookman College and the national Council of Colored Women join me in the expression of deepest grief at the loss of a foremost educator, American citizen of the highest order, and a friend.
> —Mary McLeod Bethune
> *President, Bethune-Cookman College*

> I valued the friendship of Dr. Hope more than I can ever express. I regarded him as one of the outstanding Christian leaders, not only of his own important race, but likewise of the whole people of our country. He had a large influence, not only in the educational work of America, but also in such significant movements as the Young Men's Christian Association.
> —John R. Mott
> *World Alliance of the Young Men's*
> *Christian Association*

> Deeply moved by news of homegoing of Dr. Hope, my beloved friend and one of America's greatest citizens.
> —William E. Speers
> *Chairman, General Board, Y. M. C. A*
> —Francis Harmon *General Secretary,*
> *International Committee, Y. M. C. A*

Some institutional histories highlight Trevor Arnette's tribute to Hope as most fitting,[90] while others mention that Bacote's comments synthesized and captured Hope's life and contributions.[91] Some philanthropists and GEB members such as Leo Favrot,

Trevor Arnett, and Anson Phelps Stokes also expressed a "great personal loss" and the "loss of a personal friend."[92] However, from all the tributes in the *Bulletin*, the most fitting really came from Jackson Davis, GEB's associate director, because it encapsulated Hope's essence and his significance to the affiliation, when he wrote:

> The development of Atlanta University based upon the cooperation of all the Negro colleges of Atlanta is a unique achievement in higher education in the South, and all of those who have had anything to do with it have the highest admiration for the way in which he [President Hope] brought it about step by step. His whole background and his wide experience prepared him for the opportunity which this situation presented. He understood all the complex human relationships so well that he never lost patience or tried to hurry a decision before the time was ripe for it. As a result, voluntary cooperation has proceeded without the loss of independence, and his administration closes with good will and unity of purpose prevailing because he took time to help others see the larger aims. He placed his emphasis on this larger understanding and the will to cooperate rather than upon mere organization. Atlanta University is the best example we have of cooperation with differences. Dr. Hope's passing is a tragic loss to the unfinished work which he had in mind; but the foundation which he has laid is so firm that there can be no question of the ultimate development, and those who carry on in the future will be constantly strengthened for their task by the heritage of gentleness and understanding which he leaves to Atlanta University.[93]

It is evident that Hope had unfinished business, but as Davis indicated, he laid the groundwork and a strong foundation for his successor to follow. Five years after his death, in 1941, Clark University changed its name to Clark College and joined the affiliation with the other Atlanta institutions. The name change was "to avoid confusion of having two universities in the Center," and because now, Clark was to serve as "an undergraduate college along with the other undergraduate colleges clustered around Atlanta University."[94]

In 1957, a new contract created the Atlanta University Center, with each institution holding coequal membership that included the Atlanta School of Social Work and Interdenominational Theological Center, a consortium of denominational seminaries that includes the School of Religion of Morehouse and Morris Brown Colleges, Lane College of Jackson, Tennessee, and Atlanta's Gammon Theological Seminary.[95]

7
Conclusion

> The highest trait of greatness in John Hope—a man of marked intellectual power; of noble ideals and wide capabilities; not merely a dreamer of dreams, but one endowed with the tenacity of purpose to make those dreams into realities; and yet withal, a man so simple, so gentle, so lovable, so free from narrow selfishness and mean ambition. Upon him was the hall-mark of the truest greatness—humility of spirit.[1]

John Hope attained success in his life and received numerous awards and recognition for his service in education, especially in the black community, where his contribution is evident even today in the organizations and schools that bear his name.

Hope had "an affinity for underprivileged youth and recognized the need to establish a continuing educational recreation place" for black males. He had dedicated many years of his life making plans and obtaining funds for a camp for black boys. However, his sudden death deprived him of seeing the fruition of both the Atlanta University Center and what is today known as Camp John Hope FAA-FCCLA Center.

Hope was instrumental in developing a camp for "the large number of Negro boys in the state of Georgia" in 1933. He had requested that Channing Tobias, president of Howard University and senior secretary of the Colored Work Department of the National Council of the YMCA, conduct a survey of the situation of black boys in Georgia. Tobias found there were 129,466 black boys, between the ages of 10 and 19 in Georgia, with only 22 percent living in urban areas.

In response, Hope established "the Georgia State Council for Work among Negro Boys" and served as its president. In 1934, they held a second meeting and made the decision to provide camping facilities for black boys and girls. The board of regents of the University System of Georgia acted as sponsor of the project. Later, the State Department of Education accepted the camp facility for the "New [Future] Farmers of America (FFA) and the New Homemakers of America (FHA)." Original membership consisted of New Farmers of America, Boys Club of America, Boys Scouts, 4-H Clubs, the YMCA, private schools and colleges, business and professions; later to be joined was the YWCA and the Girls Reserve. The camp's construction started in 1937 and was completed in 1938, two years after Hope's death. Today, Camp John Hope FAA-FCCLA Center is the leadership center for FFA-FCCLA (Family Career and Community Leaders of American) students across the state and is located on 226 acres of land in Macon, Georgia, and situated on Lake Lasseter.[2]

In Providence, Rhode Island, there is a John Hope Settlement House that is a part of the United Way. For 60 years, Settlement House has improved the lives of low income families in South Providence, Elmwood, and West End communities "by providing a comprehensive array of social services, advocacy, education programs[,] and recreational activities." As an indication of the importance of this service, in one year alone, "over 14,000 people turned to us for help with the struggles of poverty and with their quest for self-sufficiency and a better life." The communities it serves are "among the most diverse in both the City of Providence and the State of Rhode Island. These neighborhoods also represent the poorest in Rhode Island with the highest levels of children in poverty, low median family income, and high unemployment rates."[3]

Schools also bear the memory of John Hope. In Atlanta, Georgia, there is Hope-Hill Elementary School, a part of the Atlanta Public School System and named for John Hope and Charles Walter Hill. Hope-Hill is a Title 1 school that serves 403 inner city students (95 percent black; 5 percent Hispanic), and is "the oldest public school in Atlanta...located in the community just north of the Martin Luther King, Jr. National Historic Site and east of downtown Atlanta."[4] In Chicago, Illinois, there is the John Hope College Preparatory High School that serves grades 9–12, mostly blacks and Hispanics, with an enrollment of over 500 students.[5]

Hope also received awards and honors acknowledging his educational leadership from foundations, institutions of higher education in the United States and abroad, national organizations, and even the US military. In 1929, Hope won the William E. Harmon Foundation award for Distinguished Achievement among Negroes, commonly known as the Harmon Award—a gold medal in the education category. There is little doubt the Harmon Foundation acknowledged Hope for the work and effort he put into creating the Atlanta University System. Brown University honored Hope with the Doctor of Laws degree in 1935 for his "outstanding work in the field of education and the betterment of interracial relations." Other colleges and universities also honored Hope with the Doctor of Laws degree, including Bates College (Maine), Bucknell University (Pennsylvania), Howard University (Washington, DC), and McMaster University (Ontario, Canada).[6] In 1936, the NAACP awarded Hope with the Spingarn Medal posthumously, awarded for "the highest or noblest achievement by an American Negro during the preceding year or years."[7] The United States Maritime Commission even honored Hope on January 30, 1944, with the launching of the Liberty ship, S. S. John Hope.[8]

From all accounts, John Hope was a well-respected individual who made an impact locally and nationally. However, what is most important here is the impact he made in the lives of blacks and in the higher education of blacks. He was never one who cowered in the presence of wealthy white men or philanthropists or was a pawn in their game of capitalism. The culmination of Hope's career, educational convictions, and relationship with philanthropists paired with the philanthropists' dedication to black higher education was evident in the creation of the Atlanta University complex.

"Throughout American history, private-sector philanthropy has been a means by which philanthropic actors empower themselves, strive for a social ideal, and redefine themselves in society. Yet, the philanthropic relationship depends on both donor and recipient—and neither is truly a passive participant."[9] Every position John Hope held provided him the opportunity to strengthen his leadership skills and to develop a positive relationship with wealthy white men and philanthropists. Highlighting John Hope's involvement with the affiliation of the Atlanta institutions provided a good example of this type of relationship with philanthropists where neither he nor they were passive participants.[10] The relationship he cultivated with philanthropists was more than one of wealthy whites dominating black college leaders; a kinship and reciprocity existed between these individuals.

Gifts of themselves are bereft of purpose; as such, the greater the gift, the more tenuous is the balance between benevolence and malevolence.[11] Philanthropic giving, during the time of my research, as it is now, is no exception. When viewing philanthropic involvement in the higher education of blacks during the early twentieth century, it was necessary to reweigh the scale of the particulars. Granted, one side of the scale is loaded with obvious influences by the GEB, such as the funding appropriations to certain institutions, withholding funds, conditional grants, Florence Read's appointment to the presidency of Spelman, the Trevor Arnett Library, etc. Although these are examples of philanthropists' persuasion, one cannot view them as simple manipulation, a black-white dichotomy, without considering the dynamic growth it fueled. Clearly, the growth of black institutions belongs on the other side of the scale.

It is evident that the creation of the Atlanta University System/Center would not have come into existence without the combined efforts of philanthropists, the GEB, John Hope, and others working together. Essentially, each was needed to accomplish the task. The affiliation was a historic event; the creation of the Atlanta University System, then later Center, was even more so, as is apparent by the National Historic Preservation Society designating it as a historic district in Atlanta.[12]

At times, scholars' portrayal of the relationship between philanthropists and black leaders is one dimensional and too narrow a view to describe the human dynamics of philanthropists and black leaders, particularly in the case of John Hope. Examining the affiliation of the Atlanta institutions illustrates how John Hope transformed a situation into one of growth and development by accepting what he could get and changing it into something better. The something better is clearly the weightier side of the scales, as witnessed by the number of graduates, notable or ortherwise, from the Atlanta University System/Center (Appendix C).

Thus, philanthropists and the GEB's influence on the higher education of blacks and black college presidents, such as Hope, was not as one dimensional as to be either benevolent or manipulative. The relationship is best described as symbiotic. In symbiosis, the control mechanism of the relationship shifts back and forth, as each party defines and redefines its needs and expectations. Each side strives to reach a balance, but as is true in almost all human endeavors, balance (stasis) is nebulous and inconsistent. Thus, to limit either party to the narrow confines of manipulator or manipulated denies both parties the accolades for having established higher education opportunities for the maligned black race, particularly in Atlanta, Georgia.

Rather than minimizing discussion of the efforts made by philanthropists and individuals involved in black higher education, or simply focusing on either the philanthropists' perspective or the recipients' perspective, telling the story of the Atlanta institutions' affiliation sheds light on the evolving transformation that occurred before, during, and after the affiliation and the outcome of individuals' efforts.

A few men came from humble beginnings; some lacked formal education, yet recreated themselves as the nation's wealthiest individuals. These individuals, in turn, transformed the nation from an agrarian society to the world's leading industrial society.

Educational policies regarding blacks changed from prohibiting educational opportunities to establishing black institutions of higher education, which produced the nation's black leaders.

The South transformed from a region of segregation norms to a region of integration and democracy. Society's views and perceptions of blacks and blacks' educational achievement changed from the belief that blacks were unintelligent, uncivilized beings to individuals capable of learning and being productive citizens. Although racial issues still exist today, the United States is much different now than it was during the late 1800s and early 1900s.

Philanthropists and the GEB began their involvement with higher education for blacks on a questionable plane because they maintained the Southern caste system and accepted the South's prejudices and racism toward blacks. At its onset, the GEB mostly gave its appropriations to institutions implementing and emphasizing an industrial education curriculum. Although one cannot argue with this, what is evident is that the establishment of the GEB created "an organization which shortly became the most powerful educational foundation in the world,"[13] and had the greatest impact on the continuation of black institutions than did any other foundation. By the turn of the twentieth century, philanthropists changed their focus to include supporting institutions of higher education for blacks that had a liberal arts curriculum. During its span of almost 60 years, while dealing within a segregated society under Jim Crow laws, the GEB gave more than $41 million to black colleges and universities and aided in the affiliation that created the Atlanta University System, later the Atlanta University Center.[14]

Aside from black philanthropy and the missionary societies, Rockefeller Sr., his son Junior, and the GEB were the greatest financial benefactors of Atlanta University and its affiliated colleges, particularly Spelman College. Because of their funding appropriations, interest, and involvement, black institutions in Atlanta still exist today. John Hope, born in the South with physical features to pass as white and educated in the North, made a conscientious decision to return to the South and to make his life's mission aiding blacks and elevating their level of education and status in society. The current successes of Clark Atlanta University, Morehouse College, and Spelman College are examples of the GEB's and John Hope's aim of building up strong higher education institutions for blacks from which black leaders would emerge. These institutions are among the leading black colleges and universities, with Spelman and Morehouse Colleges having two of the richest endowments of all the black colleges.[15] Moreover, of all the black colleges, Morehouse and Spelman Colleges continue to rank as the top historically black colleges and universities,[16] and major newspapers lists them as national colleges and universities.[17]

Over the years, historians and scholars have highlighted the relationship between philanthropists and black leaders; yet much of the discussion is dichotomous with very little revealed about the outcome of these relationships. It is my hope that this book not only adds to the current literature on black higher education, but also complicates the dichotomous viewpoint between philanthropists and black college leaders. Using the affiliation of Atlanta University, Morehouse College, and Spelman College illustrates this different viewpoint by showing that there were professional relationships and personal friendships between philanthropists and John Hope. More importantly, it is my hope that this book elevates the importance of black leaders, such as John Hope, who had the fortitude and ingenuity to make a difference and the courage and conviction to stand up for the betterment of black higher education.

Why has the story of the affiliation never been told? I can only speculate. However, what I do know is reflecting on the affiliation, history, and achievements of the Atlanta institutions puts the history of black higher education into perspective by providing the opening into a wider discourse beyond agencies of manipulator and manipulated. Philanthropists' positive involvement in black higher education, positive relationships between wealthy whites and black college leaders, such as John Hope, and the story of the affiliation deserve recognition and discussion throughout the annals of the history of higher education and the higher educational achievement of blacks. The affiliation deserves a chapter alone, and to exclude it is simply unconscionable.

Appendix A

Other Strategic Locations for Cooperation among Black Institutions

The Atlanta University System was not the only location the GEB focused its attention on regarding black institutions affiliating or merging. Since most philanthropists regarded Fisk University in Nashville, Tennessee, as the "capstone" of black higher education, the GEB directed its early efforts toward building up higher education for blacks there. Fisk opened only a few months after the end of the Civil War and was the first US institution to offer liberal arts education to former slaves.[1]

However, there were philanthropists who privately preferred industrial education to liberal arts and implied that black colleges and universities should reflect such a curriculum. Julius Rosenwald, for example, wrote a letter to Abraham Flexner in 1917 and expressed his displeasure of Fisk students' demeanor and the institution's liberal arts curricular focus. "There seemed to be an air of superiority among [students]," as Rosenwald commented, "and a desire to take on the spirit of the whole university rather than the spirit which has always impressed me so at Tuskegee."[2] In response, Flexner acknowledged Rosenwald's concern and stated he felt assured, "with proper support Dr. McKenzie [would] transform the institution and make it what the colored race so badly needs—an institution where sound academic training can be obtained."[3]

Because the GEB was convinced that Fayette McKenzie, Fisk's white president, was sympathetic enough to the board's policy, they selected McKenzie and Fisk as a model for black higher education. By 1914, the GEB had given Fisk $70,000[4]; six years later, the GEB pledged $500,000 toward a $1 million endowment drive, the first of its kind.[5] Within five years, Fisk successfully completed the campaign with additional pledges from other philanthropists, the board of trustees, blacks, and other citizens in the community.[6]

During the midst of the campaign, blacks had begun in large force the "Great Black Migration," moving from the "rural South to the industrial North." This migration, as Du Bois's biographer David Levering Lewis pointed out, produced "the metropolitan dynamism undergirding the [Harlem] Renaissance."[7] The Harlem Renaissance existed from 1917 through 1935, and as Lewis explained:

> The Talented Tenth formulated and propagated a new ideology of racial assertiveness that was to be embraced by the physicians, dentists, educators, preachers, businesspeople, lawyers, and morticians who comprised the bulk of the African American affluent and influential—some ten thousand men and women out of the total population in 1929 of more than ten million.[8]

The Talented Tenth was a minority of the population who used organizations such as the NAACP and the National Urban League as vehicles to disseminate material.[9] Blacks felt that art, in its various genres, "was the means to change society in order to be accepted into it."[10] In describing the essence of the Harlem Renaissance, John Hope Franklin wrote:

> The literature of the Harlem Renaissance was for the most part, the work of a race-conscious group. Through poetry, prose, and song, the writers cried out against social and economic wrongs. They protested against segregation and lynching. They demanded higher wages, shorter hours, and better conditions of work. They stood for full equality and first-class citizenship.[11]

The height of the Renaissance was in 1924 when Charles Spurgeon Johnson, a premier sociologist and then editor of *Opportunity* magazine, "sent invitations to some dozen young and mostly unknown" black "poets and writers to attend a celebration at

Manhattan's Civic Club of the sudden outpouring of 'Negro' writings." Because of this event, the "Renaissance shifted into high gear."[12] There is little doubt the Harlem Renaissance's spirit transcended the world of academe.

As the 1920s progressed, blacks in the United States and in colleges changed; no longer would students accept being voiceless. College campuses became more liberal and allowed students to express their individuality and to influence campus policy. The nationalist tendency of the New Negro Movement manifested itself in a push for black studies and, in some cases, there was a desire for increased black control of institutions than those currently headed by whites.[13] Fisk University and its students were no exception to this movement.

Fayette McKenzie, Fisk's president, attempted to thwart and discourage students' principles of equalitarianism. He disbanded "the student government association, forbade dissent, and suspended the *Fisk Herald*," the students' publication.[14] Consequently, the alumni and students, led by W. E. B. Du Bois, attacked McKenzie's administration; and in 1925, Fisk's students protested and rioted on the campus. In a telegram to Wallace Buttrick, McKenzie briefly explained this event:

> Have just wired Mr. Cravath that Dr. Du Bois tonight bitterly attacked practically every policy of the University without largely substantial support[.] My usefulness will be largely gone.... Sixteen years ago a similar attack led to the resignation of President Merrill[.] I have done my best[.] My only personal concern is for the support of my family[.] I am not a quitter[.][15]

Evidently, McKenzie was trying to convince himself more so than Buttrick in his telegram, because not less than a year later, he resigned.[16] Some scholars maintained that after this upheaval, philanthropists were only comfortable with "Hampton, Tuskegee, and similar industrial normal schools."[17] Leroy Davis, John Hope's biographer, noted, "this uncontrolled behavior on black campuses frightened the philanthropic societies and [that philanthropists] labeled such behavior 'radical' or 'militant' and expected college presidents to keep their students in check."[18]

As evidence of this, the trustees accepted McKenzie's resignation and informed members of the GEB of his decision.[19]

Another attempt to elevate Fisk's status was with an affiliation with Meharry Medical College in 1928. The GEB, the Julius Rosenwald Fund, and others appropriated more than $1.5 million toward the cost of a new place across from Fisk. However, the hopes of the two institutions coming together in a closer degree of cooperation and giving each greater educational stature never materialized. Meharry's faculty perceived the science teaching at Fisk was inadequate; Fisk's trustees were weary of carrying an extra financial burden.[20] However, Fisk finally received its first black president years later with the appointment of Charles Spurgeon Johnson.

During the second half of the 1920s, students at Howard University also protested and were "more violent and less pious than students in the mission colleges." Students' demands included "the appointment of a [black] president, more emphasis in classes on the 'Negro experience,' fewer religious services, and relaxation of the rigid rules and strict discipline." One result of the protest was the appointment of Mordecai Johnson, a Morehouse alumni, as Howard's first black president. For some, the removal of white presidents at Fisk and Howard, and the appointment of black presidents, "epitomized the New Negro militancy" on black college campuses.[21]

Regarding another possible center for higher education, the GEB had not given much thought to Howard University's academic needs because it was a federally funded institution. As such, the GEB decided to take "no step that would weaken the responsibility of the federal government to support the institution."[22] Howard's administrators also felt that "Congress would be less inclined to rally to its support," if private foundations assumed any interest.[23] Despite this, during a capital campaign in the 1920s, Howard secured $80,000 from the GEB for construction of a new medical school building.[24]

The GEB's other attempt was prompted by Thomas Jesse Jones's suggestion to merge Straight University and New Orleans University in his 1916 study, though it did not happen until years later. By the 1920s, "the buildings and equipment of the two colleges were cramped and antiquated, and so was the hospital" at New Orleans University.[25] The two institutions were both struggling to survive and plans for a merger ensued in 1929. This was the GEB's only successful full-merger of black colleges and universities. In 1930, Straight University and New Orleans University officially formed Dillard University. Xavier University, a private Catholic institution, was also in the area; thus, having Dillard and Xavier secured higher education for blacks in New Orleans.[26]

Appendix B

Letter: John Hope to Edwin Embree (Hope's Six-Year Plan)

February 22, 1930

Mr. Edwin Embree
President
Julius Rosenwald Fund
Chicago, Illinois

Dear Mr. Embree:

Your letter of February 18 and your secretary's letter of February 18 enclosing a copy of your letter to Mr. Jerome (missent to Nashville) reached me Thursday. I have read most carefully your letter of February 12 to Mr. Jerome, and again the letter of December 7, which you wrote me after our conversation in Chicago.

2. In my recommendations for the next six years I have had in mind what Spelman College and Morehouse College are able to bring to this University venture, and I have had in mind a plan that begins with what we have and is capable of expansion and development as fast as, but not faster than, resources become available.

3. I am asking you therefore patiently to consider with me the whole situation as if you had never heard my previous discussion.

4. We have to begin with, three institutions which have for years been in the forefront of colleges for Negroes. Their traditions are wholesome and their standards for scholarship and character have been honest.

5. Simply to take account of "stock on hand," your attention is called to the figures below taken from the printed Reference List of the John F. Slater Fund—1929—(Occasional Papers No. 20):

	Teachers		College Students	Boarders	Teachers Salaries	Total Salaries
Morehouse	25	Men	391	288	36,760	49,725
*Spelman	38	Women	145	235	58,560	94,145
	63		536	523	95,320	143,870
Atlanta U.	18	Men	221	177	26,289	50,303
Fisk	38	Women	533	320	63,655	104,740
Talladega	40	"	254	240	69,000	89,800
Wiley	32	"	404	325	27,095	38,836

*The salary items for Spelman include both high school and college teachers but they are left as they indicate <u>resources</u>—available funds—of the institution.

6. When it comes to endowment resources, if we count on the successful conclusion of the present campaigns of Spelman and Morehouse—which would have been carried through if the affiliation had not occurred and which will still be completed regardless of the University scheme—we should have, before entering upon a University campaign, endowment as follows:

Morehouse College	920,000
Spelman College	3,062,000
Atlanta University	321,000
	4,303,000

7. Fortunately, we already have also a large tract of land comprising approximately 90 acres. We have some excellent buildings and equipment, and we have a library assured with maintenance, probably to be ready for use within two years.

8. For all practical purposes, these resources will be pooled in the effort to establish the University with its colleges. The

exchange of students and teachers in the junior and senior college years as well as the availability of teachers for giving University courses equalizes whatever advantage Spelman would have by making the resources of each institution contribute to the whole enterprise.

9. We begin then with an effort to strengthen all courses in the colleges. Why not? I believe it to be distinctly in the range of possibility to do this through of course it would never be possible to have every course at the top notch at one time. Practically, however, we assume they can all be improved, and we shall endeavor to improve them. In fact, this is in line with the suggestion in your letter of December 7,—"If you do agree to this (amalgamation) as a goal, then the problem is simply to provide courses in addition to those now offered at Morehouse and Spelman and to strengthen existing departments in order to make the entire Atlanta unit more serviceable."

10. We have in the affiliation the machinery necessary for developing, in the course of time, a University in the real sense, with graduate and professional schools. Our plan for the first six years includes as the immediate objective the beginning of a Graduate Department of Arts and Sciences, a Department of Education (not a Teacher's College) and a Department of Business Administration. It includes also as the expression of a desire and hope, the possibility of having a Department of Music and Fine Arts; and a Schools of Social Work on the assumption that logically the Atlanta School would become part of the University.

11. <u>Graduate Department of Arts and Science</u>. With the college curricula strengthened, with three or four new full-time appointments to the University faculty, and with professors of Morehouse and Spelman available also to offer University courses, it would be feasible to offer in 1930–31 graduate courses in English, History, Economics, and probably in Biology, chemistry, French and Mathematics. It is not a pretentious program to propose to offer in the next six years courses leading to the Master's degree in eight or ten departments.

12. <u>Department of Education</u>. It is not our idea to develop a Teachers' College along traditional lines, We purpose to have a

Practice School or Demonstration School which will be an object lesson in good and measurements, and, for training administrators, courses in supervision and administration. Our aim in this Department as set forth in the statement sent you (page 21) is as follows:

> "...graduate students who are teachers or who expect to teach would be advised to take their Master's degree not in Education but in the subject they expect to teach. In other words, in the subject-matter,—the so-called content course,—not in the method of teaching. On the other hand, the Demonstration School would offer such students an object lesson in good teaching and the Graduate Department of Education would provide instruction in principles of teaching and teaching method. The main emphasis would be on knowing something to teach and the secondary emphasis on learning how to teach it. A Master's degree in Education would be offered for persons desiring training for administrative positions in education, or for students interested mainly in research."

13. <u>Department of Economics and Business Administration</u>. You are more or less familiar with the foundation for work in business and economics. It is proposed for 1930–31 that Mr. Milton of the Morehouse faculty and Mrs. Warburton of the Spelman faculty offer graduate courses amounting roughly to the work of one full-time professor. It is proposed to develop and expand this department by the appointment of additional professors from year to year and to make this department one of the special features of the University. It is a field in which training for Negroes is greatly needed.

14. If the work in music now being done in the colleges can be expanded and some courses in fine arts begun on an undergraduate basis, it is our dream that in the not too distant future some benefactor would provide for a <u>School of Music and Fine Arts</u>.

15. <u>The School of Social Work</u> seems a reasonable expectation and I still lean to the view shared by you and me last December that this would come eventually into the University program. The School of Social Work is not financed separately and provision for its financing by the University would need to

be made separately in the same fashion on the basis of annual grants and endowment.

16. <u>Funds</u>. A University program requires money. There is no getting around that fact. When the three institutions went into combined enterprise, they took the venture on faith, to be sure, but they expected that the Boards interested in Negro education and Negro welfare generally would give liberally. The Board of Trustees of Atlanta University is willing to face the prospect. When the Executive Committee approved the program that I recommended for the six-year period, they did so with a full realization that even for the modest development proposed, several million dollars would be required. They have faith, and I have faith, that the program proposed justifies financial support.

17. Now, Mr. Embree, I know you will pardon me for saying that I wish you might have given the Atlanta situation more of your presence and time. You have visited Atlanta several times, but never (it seems to me) have you remained long enough and been sufficiently free from hurry to come into sympathetic understanding of what has already been achieved and what is now going on. In no other city have we had five colleges for Negroes. These five colleges in Atlanta, each with its own constituency with their inevitable rivalries, have yet maintained such friendly relationship and mutual respect that within a few weeks after affiliation was first broached three colleges became legally related, and cooperative activity immediately began. And all of this was done in such an admirable way that the other institutions in Atlanta, and even one in another city, are showing a disposition to relate themselves to this cooperative enterprise. This is an outcome more significant than a mere agreement of three boards of trustees. It is a generous understanding on the part of the Negro constituencies of these institutions.

18. Furthermore, as this affiliation relates to students and teachers, we have already this first year students of the three institutions associating with one another in everyday work on the three campuses. There has been a weaving together in actual practice which I think would surprise you. See Appendix A.

19. As I have said above, the three institutions in the affiliation have for years been in the forefront of colleges for Negroes.

Their record is fine in the scholarship and character of the men and women who have gone out from these institutions. Until recent years, we have not had University work among the Negro institutions except in the professions of Law, Medicine, and Theology. The work done has been definitely undergraduate work leading to the bachelor's degree, and in that field, Atlanta University, Spelman College and Morehouse College compare favorably with the best of other colleges for Negroes and Southern colleges for white people. The physical condition of Atlanta University and Morehouse College has not been what might be desired and the salaries paid have been sadly inadequate, but the teachers have remained and carried on with such devotion and loyalty that the scholarship and character of these institutions have been maintained. This fact might be accepted as a promise to expect more favorable conditions.

20. When you look well into all this, I believe your faith in the building of Atlanta University will be so great as to prevent further misgivings and hesitation on your part to give it your support. We will guide against mistakes. But if there is danger of making them, to me that is all the more reason why you should come definitely to our support at this time, assisting by your counsel and by a grant of funds from your Board.

Sincerely yours
(signed)
John Hope
JH:C

Appendix A
Exchange of Students and Teachers
1929–30
First Semester

Section 1.01 Undergraduate Courses

1	S. C.	teacher	giving	A course	at	A. U.
2	S. C.	,,s	,,	courses	,,	M. C
2	M. C.	,,	,,	,,	,,	S. C.
1	A. U.	teacher	,,	A course	,,	M. C.
12	M. C.	students	taking	courses	at	A. U.
30	M. C.	,,	,,	,,	,,	S. C.
37	S. C.	,,	,,	,,	,,	M. C.
27	A. U.	,,	,,	,,	,,	M. C.
27	A. U.	,,	,,	,,	,,	S. C.

Section 1.02 Senior-graduate Courses of Atlanta University

Courses	Teachers	Graduate	Enrollment Undergraduate
Biology			
Histology	S. C.	1	7
Neurology	M. C.	1	3
Chemistry	M. C.		10
Economics			
Corp. Finance	M. C.		8
Econ. History	S. C.		17
Education	A. U.	2	5
English			
Shakespeare	M. C.	1	17
British Poets	S. C.	1	16
French Negro Lit.	S. C.	5	5
History	M. C.		13
Latin	S. C.	5	4
Mathematics			
Proj. Geometry	M. C.		2
Diff. Equations	S. C.		5
Sociology	M. C.		9
		16	121

Source: John Hope to Edwin Embree, February 22, 1930, Atlanta University Presidential Records—John Hope Records, Atlanta University Center Robert W. Woodruff Library.

Appendix C

Notable Atlanta University System/Center Alumnus(ae)

The critical purpose for strengthening the Atlanta institutions was to provide an avenue from which black leaders would emerge. Below is a list (not exhaustive) of notable Atlanta University System/Center alumnus(ae), in various fields, from the late 1800s to the present.

Clark-Atlanta University Notable Alumni

Henry Ossian Flipper	Former slave; first black graduate of West Point in 1877, earning a commission as a second lieutenant in the US Army
Lucy Craft Laney	Educator, opened the first school for black children in Augusta, Georgia in late nineteenth century
Richard R. Wright	Valedictorian, Atlanta University's first commencement in 1876; first black paymaster in the US Army; first president of Georgia State Industrial College for Colored Youth (later, Savannah State University)
James Weldon Johnson	Educator; lawyer; diplomat; songwriter; author; anthropologist; poet; and civil rights activist
Louis Tompkins Wright	First black surgeon to head the Department of Surgery at Harlem Hospital in New York City, New York
Walter Francis White	NAACP leader; writer and one of the founders of the Harlem Renaissance

Fletcher Henderson	Pianist; bandleader; and composer; played with Louis Armstrong; Bennie Goodman; and recorded with Bessie Smith and Nina Simone
Wayman Carver	Composer; jazz flutist, one of the earliest flute soloists to perform jazz
Grace Towns Hamilton	First African American woman elected to the Georgia General Assembly; former professor and dean at LeMoyne-Owen College; former executive director of Atlanta's Urban League
Alexander Jefferson	Retired US Air Force lieutenant colonel; member of the Tuskegee Airmen, the 332nd Fighter Group
Martha S. Lewis	Former deputy commissioner for the Department of Social Services in the New York State government, in 1970s; she was the highest-ranking black official in any state government
Jo Ann Robinson	Civil rights activist; educator
Horace E. Tate	First black to earn a PhD at the University of Kentucky, doctorate in education in 1960; instrumental in bringing about the desegregation of schools in Georgia; first African American to run for mayor of Atlanta and elected to the Georgia State Senate; appointed to the National Commission on Libraries and Information Science
Horace T. Ward	Judge and first black student to challenge segregation legally at University of Georgia Law School; member of the Georgia State Senate; first black to serve on the Federal bench in Georgia, appointed by President Jimmy Carter to the United States District Court for the Northern District of Georgia
Ralph David Abernathy	Civil rights activist, associate of Martin Luther King Jr.; minister
Mary Frances Early	First black graduate of the University of Georgia; first black president of the Georgia Music Educators Association; music teacher, planning and development coordinator; divisions curriculum specialist; music resource teacher; adjunct professor at Morehouse and Spelman colleges and as a music coordinator and supervisor of Atlanta Public Schools; head of the Music Department at Clark Atlanta University.

Marva Collins	Educator; founder and director of Westside Preparatory School in Chicago, Illinois
Reatha Clark King	Scientist; philanthropist; educator; served as a research chemist for the National Bureau of Standards; chemistry professor and associate dean at York College and City University of New York; former president of Metropolitan State University; former president and executive director of the General Mills Foundation and vice president of General Mills, Inc.; former chairman of the board of trustees for the General Mills Foundation; life trustee for the University of Chicago
Hosea Williams	Civil rights leader; ordained minister; businessman; philanthropist; scientist; and politician; former executive director of Southern Christian Leadership Conference; member of Georgia General Assembly and a DeKalb county commissioner
Benjamin Brown	Civil rights activist and Georgia State Representative
Evelyn G. Lowery	Civil rights activist and leader; founder of SCLC/Women's Organizational Movement for Equality Now, Inc. (W.O.M.E.N.), the sister organization of the Southern Christian Leadership Conference
James A. Hefner	Economist; former president of Tennessee State University and Jackson State University; former provost of Tuskegee Institute; professor of economics at Morehouse College
Marvin S. Arrington Sr.	Politician and jurist; one of the first two black students to take full-time studies at the Emory University School of Law; former judge in the Superior Court of Fulton County, Georgia; and a former politician in the city of Atlanta
Otis Johnson	Two-term mayor of Savannah, Georgia
Morris Stroud	Former professional football player, tight-end for the Kansas City Chefs
Kenny Leon	Acclaimed theater director and actor
Pernessa C. Seele	Immunologist; founder and CEO of Balm in Gilead, Inc.; recipient of AU's Pathway of Excellence Award, its most outstanding graduates of all time; one of the nation's most prominent voices on issues of HIV/AIDS and other health disparities

Henry C. "Hank" Johnson	US Congressman, Georgia 4th District
Renee Blake	Director, brand strategy at Maritz
Dorothy Yancy	Retired president emeriti of Johnson C. Smith; professor emeriti of Political Science and Business
Amanda Davis	News anchor at WAGA (Fox5) in Atlanta, Georgia
Walt Landers	NFL player, former running-back with Green Bay Packards
Jody Mayfield	Composer; jazz musician; creative director for Evander Holyfield's record label, Real Deal Records; performed with musical greats such as Dizzy Gillespie, James Lloyd of Pieces of A Dream, Frank Foster, Grover Washington Jr.
Jacque Reid	Journalist; television and radio personality; former news anchor of The BET Nightly News; former co-host of the NBC New York affiliate show called "New York Live"

Morehouse College Notable Alumni

Mordecai Johnson	Educator; first black president of Howard University, Washington, DC; former professor of economics and history at Morehouse College
James M. Nabrit	Prominent civil rights attorney, argued several important arguments before the US Supreme Court; second black president of Howard University
Howard Thurman	Distinguished theologian, philosopher; civil rights leader; educator; author; former dean of Rankin Chapel at Howard University; first black dean of Marsh Chapel, Boston University
Samuel M. Nabrit	First black to receive the PhD from Brown University; former member, Atomic Energy Commission; former president of Texas Southern University; son of James M. Nabrit
Hugh M. Gloster Sr.	President emeritus, Morehouse College; founder of Association of Teachers of English in Black Colleges, later College Language Association Collective; selected as one of the 100 most effective college presidents in the United States
Thomas Kilgore Jr.	Minister; civil rights leader; pastor emeritus, Second Baptist Church; former minister at Friendship

	Baptist Church, New York; worked closely with Martin Luther King Jr.
Richard I. McKinney	Educator; philosopher; assistant professor and director of religious activities Virginia Union; former dean of the School of Religion; former president, Storer College; chairman, philosophy department, dean of the College of Arts and Sciences, Morgan State University
Nathaniel H. Bronner	Founder of Bronner Brothers Company, beauty cosmetics
Lerone Bennett, Jr.	Former executive editor, *Ebony* magazine
Samuel DuBois Cook	Educator; founder of Morehouse College's campus chapter of NAACP; taught at Southern University and Atlanta University; first black to hold a regular faculty position at Duke University; former president, Dillard University; former member of the National Council on Humanities; first black president of the Southern Political Science Association
Robert Edward Johnson	Former executive editor and associate publisher, *JET* magazine; former presidential press corp with President Richard Nixon
Martin Luther King Jr.	Nobel Peace Prize Laureate; civil rights leader; minister; president of the Southern Christian Leadership Conference
Charles Vert Willie	Distinguished professor of Education and Urban Studies, Harvard University
George W. Haley	US ambassador to Gambia; former US postal rate commissioner
Henry W. Foster Jr.	Physician; professor emeritus in the Department of Obstetrics and Gynecology at Meharry Medical College, clinical professor of Obstetrics and Gynecology at Vanderbilt University Medical Center; served as US president Bill Clinton's senior advisor on Teen Pregnancy Reduction and Youth Issues; nominee to the post of surgeon general of the United States by Clinton in 1995; past chair of the US Committee for the United Nations Population Fund; past chair of the board of directors for Pathfinder International; served two terms as chair of the board of regents of the United States National Library of Medicine

Louis W. Sullivan	Physician; businessman; founder and former president, Morehouse School of Medicine; former secretary of the US Department of Health and Human Services under President George H. W. Bush
Peter Chatard	Distinguished plastic surgeon; founder of the Chatard Surgery Center and The Aesteem Outpatient Surgery Center, Seattle, Washington
Don Clendenon	Former New York Mets outfielder; 1969 World Series MVP
Maynard H. Jackson	Politician; first black mayor of Atlanta; served three terms as mayor
Otis Moss Jr.	Minister, Olivet Institutional Baptist Church, Cleveland, Ohio; chairman, Morehouse College Board of Trustees
Major R. Owens	Retired US Congressman, New York
Lt. Gen. James R. Hall	Retired Lt. General US Army; former vice president for Campus Operations, Morehouse College
Walter E. Massey	Former president, Morehouse College; former director, National Science Foundation; former dean of the College, Brown University; former provost, University of California System
David Satcher	Director, National Center for Primary Care, Morehouse School of Medicine; former US surgeon general; former president, Meharry and the Morehouse School of Medicine
Leroy Keith, Jr.	Former chairman of the board, Carson Products; former president, Morehouse College
Abraham Davis	Author; professor of Political Science, Morehouse College
Donald R. Hopkins Sr.	Vice president, Health Programs of the Carter Center; former deputy director and acting director of the Centers for Disease Control and Prevention; former assistant professor of Tropical Public Health, Harvard School of Public Health
Harold A. Dawson Sr.	Businessman; real estate tycoon; founder of Harold A. Dawson Company
Chester A. Davenport	Businessman; founder and managing partner of Georgetown Partners, an investment firm in Bethesda, Maryland; GTE Consumer Services Corp; first black graduate of University of Georgia's Law School

Julius Coles	Former president of Africare, the oldest and largest black-led organization, providing aid to Africa; former director of the Andrew Young Center for International Development, Morehouse College; former director of the Ralph J. Bunche International Affairs Center at Howard University
Earl F. Hilliard	Former US Congressman, Alabama
Herman Cain	Author, business executive, radio host, syndicated columnist, and Tea Party activist from Georgia; former presidential candidate; former president and CEO of Godfather's Pizza; former CEO of the National Restaurant Association; former chairman of the Federal Reserve Bank, Kansas City
Robert C. Davidson, Jr.	Retired chairman and chief executive officer of Surface Protection Industries; first black to serve as board chairman, board of trustees of Art Center College of Design; among the first black board leader of a member institution within the Association of Independent Colleges of Art and Design; former director of Children's Hospital of Los Angeles
Reginald C. Lindsay	Judge; former US Federal judge, Massachusetts, nominated by President Bill Clinton, United States District Court for the District of Massachusetts
Sanford D. Bishop Jr.	Politician; former US Representative for Georgia's 2nd Congressional District
Michael L. Lomax	President and CEO, United Negro College Fund; former president, Dillard University; former president, the National Faculty
M. William Howard Jr.	Minister, Bethany Baptist Church, New Jersey; president, New York Theological Seminary; member of the Council on Foreign Relations
Arthur E. Johnson	Sr. vice president Corporate Strategic Development, Lockheed Martin
Howard E. Jeter	Former US ambassador to Nigeria; former US ambassador to Botswana
Maceo K. Sloan	Chairman, president and CEO of Sloan Financial Group, Inc. and chairman, CEO, and CIO of NCM Capital Management Group, Inc.
Calvin O. Butts III	President of State University of New York College at Old Westbury; pastor of Abyssinian Baptist Church in the City of New York, nationally renowned

Samuel L. Jackson	Academy-award nominee; stage and film actor
Roderic I. Pettigrew	Physician; nuclear physicist, National Institutes of Health
Robert R. Jennings	President of Lincoln University; former president of Alabama Agricultural and Mechanical University
Ralph B. Everett, Esq.	President and CEO of the Joint Center for Political and Economic Studies
Robert Michael Franklin	Former president, Morehouse College; presidential fellow and professor, Emory University, former president of the Interdenominational Theological Seminary (ITC)
Bill G. Nunn III	Actor
Charles David "C. D." Moody	President and chief executive officer of C. D. Moody Construction Company, Inc.
Edwin C. Moses	Olympic gold medalist; financial consultant
Jeh Johnson	Civil and criminal attorney; general counsel of the Department of Defense, US Department of Defense
John Silvanus Wilson Jr.	Current president of Morehouse College; former exective director of the White House Initiative on historically black colleges and universities, appointed by President Barack Obama; former director of Massachusetts Institute of Technology's Foundation Relations; former executive dean of George Washington University's Virginia campus and former associate professor of higher education in the Graduate School of Education
Shelton "Spike" Lee	Filmmaker and president, 40 Acres & A Mule
Robert L. Mallett	Visiting professor of law, Georgetown University; former executive vice president and general counsel, Public and Senior Markets Group, a division of United Health Group; former senior vice president, Worldwide Policy & Public Affairs, Pfizer Inc; former deputy secretary, US Department of Commerce
Cameron Moody	Director of the White House Office of Administration, executive office of the president, appointed by President Barack Obama; former deputy CEO for operations for the Democratic National Convention (2008, 2004 and 2000) and former deputy director of transportation for the 1996 Democratic National Convention.

Nelson Bowman III	Executive director of development at Prairie View A&M University; author of *Engaging Diverse College Alumni, A Guide to Fundraising at Historically Black Colleges and Universities*, and *Unearthing Promise and Potential: Our Nation's Historically Black Colleges and Universities*, recipient of the John Grenzebach Award for Outstanding Research in Philanthropy for Educational Advancement, presented by Council for the Advancement and Support of Education (CASE)
Nima A. Warfield	First black Rhodes Scholar from a historically black college and university

Spelman College Notable Alumnae

Alberta Williams King	Mother of Martin Luther King Jr.
Selena Sloan Butler	Founder of first black parent-teacher organization, the National Congress for Colored Parents & Teachers; cofounder the National Parent-Teacher Association
Blanche Armwood	Educator; activist; first black woman in the State of Florida to graduate from an accredited law school; Armwood High School in Tampa, FL, is named in her honor
Sue Bailey Thurman	Founder and first chairperson, National Council of Negro Women's National Library
Janet Bragg	Aviation pioneer; first black female to obtain a commercial pilot license
Clara Stanton Jones	First black president of the American Library Association
Dovey Johnson Roundtree	Trial attorney; military veteran; civil rights pioneer; Landmark case, *Sarah Keys v. Carolina Coach Company (1955)*
Eva Rutland	Author, *When We Were Colored: A Mother's Story*; winner of the 2000 Golden Pen Lifetime Achievement Award; author of more than 20 Romance novels
Mattiwilda Dobbs	Opera singer; board of directors for the Metropolitan Opera and the National Endowment for the Arts
Mary Barksdale	Past president, Jack and Jill of America, Inc.
Christine King Farris	Public speaker and educator; teacher at Spelman College; eldest and only living sibling of the late Rev. Martin Luther King Jr.

Ella Gaines Yates	First black director of the Atlanta-Fulton Public Library System
Mary McKinney Edmonds	Former vice provost and dean of student affairs; emeritus at Stanford University
Audrey F. Manley	Former acting surgeon general of the United States; president emeriti of Spelman College
Alexine Clement Jackson	Former national president of the YWCA; former chair, Susan G. Komen for the Cure
Marian Wright Edelman	Founder of the Children's Defense Fund; MacArthur Fellow; Heinz Award; Presidential Medal of Freedom
Rubye Robinson	Former civil rights activist; former executive secretary of Student Nonviolent Coordinating Committee
Marcelite J. Harris	First black female to obtain the rank of general in the United States Air Force
Alice Walker	Pulitzer Prize winning novelist, *The Color Purple*
Aurelia Brazeal	Retired US ambassador to Ethiopia and Kenya; Department of State
Elynor A. Williams	Former vice president of Public Responsibility at Sara Lee Corporation
Beverly Guy-Sheftall	Author; feminist scholar; English professor, Spelman College; founder of the Women's Research and Resource Center at Spelman College; cofounder of *SAGE: A Scholarly Journal on Black Women*; former trustee, Dillard University
Ruth A. Davis	24th director general of the United States Foreign Service; former director, Foreign Service Institute and two-time recipient of the President's Award for Distinguished Federal Civilian Service
J. Veronica Biggins	Managing partner of Diversity and Sr. partner, Heidrick & Struggles; former director for AirTran Airway; former director of presidential personnel at the White House for President Bill Clinton
Bernice Johnson Reagon	Founder of Sweet Honey in the Rock; MacArthur Fellow; professor emeritus American University; curator emeritus, Smithsonian Institute National Museum American History; National Humanities Medal; Heinz Award
Yvonne R. Jackson	Former chief human resources officer at three Fortune 500 companies-Pfizer, Inc., Compaq Computer Corporation, and Burger King Corporation

LaTanya Richardson	Actress, *U. S. Marshalls*, *The Fighting Temptations*; wife of actor Samuel L. Jackson, Morehouse College alumni
Pearl Cleage	Novelist, playwright, poet, essayist, and journalist
Tina McElroy Ansa	Author, *Baby of the Family*, *Ugly Ways*, *The Hand I Fan With*, and *You Know Better*
Kathleen McGee-Anderson	Television producer and playwright, *Soul Food*, *Lincoln Heights*, *Touched by An Angel*, *Any Day Now*
Sheryl Riley Gripper	Four-time Emmy Award winner and founder of the Black Women Film Network
Varnette Honeywood	Painter, author and businesswoman; creator of the Little Bill character
Virginia Davis Floyd	Vice president of PROMETRA International, and executive director of PROMETRA USA; former director of Human Development & Reproductive Health for the Ford Foundation
Deborah Prothrow-Stith	First female commissioner of Public Health for the Commonwealth of Massachusetts; associate dean and professor of Public Health Practice at the Harvard School of Public Health
Evelynn M. Hammonds	Dean of Harvard College; professor of the History of Science and of African and Black Studies at Harvard University; founding director of the Center for the Study of Diversity in Science, Technology and Medicine at Massachusetts Institute of Technology
Sibyl Avery Jackson	Award-winning author; screenwriter; executive producer; former PR spokesperson for one of the nation's leading wireless companies; former researcher/editor in the Oral History Program at the Lyndon Baines Johnson Library
Jerri DeVard	Advisor for Nokia; former chief marketing officer, Nokia; served as the chief marketing officer, executive vice president and member of Nokia Leadership Team of Nokia Corporation; former chief marketing officer at Citigroup
Brenda V. Smith	Professor at the Washington College of Law at American University; project director for the United States Department of Justice, National Institute of Corrections Cooperative Agreement

	on Addressing Prison Rape; appointed to the National Prison Rape Elimination Commission by the United States House of Representatives Minority Leader, Nancy Pelosi (D-Calif.)
Rolonda Watts	Journalist, actress; author; former talk show host
Kimberly B. Davis	Managing director of Global Philanthropy, president of the JPMorgan Chase Foundation, and a member of the executive committee
Linda Goode Bryant	Documentary filmmaker, *Flag Wars*; Peabody Award winner and 2004 Guggenheim Fellow
Tanya Walton Pratt	First black judge in Indiana's history, United States District Court appointed by President Barack Obama
Rosalind Gates Brewer	First black female chief executive officer and president of Sam's Club Segment at Wal-Mart Stores; *Forbes's* #50 Most Powerful Women in the World; former executive vice president, Walmart Stores, Inc. and president Walmart Stores South, USA; chair—board of directors, Spelman College; board of directors, Lockheed Martin
Traci S. Jackson	Global Client Relationship Manager of Orange Business Services, a global IT and communications services provider, with services available in 220 countries and a local presence in 166.
Jacqueline Calhoun Marshall	First black and female VP Strategic Accounts K-12 Technology Group/Solutions with Pearson Education, the world's leading education publishing and technology company
Shaun Robinson	Co-anchor, Access Hollywood; former host, TV One Access; contributing reporter to The Today Show, MSNBC, CNN and NBC's Nightly News; award-winning journalist, author, *Just As I Am*
Renee Chube Washington	Chief operating officer of USA Track & Field; past president of the Junior League of Indianapolis; former deputy associate general counsel and acting associate general counsel, US Department of Labor
Bernice King	Minister; former resident, SCLC; daughter of Martin Luther King Jr.
Mary A. Gordon	Vice president of manufacturing US Smokeless Tobacco Company; former VP of Manufacturing, Philip Morris

Noliwe Rooks	Author; associate professor at Cornell University; professor, associate director of the Center for Black Studies at Princeton University and the founding coordinator of the Center's Urban Education Reform Initiative
Adrienne-Joi Johnson	Actress; choreographer; fitness coach
Cassi Davis	Actress, *House of Payne*
Renita Barge Clark, M.D.	Notable physician in Detroit, MI; founder and president, Cotillion Society of Detroit
Sharmell Sullivan	Professional wrestling valet and occasional wrestler; wife of professional wrestler Booker T; Miss Black America, 1991
Traci Lynn Blackwell	Vice president of Current Programming, the CW Television Network
Tayari Jones	Author, *Leaving Atlanta* and *The Untelling*
Angela M. Banks	Professor of Law, William & Mary Law School, noted Immigration Law expert; former editor of the *Harvard Law Review* and the *Harvard International Law Journal*
Tanika Ray	Actress; television personality
Celeste Watkins-Hayes	Associate professor of Sociology and Black Studies at Northwestern University and chair of the Department of Black Studies
Tia Fuller	Jazz saxophonist; composer; educator; member of Beyoncé's all-female band
Danica Tisdale	Fellowships coordinator, Center for Global Education at Claremont McKenna College; first black Miss Georgia, 2004
Keshia Knight Pulliam	Actress, *The Cosby Show, House of Payne*
Kristen Jarvis	Special assistant for scheduling and traveling aide to First Lady Michelle Obama
Phire Dawson	Actress; model; "Barker's Beauty" on *The Price Is Right*
Betty Davis	Former meteorologist, The Weather Channel
Dazon Dixon Diallo	Founder and CEO SisterLove, Inc.

Notes

Introduction

1. Leroy Davis, *A Clashing of the Soul: John Hope and the Dilemma of African American Leadership and Black Higher Education in the Early Twentieth Century,* with a foreword by John Hope Franklin (Athens, Georgia: University of Georgia Press, 1998), 297.
2. Atlanta University Trustees Minutes, February 25, 26, 1929, box 89, folder 2, John Hope Records, Atlanta University Center Robert W. Woodruff Library, Atlanta, Georgia. (Hereafter designated as Hope Records and AUC).
3. "Atlanta University: Affiliation in University Plan," box 96, folder 6, Hope Papers, AUC; "Charter of Atlanta University," State of Georgia, April 1, 1929, box 89, folder 1, ibid.
4. Clifford M. Kuhn, Harlon E. Joye, and E. Bernard West, *Living Atlanta: An Oral History of the City, 1914–1948,* foreword by Michael Lomax (Athens, Georgia: University of Georgia Press, 1990), 158, 166; Clarence A. Bacote, *The Story of Atlanta University: A Century of Service, 1865–1965* (New Jersey: Princeton University Press, 1969), 245–249; and Florence M. Read, *The Story of Spelman College* (New Jersey: Princeton University Press, 1961), 206–208.
5. David Levering Lewis, *W. E. B. Du Bois: Biography of a Race, 1868–1919* (New York: Henry Holt and Company, 1993), 241; William H. Watkins, *The White Architects of Black Education: Ideology and Power in America, 1865–1954* (New York: Teachers College, Columbia University, 2001), 23.
6. James D. Anderson, *The Education of Blacks in the South, 1860–1935* (Chapel Hill: University of North Carolina Press, 1988), 238. Industrial philanthropy refers to foundations such as the Peabody Educational Fund, the Slater Fund, Anna T. Jeanes Foundation, Phelps-Stokes Fund, Carnegie Foundation, Laura Spelman Rockefeller Memorial Fund, Julius Rosenwald Fund, and the General Education Board. W. E. B. Du Bois, *The Souls of Black Folks,* with an introduction by Herb

Boyd (New York: Modern Library, Modern Library Edition, 1996), 53, 58; Carter G. Woodson, *The Mis-Education of the Negro*, with an introduction by H. Khalif Khalifah (Newport News, Virginia: United Brothers & Sisters Graphics & Printing, 1992), 27. This is the complete text as published in 1933. Du Bois argued that industrialists were interested in keeping blacks ignorant and disfranchised by providing only industrial education. Du Bois further maintained that the "money-makers" wished to use blacks as laborers. Similarly, Woodson argued that the system by which blacks were educated was one that perpetuated enslavement. The system Woodson referred to was one totally dominated by whites (e.g., funds, teachers, college presidents, etc.). Ibid., 276. It is noteworthy to mention Anderson supplied examples of blacks having agency on the K-12 educational level; blacks assisted in establishing schools and school systems for their own. See Anderson, *Education of Blacks in the South*, 148, Chap. 1, "Ex-Slaves and the Rise of Universal Education in the South, 1860–1880," and Chap. 5, "Common Schools for Black Children, 1900–1935." For this book, I define agency as "the assumed ability for individuals to shape the condition of their lives." Meredith D. Gall, Walter R. Borg, and Joyce P. Gall, *Educational Research: An Introduction*, 6th ed. (White Plains, New York: Longman, 1996), 610.
7. Merle Curti and Roderick Nash, *Philanthropy in the Shaping of American Higher Education* (New Jersey: Rutgers University Press, 1965), 168, 185; Dwight Oliver Wendell Holmes, *The Evolution of the Negro College* (New York: Arno and The New York Times, 1969), 7; and Horace Mann Bond, *The Education of the Negro in the American Social Order* (New York: Octagon Books, 1970), 150.
8. Marybeth Gasman and Katherine Sedgwick, *Uplifting a People. Essays on African American Philanthropy and Education* (New York: Peter Lang, 2005). Particularly, See Chap. 1–3.
9. Edward A. Jones, *A Candle in the Dark: A History of Morehouse College* (Valley Forge, Pennsylvania: Judson, 1967), 121.
10. Ibid., 85; Davis, *Clashing of the Soul*, 186.
11. Rayford Logan, *The Dictionary of American Negro Biography*, ed. Rayford Logan and Michael R. Winston (New York: W. W. Norton, 1982), 323. See Davis, *Clashing of the Soul*, 256–263; Kuhn, Joye, and West, *Living Atlanta*, 131. Booker T. Washington High School in Atlanta, Georgia, was established in 1924 as Atlanta's first public high school for blacks.
12. Davis, *Clashing of the Soul*, 260, 314; Logan, "John Hope," *Dictionary of American Negro Biography*, 323.
13. Davis, *Clashing of the Soul*, 266,
14. Eric Anderson and Alfred A. Moss Jr., *Dangerous Donations: Northern Philanthropy and Southern Black Education, 1902–1930*, foreword by Louis R. Harlan (Missouri: University of Missouri Press, 1990), 214.

15. For other examples of works using a single event as a departure to discuss cultural or historic events, see Clifford Geertz, "Deep Play on the Balinese Cockfights," *Daedelus* 101 (Winter 1972), 1–37; Simon Schama, *Dead Certainties: Unwarranted Speculations* (New York: Vintage Books, 1991), and Mark Bauerlein, *Negrophobia, A Race Riot in Atlanta, 1906* (San Francisco: Encounter Books, 2001).
16. Jacques Barzun and Henry F. Graff, *The Modern Researcher* (New York: Harcourt Brace Jovanovich, 1992), 253–254.
17. Andrew Carnegie, "Wealth," *North American Review*, June 1889 [journal on-line], Cornell University Library, Division of Rare and Manuscript Collections, accessed April 11, 2001, http://cdi.library.cornell.edu; John D. Rockefeller Sr., *Random Reminiscences of Men and Events* (Garden City, New York: Doubleday, Page & Company, 1913).
18. John Hope, "Autobiographical Sketch," July 22, 1934, box 65, folder 3, Hope Records AUC. Hope stated his only purpose for writing this sketch was so his two sons "might know him better." However, he admitted that he probably would not tell everything.
19. Ron Chernow, *Titan: The Life of John D. Rockefeller, Sr.* (New York: Random House, 1998); Ridgely Torrence, *The Story of John Hope*, with an introduction by Rayford Logan (New York: Macmillan, 1948; reprint, New York: Arno and The New York Times, 1969); and Davis, *Clashing of the Soul*.
20. James D. Anderson, "Philanthropic Control over Private Black Higher Education," in *Philanthropy and Cultural Imperialism*, ed. Robert F. Arnove (Bloomington, Indiana: Indiana University Press, 1980), 152; Anderson, *Education of Blacks in the South*; Anderson and Moss Jr., *Dangerous Donations*; Curti and Nash, *Philanthropy in the Shaping of American Higher Education;* and Raymond B. Fosdick, Henry F. Pringle, and Katherine Douglas Pringle, *Adventures in Giving: The Story of the General Education Board* (New York: Harper & Row, 1962).
21. Bond, *Education of the Negro in the American Social Order*; John Hope Franklin, *From Slavery to Freedom: A History of American Negroes*, 2nd ed. (New York: Alfred A. Knopf, 1964); Kuhn, Joye, and West, *Living Atlanta*; Lewis, *W. E. B. Du Bois*.
22. Bacote, *Story of Atlanta University*; Benjamin Brawley, *The History of Morehouse College* (Atlanta, Georgia: Morehouse College, 1917); Jones, *Candle in the Dark*; and Read, *Story of Spelman College*.

I Historical Backdrop

1. Cornel West, *Race Matters* (Boston: Beacon, 1993), 3.
2. John D. Rockefeller Sr., for example, founded the Standard Oil Trust in 1863 and built it up through 1868, the same year as John

Hope's birth, to become the largest oil refinery in the world. In 1870, the same year Georgia became the last Confederate state readmitted to the Union, Rockefeller renamed his trust to Standard Oil Company. By the late 1870s, Rockefeller's wealth was worth more than "$5 million" and his "Standard Oil stock alone was by then worth $18 million." Ron Chernow, *Titan: The Life of John D. Rockefeller, Sr.* (New York: Random House, 1998), 217.
3. Chernow, *Titan*, 9.
4. John D. Rockefeller Sr., *Random Reminiscences of Men and Events* (Garden City, New York: Doubleday, Page & Company, 1913), 33, 35.
5. Ibid., 77, 87; Chernow, *Titan*, 17.
6. Rockefeller Sr., *Random Reminiscences*, 34.
7. Chernow, *Titan*, 19.
8. Rockefeller Sr., *Random Reminiscences*, 146.
9. Merle Curti, "The History of American Philanthropy as a Field of Research," *American Historical Review* 62 (1957), 353.
10. Rockefeller Sr., *Random Reminiscences*, 146; Chernow, *Titan*, 177.
11. Rockefeller Sr., *Random Reminiscences*, 142.
12. Julian B. Roebuck and Komanduri S. Murty, *Historically Black Colleges and Universities: Their Place in American Higher Education* (Westport, Connecticut: Praeger, an imprint of Greenwood Publishing Group), 23.
13. Willard Range, *The Rise and Progress of Negro Colleges in Georgia, 1865–1949* (Athens, Georgia: University of Georgia, 1951), 19.
14. John Hope Franklin, *From Slavery to Freedom: A History of American Negroes*, 2nd ed. (New York: Alfred A. Knopf, 1964), 538.
15. Vernon L. Wharton, "Jim Crow Laws and Miscegenation," in *The Origins of Segregation: Problems in American Civilization*, ed. Joel Williamson (Boston: D. C. Heath, 1968), 14.
16. John H. Stanfield, *Philanthropy and Jim Crow in American Social Science* (Westport, Connecticut: Greenwood, 1985), 8.
17. Ibid. Stanfield explained that Jim Crow was a "variant of apartheid which emphasized legal and psychological separation of the races; prohibition of interracial marriages, separate health, transportation, and educational facilities; racially defined occupations; highly ritualized racial etiquette in public spheres; and violent treatment and usurpation of the civil rights of racial minorities." Bennett explained the term Jim Crow had "become a part of the American language by 1838 and was used [derogatorily] as a synonym for Negro–a noun, a verb, and adjective, a 'comic' way of life." Lerone Bennett, *Before the Mayflower: A History of Black America*, 4th ed. (Chicago: Johnson, 1969), 221.
18. C. Vann Woodward, "Why Negroes Were Segregated in the South," in *The Origins of Segregation: Problems in American Civilization*, ed. Joel Williamson (Boston: D. C. Heath, 1968), 53.

19. C. Vann Woodward, "Folkways, Stateways, and Racism," in *The Segregation Era, 1863–1954*, ed. Allen Weinstein and Frank Otto Gatell (New York: Oxford University Press, 1970), 79–80. This was abridged from C. Vann Woodward, *The Strange Career of Jim Crow*, 2nd ed. (New York: Oxford University Press, 1966).
20. W. E. B. Du Bois, *The Souls of Black Folks*, with an introduction by Herb Boyd (New York: Modern Library, Modern Library Edition, 1996), 5.
21. Frantz Fanon, *Black Skin, White Masks*, trans. Charles Lam Markmann (New York: Grove, 1967), 211.
22. Frantz Fanon, *The Wretched of the Earth*, trans. Constance Farrington (New York: Grove, 1963), 250; David P. Ausubel, "Ego Development Among Segregated Negro Children," *Mental Health and Segregation*, ed. Martin M. Grossack (New York: Springer, 1963), 35. Ausubel found in his study of black children that a black child "inherits caste status and almost inevitably acquires the negative self-esteem that is the realistic ego reflection of such status." Furthermore, he concluded unpleasant contacts with whites and with institutionalized symbols of cast inferiority and more directly through mass media, individuals gradually become aware of the social significance of racial membership.
23. Gunnar Myrdal, *An American Dilemma: The Negro Problem and Modern Democracy*, vol. 2, with a new introduction by Sissela Bok (New York: Harper & Row, 1944, 1962; reprint, New Brunswick, NJ: Transaction Publishers, 1996), 689 (page citations are to the reprinted edition).
24. Woodward, "Why Negroes Were Segregated in the New South," 51.
25. Martin Grossack, "Introduction: Segregation and Its Meaning," in *Mental Health and Segregation*, ed. Martin M. Grossack (New York: Springer, 1963), 1; Herbert Aptheker, *Afro-American History, the Modern Era: A Pioneering Chronicle of the Black People in Twentieth-Century America* (Secacus, New Jersey: Citadel, 1971), 35.
26. Mark Bauerlein, *Negrophobia, A Race Riot in Atlanta, 1906* (San Francisco: Encounter Books, 2001), 31–32. See also, Clifford M. Kuhn, Harlon E. Joye, and E. Bernard West, *Living Atlanta: An Oral History of the City, 1914–1948*, foreword by Michael Lomax (Athens, Georgia: University of Georgia Press, 1990).
27. For a lengthy discussion of segregational practices in the South, see Bauerlein, *Negrophobia*, 289; Franklin, *From Slavery to Freedom*; Charlayne Hunter-Gault, *In My Place* (New York: Farrar Straus Giroux, 1992); and Myrdal, *American Dilemma*.
28. Because it is the purpose of this book to highlight John Hope's involvement and accomplishments related to the affiliation of the Atlanta institutions and not to produce another biography, I only use relevant information.

29. John Hope, Autobiographical Sketch, July 22, 1934, box 65, folder 3, Hope Records, AUC.
30. Torrence, *Story of John Hope*, 14.
31. Ibid., 15.
32. Ibid., 17; Davis, *Clashing of the Soul*, 3. Torrence explained how James Hope was vehement about redeeming his father's failure in a cotton mill in Scotland, which was the trigger that sent Hope South "to the very source of cotton." In 1945, Hope and other associates created the Augusta Manufacturing Company, which was a pioneer mill in Augusta and one of the first in the South. Torrence, *Story of John Hope*, 21. Davis added that Augusta was the second largest city in Georgia and cotton dominated its commerce. Davis, *Clashing of the Soul*, 3.
33. Davis, *Clashing of the Soul*, 10.
34. Although literature, even Davis, identified Fanny and John Hope as mulattos, technically they were quadroons, having one-fourth black blood and not half as does a mulatto. One would have to trace back several generations to find a pure black male in this family's history. John Hope describes his mother as a "quadroon." John Hope, Autobiographical Sketch, July 22, 1934, box 65, folder 3, Hope Records, AUC.
35. Torrence, *Story of John Hope*, 6.
36. Ibid., 8.
37. Ibid., 20, 27. Torrence also indicated that this listing "in view of the usual southern refusal to acknowledge the alliance of colored women and a white man" was strikingly extreme. However, Torrence believed that Newton married Fanny in South Carolina where it was legal. Davis also espoused that mulattos during this time "maintained more than cordial relations with their white benefactors." Davis, *Clashing of the Soul*, 8. Lewis asserted that mulattos lived within an enclave and "sometimes lived privileged lives," however, after the Civil War these mulattos were "treated the same as other blacks not unless they passed for white." David Levering Lewis, *W. E. B. Du Bois: Biography of a Race, 1868–1919* (New York: Henry Holt and Company, 1993), 254.
38. Davis, *Clashing of the Soul*, 8–11; Lewis, *W. E. B. Du Bois*, 253–254; Torrence, *Story of John Hope*, 20–25, 28; and John Hope, Autobiographical Sketch, July 22, 1934, box 65, folder 3, Hope Records, AUC.
39. John Hope, Autobiographical Sketch.
40. Torrence, *Story of John Hope*, 39.
41. Davis, *Clashing of the Soul*, 78.
42. John Hope, Autobiographical Sketch, July 22, 1934, box 65, folder 3, Hope Records, AUC.
43. Davis, *Clashing of the Soul*, 78; Torrence, *Story of John Hope*, 63.
44. Rayford Logan, "John Hope," in *The Dictionary of American Negro Biography*, ed. Rayford Logan and Michael R. Winston

(New York: W. W. Norton, 1982), 322; John Hope, Autobiographical Sketch, July 22, 1934, box 65, folder 3, Hope Records, AUC; Torrence, *Story of John Hope*, 65–68; and Clarence A. Bacote, *The Story of Atlanta University: A Century of Service, 1865–1965* (New Jersey: Princeton University Press, 1969), 273. It is worthy to note that one of Hope's primary teachers was Lucy Laney, one of the first graduates from Atlanta University's Normal Department. Hope also received help with his schoolwork from is half-sister Georgia (Sissie) Newton when she came home from Atlanta University's Lower Normal Department.

45. Davis, *Clashing of the Soul*, 39; Torrence, *Story of John Hope*, 74. Rev. John Dart, a black Baptist minister in Augusta and friend of Hope's aunt and uncle, encouraged Hope to return to school and to attend Worcester. Dart also assisted him spiritually and financially. Torrence, *Story of John Hope*, 68–69.
46. Davis, *Clashing of the Soul*, 47; Torrence, *Story of John Hope*, 83. In remembering Edward Soloman's generosity, Hope named his first son Edward in honor of him. Davis, *Clashing of the Soul*, 47, 124.
47. "A Negro Educator," Interview with John Hope, April 8, 1931, box 65, folder 3, Hope Records, AUC (interviewer is unknown); Davis, *Clashing of the Soul*, 41; and Torrence, *Story of John Hope*, 87. According to Torrence, Hope received a scholarship to Brown obtained by Daniel Webster Abercrombie, principal of Worcester and a trustee of Brown University.
48. "History: Almost Two and a Half Centuries of History," Brown University, accessed August 18, 2012, http://www.brown.edu/about/history.
49. Davis, *Clashing of the Soul*, 51. Hope used the terms "higher education" and "liberal arts education" interchangeably. Davis explained, liberal arts to Hope meant "training of the mind in the various realms of knowledge," based "first [on] well-grounded principles," 90.
50. Bacote, *Story of Atlanta University*, 274; Davis, *Clashing of the Soul*, 54, 64; and Torrence, *Story of John Hope*, 97.
51. Logan, "John Hope," 322; Torrence, *Story of John Hope*, 106. Torrence explained that Hope would have preferred the higher salary offered by Washington, but the fact that he desired to teach the classics and be in Georgia demonstrated Hope was not "one to be moved selfishly." Hope also felt his services were needed more at Roger Williams.
52. Davis, *Clashing of the Soul*, 66. Daniel W. Phillips established Roger Williams University in 1867 as Nashville Institute. Phillips was a white Baptist minister in Nashville and member of the American Baptist Home Missionary Society. Phillips taught black ministers in his home, but the classes outgrew that space. By 1883, the Institute found a permanent location and was incorporated as Roger Williams University. Ibid, 69–70. Roger Williams University no longer exists. Franklin explained while some of the larger

philanthropic agencies continued to support black higher education institutions in the twentieth century, the contributions of wealthy philanthropists of the North declined noticeably. Consequently, smaller private institutions either curtailed their programs or closed down altogether (e.g., Walden University and Roger Williams University). Franklin, *From Slavery to Freedom*, 538. Also, see Edward A. Jones, *A Candle in the Dark: A History of Morehouse College* (Valley Forge, Pennsylvania: Judson, 1967), 76.
53. Torrence, *Story of John Hope*, 106; "Roger Williams University," Tennessee State University, Library and Archives [digital], accessed August 16, 2012, ww2.tnstate.edu/library/digital/roger.htm.
54. John Hope, Autobiographical Sketch, July 22, 1934, box 65, folder 3, Hope Records, AUC; John Hope, Biographical Sketch, ibid. The AUC archivist believed Torrence wrote the autobiographical sketch and indicated that Hope had the opportunity of working with the *Providence Journal* after he graduated from Brown and further his journalism career. The faculty advisory committee at Brown secured this job for him; however, in taking the position, Hope would have had to pass for white, which he opted not to do. He was adamant about returning to the South and "finding work among the Negro race." Davis, *Clashing of the Soul*, 64–65.
55. Davis, *A Clashing of the Soul*, 71.
56. Ibid., 72.
57. Torrence, *Story of John Hope*, 111, 114; Bacote, *Story of Atlanta University*, 262. Bacote was not only hired by Hope but was also the first faculty member hired at Atlanta University, in the history department, once the affiliation took place.
58. John Hope, quoted in Torrence, *Story of John Hope*, 114–115; John Hope, quoted in Davis, *Clashing of the Soul*, 87. See Lewis, *W. E. B. Du Bois*, 255–256.
59. John Hope, quoted in Torrence, *Story of John Hope*, 115.
60. Davis, *Clashing of the Soul*, 100; Torrence, *Story of John Hope*, 115, 122.
61. Davis, *Clashing of the Soul*, 106–107; Jones, *Candle in the Dark*, 74; and Lewis, *W. E. B. Du Bois*, 253.
62. Davis, *Clashing of the Soul*, 103.
63. Ibid., 106–109; Torrence, *Story of John Hope*, 130.
64. Booker T. Washington to William Baldwin Jr., March 28, 1902, box 722, folder 7427, General Education Board Archives, Rockefeller Archive Center, Sleepy Hollow, New York. (Hereafter, designated as GEB and RAC). Washington wanted Baldwin, then president of Long Island Railroad, to know and possibly publish the fact that the distributions of school funds were not as equal between the races as the South tried to indicate it was. Washington gave the following example of difference in Wilcox Co., Alabama: $600 for 75 white students in one school and $295 for 290 black students in

three black schools. The point was "whites receive practically $8 per child and the colored $1 per child."
65. Bacote, *Story of Atlanta University*, vii; Kuhn, Joye, and West, *Living Atlanta*, 152; Dwight Oliver Wendell Holmes, *The Evolution of the Negro College* (New York: Arno and The New York Times, 1969), 11; and Roebuck and Murty, *Historically Black Colleges*, 3. Roebuck and Murty define black colleges and universities, more contemporarily referred to as historically black colleges and universities (HBCUs), as "academic institutions established prior to 1964 whose principal mission was, and still is, the education of black Americans."
66. James D. Anderson, *The Education of Blacks in the South, 1860–1935* (Chapel Hill: University of North Carolina Press, 1988); Eric Anderson and Alfred A. Moss Jr., *Dangerous Donations: Northern Philanthropy and Southern Black Education, 1902–1930*, foreword by Louis R. Harlan (Missouri: University of Missouri Press, 1990); Horace Mann Bond, *The Education of the Negro in the American Social Order* (New York: Octagon Books, 1970); Merle Curti and Roderick Nash, *Philanthropy in the Shaping of American Higher Education* (New Jersey: Rutgers University Press, 1965); Franklin, *From Slavery to Freedom*; Roebuck and Murty, *Historically Black Colleges and Universities*; Myrdal, *American Dilemma*; Carter G. Woodson, *The Education of the Negro Prior to 1861: A History of the Education of the Colored People in the United States from the Beginning of Slavery to the Civil War* (Washington, DC: Associated, 1969); and Carter G. Woodson, *The Mis-Education of the Negro*, with an introduction by H. Khalif Khalifah (Newport News, Virginia: United Brothers & Sisters Graphics & Printing, 1992).
67. Booker T. Washington, W.E. Burghardt DuBois, Charles W. Chesnutt, Wilford H. Smith, H.T. Kealing, Paul Laurence Dunbar, and T. Thomas Fortune, et. al., *The Negro Problem*, with a preface by August Meier (New York: Arno Press and the New York Times, 1969).
68. W. E. B. Du Bois, "The Hampton Idea," *The Education of Black People: Ten Critiques, 1906–1960*, ed. Herbert Aptheker (New York: Monthly Review, 2001), 25–26. This was part of the 1906 speech Du Bois gave at a conference at Hampton Institute that focused on "negro education."
69. Du Bois, *Souls of Black Folks*, 94.
70. W. E. B. Du Bois, "The Jubilee of the New South," *Century Magazine*, January 1896, 470.
71. Edgar G. Epps, in *College in Black and White: African American Students in Predominantly White and in Historically Black Public Universities*, ed. Walter R. Allen, Edgar G. Epps, and Nesha Z. Haniff, with a foreword by Edgar G. Epps (New York: State University of New York Press, 1991), xiii. Although, at times, I

briefly discuss and mention the ideological differences between providing blacks with either industrial education or classical education, it is not the major focal point here. Many scholars have discussed this in detail. See Anderson, *Education of Blacks in the South;* Bond, *Education of the Negro in American Social Order;* Du Bois, "Of the Training of Men," *Souls of Black Folks;* Du Bois, "The Talented Tenth," *The Negro Problem,* 33–75; Franklin, *From Slavery to Freedom;* Lewis, *W. E. B. Du Bois;* Robert C. Morris, *Reading, 'Riting, and Reconstruction: The Education of Freedmen in the South, 1861–1870* (Chicago: University of Chicago Press, 1976, reprinted 1981); Myrdal, *American Dilemma;* Booker T. Washington, "Industrial Education for the Negro," *The Negro Problem,* 7–29; Michael Bieze, *Booker T. Washington and the Art of Self-Representation* (New York: Peter Lang, 2008); and Michael Scott Bieze and Marybeth Gasman, ed., *Booker T. Washington Rediscovered* (Baltimore: Johns Hopkins, 2012).

72. Holmes, *Evolution of the Negro College,* 11–15; Dwight Oliver Wendell Holmes, "The Beginning of the Negro College," *Journal of Negro Education* 3 (April 1934): 168–193.

73. Franklin, *From Slavery to Freedom,* 302–303; Roy E. Finkenbine, "Law, Reconstruction, and African American Education," in *Charity, Philanthropy, and Civility in American History,* ed. Lawrence J. Friedman and Mark D. McGarvie (New York: Cambridge University Press, 2003), 162–163, 166.

74. Holmes, *Evolution of the Negro College,* 11–15; James D. Anderson, "Philanthropic Control over Private Black Higher Education," in *Philanthropy and Cultural Imperialism,* ed. Robert F. Arnove (Bloomington, Indiana: Indiana University Press, 1980), 152; and Anderson, *Education of Blacks in the South,* 241. Missionary philanthropy consisted of the American Missionary Association, the Freedman's Aid Society of the Methodist Episcopal Church, the American Baptist Home Mission Society, the Freedmen's Missions of the United Presbyterian Church, the American Church Institute for Negroes of the Protestant Episcopal Church, the United Christian Missionary Society of the Disciples of Christ, and Sisters of the Blessed Sacrament of Pennsylvania of the Roman Catholic Church. Black philanthropy consisted of the African Methodist Episcopal, the African Methodist Episcopal Zion, the Colored Methodist Episcopal Churches, and the Negro Baptist Conventions. Because this book involves Atlanta University (Congregational, later nondenominational), Morehouse College (Baptist), and Spelman College (Baptist), most of the emphasis herein is on the American Missionary Association, the American Baptist Home Mission Society, and the Negro Baptist Conventions. Anderson, "Philanthropic Control over Private Black Higher Education," 152.

75. Finkenbine, "Law, Reconstruction, and African American Education," 164–166.

76. Anderson, *Education of Blacks in the South*, 241. The definition of classical and liberal arts education has changed over time. Generally, liberal education is defined as "the cultivation of the intellect," according to John Henry Newman, with the object being "intellectual excellence." John Henry Newman, *The Idea of a University*, edited and with an introduction by Martin J. Svaglic (Notre Dame, Indiana: University of Notre Dame Press, 1982). Specifically, in the 1880s, as Anderson explained, New England classical, liberal curriculum entailed different courses on different levels. Elementary levels studied reading, spelling, writing, grammar, diction, history, geography, arithmetic, and music. Normal departments studied Standard English curriculum with additional courses in orthography, map drawing, physiology, algebra and geometry, and theory and practice of teaching. The college curriculum varied slightly among institutions, but the classical course leading to a bachelor's degree usually required Latin, Greek, mathematics, science, philosophy, and, in a few cases, one modern language. Anderson, *Education of Blacks in the South*, 28–29. More contemporarily, the purpose of a liberal arts education, as Christie Farnham explained, is "to discipline and furnish the mind, develop character, and enrich life by encouraging future learning." Christie Anne Farnham, *The Education of the Southern Belle: Higher Education and Student Socialization in the Antebellum South* (New York: New York University Press, 1994), 69.
77. Morgan to Buttrick, January 31, 1901, box 717, folder 7392, American Baptist Home Mission Society, 1901–1909, GEB, RAC.
78. Atlanta University, October 1929, *Spelman Messenger*, Spelman College Archives; The Atlanta University Affiliation, May 1933, *Bulletin of the Association of American Colleges*, 2–6; Bacote, *Story of Atlanta University*, vii; and Kuhn, Joye, and West, *Living Atlanta*, 152.
79. Thomas J. Morgan to Wallace Buttrick, January 31, 1901, box 717, folder 7392, American Baptist Home Mission Society, 1901–1909, GEB, RAC. These are some of Morgan's thoughts on "Forty Years' Work for the Negroes by the Home Mission Society."
80. Ibid. Also see Frederick Rudolph, *The American College and University: A History* (Athens, Georgia: University of Georgia, 1962); Laurence Veysey, *The Emergence of the American University* (Chicago: University of Chicago Press, 1965). These histories of higher education in the United States provided not only details about the creation of colleges and universities in this country but also illustrated the lack of access for blacks to matriculate in higher education.
81. Bacote, *Story of Atlanta University*, 4; Davis, *Clashing of the Soul*, 109.
82. Bacote, *Story of Atlanta University*, vii.
83. Ibid., 4–13.

84. Ibid., 6–8.
85. Ibid., 13.
86. Historical Statement: Atlanta University, box 96, folder 6, Hope Records, AUC.
87. Ibid.
88. Ibid., 15.
89. Ibid., 16, 23. Bacote asserted Ware and other members of the Yale University class of 1863 desired a motto "that would reflect the training and inspiration they received from their Alma Mater." Furthermore, Bacote explained this Yale spirit brought by its graduates would become "for Negro men and women of the South the Atlanta University spirit."
90. Ibid., 16; Range, *Rise and Progress of Negro Colleges*, 21.
91. Historical Statement: Atlanta University, box 96, folder 6, Hope Records, AUC; Atlanta University, *Spelman Messenger*, October 1929, Spelman College Archives (Hereafter designated as SCA); and Bacote, *Story of Atlanta University*, 64.
92. Bacote, *Story of Atlanta University*, 17, 22, 24.
93. John Mercer Langston, quoted in Bacote, *Story of Atlanta University*, 21.
94. Edmund Asa Ware, quoted in Bacote, *Story of Atlanta University*, 15, 23.
95. Range, *Rise and Progress of Negro Colleges*, 23. Also, see Anderson and Moss Jr., *Dangerous Donations*, 19; Franklin, *From Slavery to Freedom*, 378.
96. Range, *Rise and Progress of Negro Colleges*, 23.
97. Historical Statement: Atlanta University, box 96, folder 6, Hope Records, AUC; Atlanta University, *Spelman Messenger*, October 1929, SCA. Much of the literature also described White as a "Negro minister," however, Jones and other historians explained White was not black. Although White's lineage easily caused confusion, Jones's interview with White's eldest daughter, in 1964, sheds light on the subject. White, as Jones explained, was ethnically "the product of several generations of mating between white men and [Cherokee] Indian women." White's mother was a Cherokee Indian. It is unclear whether the father's surname was White, or if the name was given to indicate his ethnicity. Another area that possibly caused confusion concerning White's ethnicity stemmed from White's own marriage and adult life. White married a black woman with whom he had 11 children and "identified himself proudly with the Negroes despite his non-Negro parentage." Since White and his wife, at the time, could not live openly as husband and wife, he decided to live with her as a black man in her mistress's house. It was not until after their fourth child was born did the two venture out on their own, buy a house, and live openly as husband and wife. Jones, *Candle in the Dark*, 20–21, 25. Also see Lewis, *W. E. B. Du Bois*, 255.

98. Jones, *Candle in the Dark*, 19. See Benjamin Brawley, *History of Morehouse College* (College Park, Maryland: McGrath, 1917; reprinted 1970), 14. During a journey from the North back to the South, Coulter had attended the National Theological Institute and University, an institute organized by Edmund Turney.
99. Brawley, *History of Morehouse College*, 16; Jones, *Candle in the Dark*, 24–26.
100. Historical Statement: Atlanta University, box 96, folder 6, Hope Records, AUC; Jones, *Candle in the Dark*, 31, 32, 34, 37; and Atlanta University, *Spelman Messenger*, October 1929, SCA.
101. Jones, *Candle in the Dark*, 37. Jones indicated that the motto for the seminary did not appear in any catalogues until the academic year 1895–1896. In this year, the motto was written in English: "And There Was Light"; whereas, in subsequent catalogues, it appeared in Latin: "*Et Facta Est Lux*." Jones, ibid., 64–65. Florence Read explained people endearingly referred to Frank Quarles as "Father Quarles." His church, Friendship Baptist, was founded three years after emancipation with its first members being former slaves. Moreover, Read asserted, by 1881, Friendship had 1,500 members and by this time, Quarles had become "influential in the educational and civic life as well as in the religious life of Georgia." Florence M. Read, *The Story of Spelman College* (New Jersey: Princeton University Press, 1961), 42.
102. Jones, *Candle in the Dark*, 38–39; Brawley, *History of Morehouse College*, 36–37.
103. Jones, *Candle in the Dark*, 45. There were no institution for black females until Spelman was established; Bennett College was established for females after Spelman. Bennett was founded in 1873 as Bennett Seminary. The seminary was chartered in 1889 as a coeducational college and was renamed Bennett College. In 1926, it was reorganized again as a college for women. Levrin Hill, ed., *Black American Colleges & Universities: Profiles of Two-Year, Four Year, & Professional Schools*, (Detroit, Michigan: Gale Research, Inc., 1994), 437; Roebuck and Komanduri, *Historically Black Colleges and Universities*, 65.
104. Read, *Story of Spelman College*, 13–30. Read explained that Catherine Beecher's "The Duty of American Women to Their Country," and the historic "Women's Rights Convention" in 1848 stirred Packard and Giles's "urgent need to educate and to convert [free people and Indians] to the Christian way of life." In 1877 Packard, Giles, and other women formed the Women's American Baptist Homes Mission Society as an auxiliary to the ABHMS. Packard, according to Read, "wrote the legal document applying for incorporation and called the first meeting thereafter." Read, ibid., 31.
105. Ibid., 32–33.
106. College History, 2000–2001, *Spelman College Bulletin*, 5. (Hereafter, designated as *SCB*). See Yolanda Watson-Moore, *Training the*

Head, the Hand, and the Heart: The Evolution of the Academic Curriculum of Spelman College, (1881–1953) (PhD diss., Georgia State University, 2000), 7–8; Read, *Story of Spelman College*, 35. New Orleans University and Straight Institute later merged and formed Dillard University.

107. Read, *Story of Spelman College*, 42.
108. Ibid., 43, 45, 50; College History, 2000–2001, *SCB*, 5. After holding meetings with other black ministers and individuals such as Joseph Robert, president of Atlanta Baptist Seminary, they granted the acceptance of a school. Individuals of varying churches solicited students from the church community and from going door-to-door. Range indicated the women were from 30 to 35 years of age. Range, *Rise and Progress of Negro Colleges*, 51. Watson-Moore indicated that individuals such as William White opposed females under the age of 15; thus, after receiving pressure from him and a committee of black ministers, Packard and Giles "sent all of the children away." Watson-Moore, *Training the Head, the Hand, and the Heart*, fn. 11, 40. Watson also pointed out the early curriculum at the Female Seminary did not "feature the practical and classical curriculum which pervaded many women's educational institutions of the period." Watson-Moore, *Training the Head*, 10, 54; Range, *Rise and Progress of Negro Colleges*, 51.
109. Chernow, *Titan*, 307; *General Education Board: An Account of Its Activities, 1902–1914* (New York: General Education Board, 1915), 6.
110. Chernow, *Titan*, 240; College History, 2000–2001, *SCB*, 5; and Read, *Story of Spelman College*, 64.
111. Read, *Story of Spelman College*, 77–79.
112. College History, 2000–2001, *SCB*, 5; Read, *Story of Spelman College*, 70–71, 73, 75; Range, *Rise and Progress of Negro Colleges*, 52; Chernow, *Titan*, 240–241; and Henry Morehouse, quoted in Read, *Story of Spelman College*, 79.
113. Anderson, *Education of Blacks in the South*, 68; Kenneth Rose, "John D. Rockefeller, the American Baptist Education Society, and the Growth of Baptist Higher Education in the Midwest," 4, the Rockefellers Archives, accessed July 10, 2012, www.rockarch.org/publications/resrep/rosel.pdf.
114. John D. Rockefeller Sr., as quoted in Chernow, *Titan*, 240; Rose, "John D. Rockefeller," 12.
115. Chernow, *Titan*, 240.
116. Raymond B. Fosdick, *John D. Rockefeller, Jr.: A Portrait* (New York: Harper & Brothers, 1956), 15; Chernow, *Titan*, 90.
117. "Atlanta University," *Spelman Messenger*, October 1929, SCA; Raymond B. Fosdick, Henry F. Pringle, and Katherine Douglas Pringle, *Adventures in Giving: The Story of the General Education Board* (New York: Harper & Row, 1962), 5; and Fosdick, *John D. Rockefeller, Jr.*, 117–120.

118. Lewis, *W. E. B. Du Bois*, 215.
119. Ibid., 238, 252; Davis, *Clashing of the Soul*, 110–112. Davis stated that Du Bois was convinced that "reasoned study and analysis, not religion, would break down the walls of discrimination." Hope believed in "the importance of scientific study." Both men "promoted Western culture as a fundamental basis of good character."
120. Bacote, *Story of Atlanta University*, 132; Lewis, *W. E. B. Du Bois*, 215. Lewis explained how Du Bois used student's research papers as building blocks for the Atlanta University's Conference of Negro Problem, a series of studies under Du Bois's direction.
121. Bacote, *Story of Atlanta University*, 130; Lewis, *W. E. B. Du Bois*, 198, 224. Lewis affirmed Du Bois received national and international recognition for his work and became "the second most sought-after spokesperson for his race after Booker T. Washington."
122. Lewis, *W. E. B. Du Bois*, 201, 202, 203. This essay, as Lewis explained, "challenged the giants of contemporary sociology and declared that the discipline's methodology was based on theoretical fallacies that ignored the ineradicable element of human chance in human affairs." Furthermore, Lewis pointed out that Du Bois created his own definition of sociology, "the science that seeks [to measure] the limits of Chance in human conduct."
123. Lewis, *W. E. B. Du Bois*, 202. By not basing his methodological framework on theory, Du Bois set out to redefine sociological studies from an historical perspective. *The Philadelphia Negro*, Lewis wrote, "recounted the ascent through slavery and adversity by the late-seventeenth-century Africans in the city until their progress was sharply checked, temporarily, by European migration in the mid-nineteenth; then through their rise and fall again later in the century–due, in part, to an influx of southern black folk." Ibid., 203.
124. Ibid., 220. Some of Du Bois's published works while on the faculty of Atlanta University were: *The Negro Artisan* (1902), *The Negro Church* (1903), *The Souls of Black Folks* (1903), *The Negro American Family* (1908), *The College-Bred Negro* (1910), and *The Negro Common School* (1911). Lewis, *Du Bois*, 221.
125. Ibid., 223–225.
126. Bacote, *Story of Atlanta University*, 137.
127. Franklin, *From Slavery to Freedom*, 433–435. Franklin elaborated on these riots in such places as Springfield, Ohio (1904), Brownsville, Texas (1906), Atlanta, Georgia (1906), and Springfield, Illinois (1908).
128. Bauerlein, *Negrophobia*, 61.
129. Woodward, "Folkways, Stateways, and Racism," 73–92.
130. Franklin, *From Slavery to Freedom*, 383, 538. Franklin pointed out that by 1933, there were more than 38,000 blacks receiving collegiate instruction, and 97 percent were in colleges in the South. Ibid., 539.

131. Ibid., 378; Anderson, *Education of Blacks in the South*, 242–252, 277–278; Anderson, "Philanthropic Control over Private Black Higher Education," 158; Bacote, *Story of Atlanta University*, 258; and Myrdal, *American Dilemma*, 880.
132. Franklin, *From Slavery to Freedom*, 378; Curti and Nash, *Philanthropy in the Shaping of American Higher Education*, 239.

2 Mythical Phoenix and the Ashes It Spreads

1. Laurence Veysey, *The Emergence of the American University* (Chicago: University of Chicago Press, 1965), 3.
2. James D. Anderson, "Philanthropic Control over Private Black Higher Education," in *Philanthropy and Cultural Imperialism*, ed. Robert F. Arnove (Bloomington, Indiana: Indiana University Press, 1980), 154–155, 163; James D. Anderson, *The Education of Blacks in the South, 1860–1935* (Chapel Hill: University of North Carolina Press, 1988), 241.
3. Anderson, "Philanthropic Control over Private Black Colleges," 173, 163; Atlanta University: Purpose of Atlanta University, box 96, folder 6, Hope Records, AUC; Wallace Buttrick to John D. Rockefeller Jr., February 14, 1914, box 203, folder 1937, Oswald Villard, 1903–1954, GEB, RAC; *General Education Board: An Account of Its Activities, 1902–1914* (New York: General Education Board, 1915), 208; and Raymond B. Fosdick, Henry F. Pringle, and Katherine Douglas Pringle, *Adventures in Giving: The Story of the General Education Board* (New York: Harper & Row, 1962), 88–89.
4. Herbert Spencer, quoted in Stewart H. Holbrooke, *The Age of the Moguls* (Garden City, New York: Doubleday, 1952), 88.
5. Bradley W. Bateman, "Clearing the Ground: The Demise of the Social Gospel Movement and the Rise of Neoclassicism in American Economics," *History of Political Economy*, Winter 1998, 29–52.
6. Ronald C. White Jr., *Liberty and Justice for All: Racial Reform and the Social Gospel*, with a foreword by James M. McPherson (New York: Harper & Row, 1990), xx, xxi.
7. Bateman, "Clearing the Ground," 29–52.
8. Veysey, *Emergence of the American University*, 124.
9. Edwin Embree, "Rockefeller Foundation," 1930, box 1, folder 3, Edwin Embree Papers, Rockefeller Archive Center, Sleepy Hollow, New York. (Hereafter, designated as Embree Papers and RAC); Alice Fleming, *Ida Tarbell: First of the Muckrakers* (New York: Thomas Y. Crowell, 1971), 112, 126–127. In 1906, President Theodore Roosevelt condemned reckless and irresponsible journalists who only reported the "bad side of things" and took advantage of the

public's response to Tarbell's expose by writing in the interest of sensationalism. He compared these individuals with the character in John Bunyan's *Pilgrim's Progress* and called them "muckrakers." Though Roosevelt also praised those writers who were attacking "legitimate social ills," he did not distinguish the term between the two; thus, "muckraker" eventually became a term applied to those journalists, like Tarbell, "who were working on behalf of reform." Fleming indicated, "The insult was transformed into a term of approval, and Ida, who had at first resented being called a muckraker, came to accept the title as a badge of distinction."
10. Fleming, *Ida Tarbell*, 104, 122.
11. John D. Rockefeller Sr., *Random Reminiscences of Men and Events* (Garden City, New York: Doubleday, Page, 1913), 58; Ron Chernow, *Titan: The Life of John D. Rockefeller, Sr.* (New York: Random House, 1998), xxi; and Holbrook, *Age of the Moguls*, 67.
12. Holbrook, *Age of the Moguls*, 139.
13. Chernow, *Titan*, 9. Carnegie was born in 1835, Gould in 1836, Morgan in 1837, and Rockefeller Sr. in 1839.
14. Veysey, *Emergence of the American University*, 348.
15. Andrew Carnegie, "Wealth," *North American Review* 148 (June 1889), Cedar Falls, Iowa: University of Northern Iowa, Cornell University Library, Division of Rare and Manuscript Collection, accessed April 11, 2001, http://cdi.library.cornell.edu.
16. Andrew Carnegie, "The Best Fields of Philanthropy," *North American Review* 149 (December 1889), Cedar Falls, Iowa: University of Northern Iowa, ibid.
17. John D. Rockefeller Sr., quoted in Kenneth Rose, "The Rockefeller Foundation: A History; Introduction" (New York: The Rockefeller Foundation), accessed April 23, 2001, http://rockfound.org.
18. Rockefeller Sr., *Random Reminiscences*, 157.
19. John Ensor Harr and Peter J. Johnson, *The Rockefeller Conscience: An American Family in Public and in Private* (New York: Charles Scribner's Sons, Macmillian, 1991), xiv.
20. Veysey, *Emergence of the American Universities*, 3. The idea of erecting Cornell University grew from the Morrill Land Grant Act (1862), which appropriated public land to aid state agricultural and mechanical colleges, and Ezra Cornell's discussions with Andrew White, who later became the first president of Cornell University. In 1865, White introduced the bill to the Senate, and in April of that year, the bill passed. Cornell endowed the university through a gift of $500,000, which added to the sum realized by Cornell's purchase of the Morrill land strip from the state. Cornell University was established with all of the aspects Ezra Cornell felt most important in life: concern for education, interest in agriculture, and a philanthropic impulse. "Ezra Cornell: A Nineteenth-Century Life," Cornell University Library, Division of Rare and Manuscript Collections, accessed April 16, 2001, http://

rmc.library.cornell.edu/ezra-exhibit/entrance.html. Johns Hopkins left a large endowment to fund several institutions of higher education. In 1867, six years before his death, Hopkins left $7 million in his will to organize two corporations, one for a hospital and one for a university. Equally divided, this fund led to the establishment of Johns Hopkins University in 1876, Johns Hopkins Hospital in 1889, and later Johns Hopkins Medical School in 1893. "Who is Johns Hopkins," Johns Hopkins University Library, accessed April 16, 2001, http://webapps.jh.edu/jhuniverse/information_about_hopkins.

21. Carnegie, "The Best Fields of Philanthropy," 682–699. The death of Leland and Jane Stanford's only son, Leland Jr., resulted in their desire to erect an educational institution in his memory. However, the desire was to build a university that was unlike the institutions in the East: nontraditional (coeducational), nondenominational, and practical, producing cultured and useful citizens. In 1885, when Stanford University opened, it was distinct from the other leading institutions. David Starr Jordan, a leading scientific man of the time, was president; its student body consisted of both males and females; and the curriculum followed the German model of providing graduate and undergraduate instruction that stressed research along with teaching. Leland Stanford, "The Founding of the University," Stanford University, access April 9, 2001, http://www.stanford.edu/home/stanford/history/begin.html.

22. Veysey, *Emergence of the American University*, 57–120. Charles Eliot, president of Harvard, and Andrew D. White, president of Cornell, were the leaders in making utility the key to and the acceptance of college education in the American scheme of things. Through the elective system, Harvard offered a broadened program in the liberal arts, placing more emphasis on natural and physical subjects (e.g., modern languages, history, etc.). White leaned more toward the combination of liberal arts, scientific, and vocational training. However, neither of the men initially urged an emphasis on research; Ibid., 68–95.

23. Veysey noted that Harvard did not exclude minority students (e.g., blacks and Jews) who passed the entrance exam. However, President Eliot did not necessarily approve of social interaction between the races and held stereotypical views of Jewish students. Veysey, *American University*, 92. Conversely, Ezra Cornell, founder of Cornell University, took measures so as not to exclude women and blacks. In 1869, Cornell wrote, "There is a great reform required in the education and habits of females. Please study the subject and see what can be done for them." Ezra Cornell to Mattie Curran, July 24, 1869, in "Ezra Cornell: A Nineteenth-Century Life," Cornell University Library, Division of Rare and Manuscript Collections, accessed April 16, 2001, http://rmc.library.cornell.edu/ezra-exhibit/entrance.html.

24. Veysey, *American University*, 126. Veysey explained that most American universities did not initially implement the German model; instead, most implemented utilitarian curricula, causing contrasting methods in the teaching field for those who trained in the United States and those trained abroad. There was a difference, however, between American universities and German universities, as Veysey explained, "German rhetoric about academic purpose appears to have centered upon three quite different conceptions: first, on the value of non-utilitarian learning, freely pursued without regard to the immediate needs of the surrounding society (hence "pure" learning, protected by *Lehrfreheit*); second, on the value of *Wissenschaft*, or investigation and writing in a general sense, as opposed to teaching (*Wissenschaft* did not necessarily connote empirical research; it could just as easily comprehend Hagelian philosophy); finally, on their epistemological side, German statements of academic aim continues to run toward some form of all-encompassing idealism." Since learning in the late nineteenth century in the United States was of utilitarian orientation, there were only two universities dominated by the ideal of scientific research and established as centers for graduate study when they opened: Johns Hopkins University (1876) and Clark University (1889); institutions such as Harvard and Columbia were in the process of transforming into universities. Lawrence A. Cremin, "The Education of the Educating Profession," *The History of Higher Education*, 2nd ed., ASHE Reader Series, ed. Lester F. Goodchild and Harold S. Wechsler (Boston, Massachusetts: Pearson Custom, 1997), 403.
25. Merle Curti and Roderick Nash, *Philanthropy in the Shaping of American Higher Education* (New Jersey: Rutgers University Press, 1965), 213.
26. Wickliffe Rose, "Summary of Operations of the Peabody Education Fund," June 20, 1916, folder 5, box 1, Wickliffe Rose Papers, RAC. In 1910, Rose was elected president of the George Peabody College for Teachers. In 1913, he became a trustee for the GEB and later, in 1925, became president of the GEB. Rose noted that during the 47 years of the fund's operation, "the Trustees contributed from the income of the Fund toward the encouragement of public education in the Southern states about three and three-quarter million dollars." See Horace Mann Bond, *The Education of the Negro in the American Social Order*, 130–144; Curti and Nash, *Philanthropy in the Shaping of American Higher Education*, 173; Fosdick, Pringle, and Pringle, *Adventures in Giving*, 3; John Hope Franklin, *From Slavery to Freedom: A History of American Negroes*, 2nd ed. (New York: Alfred A. Knopf, 1964), 378–384; and Gunnar Myrdal, *An American Dilemma: The Negro Problem and Modern Democracy*, vol. 2, with a new introduction by Sissela Bok (New York: Harper & Row, 1944, 1962; reprint, New Brunswick, NJ: Transaction Publishers, 1996), 890.

27. *General Education Board*, 9. During its operation, the three general agents for the Peabody Fund were Barnes Sears, J. L. M. Curry, and Wickliffe Rose.
28. Dwight Oliver Wendell Holmes, *The Evolution of the Negro College* (New York: Arno and The New York Times, 1969), 164–165.
29. John E. Fisher, *The John F. Slater Fund: A Nineteenth Century Affirmative Action for Negro Education* (Lanham, Maryland: University Press of America, 1986), 3.
30. Bond, *Education of the Negro in the American Social Order*, 130–144; Curti and Nash, *Philanthropy in the Shaping of American Higher Education*, 173; Roy E. Finkenbine, "Law, Reconstruction, and African American Education," in *Charity, Philanthropy, and Civility in American History*, ed. Lawrence J. Friedman and Mark D. McGarvie (New York: Cambridge University Press, 2003), 167; Fosdick, Pringle, and Pringle, *Adventures in Giving*, 3; Franklin, *From Slavery to Freedom*, 378–384; and Myrdal, *American Dilemma*, 890.
31. Franklin, *From Slavery to Freedom*, 379.
32. *General Education Board*, 10; Fosdick, Pringle, and Pringle, *Adventures in Giving*, 103. Bishop Haygood, J. L. M. Curry, Wallace Buttrick, and James H. Dillard served in succession as general agents of the Slater Fund.
33. Holmes, *Evolution of the Negro College*, 163–164.
34. Curti and Nash, *Philanthropy in the Shaping of American Higher Education*, 173.
35. *General Education Board*, 11; "The Phelps-Stokes Fund: Celebrating Our 90th Year," accessed July 28, 2003, http://www.psfdc.org; Holmes, *Evolution of the Negro College*, 164–172, 176–178; and Myrdal, *American Dilemma*, 890–891.
36. Carnegie, "The Best Fields of Philanthropy," 685.
37. Bernard Alderson, *Andrew Carnegie: The Man and His Work* (New York: Doubleday, Page, 1908), 155.
38. Louis M. Hacker, *The World of Andrew Carnegie, 1865–1901* (Philadelphia and New York: J. B. Lippincott, 1968), 364–367; "History of Carnegie Mellon," http://www.cmu.edu/home/about/about_history.html; and Ellen Condliffe Lagerman, "Surveying the Professions," in Goodchild and Wechsler, *History of Higher Education*, 394–402.
39. Anderson, *Education of Blacks in the South*, 91; Myrdal, *American Dilemma*, 890–891. The Carnegie Corporation sponsored Myrdal's study.
40. Roger L. Geiger, "Research, Graduate Education and the Ecology of American Universities: An Interpretive History," in Goodchild and Wechsler, *History of Higher Education*, 280.
41. W. Bruce Leslie, "The Age of the College," in Goodchild and Wechsler, *History of Higher Education*, 337. Also see the Carnegie

Foundation for the Advancement of Teaching, *Missions of the College Curriculum*, (San Francisco: Jossey-Bass, 1977).
42. John S. Brubacher and Willis Rudy, "Professional Education," in Goodchild and Wechsler, *History of Higher Education*, 385. See Hugh Hawkins, "Toward System," in Goodchild and Wechsler, *History of Higher Education*, 318–328; W. Bruce Leslie, "The Age of the College," in Goodchild and Wechsler, *History of Higher Education*, 333–343; and Lawrence A. Cremin, "The Education of the Educating Professions," in Goodchild and Wechsler, *History of Higher Education*, 403–412.
43. Chernow, *Titan*, 491–492.
44. Rose, "The Rockefeller Foundation".
45. John D. Rockefeller Jr. to William H. Baldwin Jr., March 1, 1902, Appendix II, in *General Education Board*, 216.
46. Fosdick, Pringle, and Pringle, *Adventures in Giving*, 1; Franklin, *From Slavery to Freedom*, 380; and *General Education Board*, 11, 196.
47. *General Education Board*, 4.
48. Chernow, *Titan*, 472–479, 484, 489, 491, 596; Rose, "The Rockefeller Foundation. This introduction indicated that the Rockefeller Foundation has given "more than $2 billion to thousands of grantees worldwide and has assisted directly in the training of nearly 13,000 Rockefeller Foundation Fellows."
49. Harr and Johnson, *Rockefeller Conscience*, 6.
50. Raymond B. Fosdick, *John D. Rockefeller, Jr.: A Portrait* (New York: Harper & Brothers, 1956), 61.
51. John D. Rockefeller Jr. to John D. Rockefeller Sr., February 11, 1919, in *"Dear Father"/"Dear Son:" Correspondence of John D. Rockefeller and John D. Rockefeller, Jr*, ed. Joseph W. Ernst (New York: Fordham University Press in cooperation with Rockefeller Archive Center, 1994), 90.
52. "Rockefeller Brothers Fund," the Rockefeller Foundation, accessed April 23, 2001, http://www.rbf.org. The Rockefeller Brothers Fund was established in 1940 and dedicated "to promote the well-being of all people in the transition to global interdependence." This is a philanthropic organization established by John D. Rockefeller Jr.'s five sons (John D., 3rd, Winthrop, Laurence, David, and Nelson) and daughter (Abby Rockefeller Mauze); they shared a source of advice and research on charitable activities and combined some of their philanthropies.
53. Fosdick, *John D. Rockefeller, Jr.*, 16, 373, 41. Rockefeller Sr. bought Junior a scholarship for a student at Hampton. Fosdick indicated that Junior and this student remained in contact for a number of years.
54. Chernow, *Titan*, 481–483; Curti and Nash, *Philanthropy in the Shaping of American Higher Education*, 215; Fosdick, *John D. Rockefeller, Jr.*, 117; Allan Nevins, *John D. Rockefeller: The Heroic*

Age of American Enterprise, vol. 2 (New York: Charles Scribner's Sons, 1940), 482–484; and Clarence A. Bacote, *The Story of Atlanta University: A Century of Service, 1865–1965* (New Jersey: Princeton University Press, 1969), 248.
55. Chernow, *Titans*, 482.
56. Henry St. George Tucker, quoted in Chernow, *Titan*, 483.
57. Rockefeller Sr., *Random Reminiscences*, 6.
58. Frederick Gates, quoted in Edwin Embree to Clarence Day, August 21, 1925, box 1, folder 3, Embree Papers, RAC. Junior, Gates, and Murphy met and discussed ways in which Rockefeller Sr. could distribute his wealth. In correspondence with his father, Junior recommended his father direct his funds to the University of Chicago, the Rockefeller Institute of Medical Research, and the GEB. Furthermore, Junior recommended using the GEB as the trustee for all corporations. John D. Rockefeller Jr. to John D. Rockefeller Sr., January 24, 1907, box 1, folder 14, John D. Rockefeller Jr., Personal Papers, RAC.
59. Chernow, *Titan*, 484; *General Education Board*, 3.
60. Edwin Embree to Clarence Day, August 21, 1925, box 1, folder 3, Embree Papers, RAC.
61. Ibid.
62. Anderson, *Education of Blacks in the South*, 97. See "Training the Apostles of Liberal Culture," ibid., 238–278.
63. *General Education Board*, 3.
64. *General Education Board*. Frederick T. Gates, William H. Baldwin Jr., Jabez L. M. Curry, Robert Ogden, Daniel C. Gilman, Walter H. Page, George F. Peabody, and Albert Shaw officially submitted the articles of association. See "An Act to Incorporate the General Education Board," Appendix II, ibid., 212–215. The two additional members were Rockefeller Jr. and Wallace Buttrick, trustee and secretary, respectively.
65. *General Education Board*, 4–5.
66. Ibid., 7; Fosdick, Pringle, and Pringle, *Adventures in Giving*, 7–8; and Frederick T. Gates, quoted in ibid., 9.
67. Rockefeller, *Random Reminiscence*, 166.
68. Kenneth Rose, "John D. Rockefeller, the American Baptist Education Society, and the Growth of Baptist Higher Education in the Midwest," 12, the Rockefeller Archives, accessed July 10, 2012, www.rockarch.org/publications/resrep/rosel.pdf.
69. *General Education Board*, 15.
70. Ibid., 108–109.
71. Ibid., 109–111.
72. Ibid., 111.
73. Ibid., 104.
74. Ibid., 105.
75. Ibid., 155.
76. Ibid., 18, 22.

77. Fosdick, Pringle, and Pringle, *Adventures in Giving*, 7, 15, 26–27.
78. *General Education Board*, 15. Also see, Frederick Gates to Messrs. Wallace Buttrick and Starr J. Murphy, June 30, 1905, Appendix II, ibid., 218–219.
79. Fosdick, Pringle, and Pringle, *Adventures in Giving*, 88–89; Chernow, *Titan*, 486; John D. Rockefeller Jr. to General Education Board, February 5, 1905, Appendix II, in *General Education Board*, 219; and John D. Rockefeller Jr. to General Education Board, June 29, 1909, ibid., 221–222. This amount, as Chernow equated, was the equivalent of $500 million in 1998. However, it is equivalent to over $739 million in 2010.
80. Anderson, *Education of Blacks in the South*, 136; *General Education Board*, 191, 193.
81. *General Education Board*, 193; Report on the Field of Negro Education in the Southern States, March 1911, box 353, folder 3651, GEB, RAC. On the contrary, Anderson maintained that industrialist, such as William Baldwin Jr. "opposed the development of black higher education" and felt "higher education ought to direct black boys and girls to places in life that were congruent with the South's racial caste system"; Anderson, *Education of Blacks in the South*, 247–248.
82. *General Education Board*, 193, 194, 199.
83. Ibid., 81–87, 203. By 1914, the GEB had given $555,781 in appropriations to the following black industrial institutions: Hampton Institute ($138,000), Tuskegee Institute ($135,483), Spelman Seminary ($196,913), and other institutions ($85,385).
84. Report on the Field of Negro Education, March 1911, box 353, folder 3651, GEB, RAC, 9–10.
85. Myrdal, *American Dilemma*, 899.
86. Lewis, *W. E. B. Du Bois*, 221, 548.
87. Du Bois to Buttrick, March 31, 1905, box 49, folder 442, Ga 80 Atlanta University, GEB, RAC.
88. Ibid.; Du Bois to Buttrick, April 3, 1906, ibid.; Du Bois to Buttrick, March 15, 1910, box 49, folder 443, Ga 80 Atlanta University, ibid.; Buttrick to Du Bois, March 17, 1910, ibid.; Du Bois to Buttrick, 9, May 1910, ibid.; and Buttrick to Du Bois, May 13, 1910, ibid.
89. W. E. B. Du Bois to Wallace Buttrick, October 8, 1907, box 49, folder 443, Ga 80 Atlanta University, 1907–1911, GEB, RAC. Du Bois's quote is written grammatically as it appeared in his letter to Buttrick.
90. Buttrick to Du Bois, October 11, 1907, box 49, folder 443, Ga 80 Atlanta University, 1907–1911, GEB, RAC.
91. Anderson, *Education of Blacks in the South*, 251–252; Franklin, *From Slavery to Freedom*, 538–539; and Eric Anderson and Alfred A. Moss Jr., *Dangerous Donations: Northern Philanthropy and Southern Black Education, 1902–1930*, foreword by Louis R. Harlan (Missouri: University of Missouri Press, 1990), 205–206.

92. John D. Rockefeller Jr. to Wallace Buttrick, February 2, 1914, box 353, folder 3651, GEB, RAC.
93. Atlanta University: Purpose of Atlanta University, box 96, folder 6, Hope Records, AUC.
94. Wallace Buttrick to John D. Rockefeller Jr., February 5, 1914, box 203, folder 1937, Oswald Villard, 1903–1954, GEB, RAC.
95. *General Education Board*, 208.
96. Buttrick to Rockefeller Jr., February 5, 1914, box 203, folder 1937, Oswald Villard, 1903–1954, GEB, RAC.
97. *General Education Board*, 209.
98. Both Morehouse and Spelman Colleges received money from the GEB by 1914. Benjamin Brawley, *The History of Morehouse College* (Atlanta, Georgia: Morehouse College, 1917), 107; John D. Rockefeller Jr. to the General Education Board, March 23, 1906, box 39, folder 360, Ga 10 Spelman College, 1902–1965, GEB, RAC; Abraham Flexner to John D. Rockefeller Jr., September 21, 1914, box 40, folder 362, ibid.; and Booker T. Washington to Andrew Carnegie, November 13, 1909, *The Booker T. Washington Papers*, 196.
99. Anson Phelps Stokes to Edward T. Ware, February 10, 1915, box 49, folder 444, Ga 80 Atlanta University, GEB, RAC.
100. W. T. B. Williams, "Report on Atlanta University," April 9, 1918, box 49, folder 444, Ga 80 Atlanta University, GEB, RAC.

3 John Hope: Hallmark of the Truest Greatness

1. John Hope Franklin, in Leroy Davis, *A Clashing of the Soul: John Hope and the Dilemma of African American Leadership and Black Higher Education in the Early Twentieth Century*, with a foreword by John Hope Franklin (Athens, Georgia: University of Georgia Press, 1998), ix.
2. For example, when I presented a paper on the Atlanta University affiliation at the Association for the Study of Higher Education (ASHE) conference, the discussant began his critique of my paper by addressing what I had presented on John Hope Franklin rather than John Hope. He repeatedly said this though it was clear I was discussing John Hope. Eventually, he corrected himself.
3. Franklin, in Davis, *Clashing of the Soul*, x.
4. Davis, *Clashing of the Soul*, xxiv.
5. Raymond B. Fosdick, Henry F. Pringle, and Katherine Douglas Pringle, *Adventures in Giving: The Story of the General Education Board* (New York: Harper & Row, 1962), 197; Wallace Buttrick to John Hope, June 10, 1906, box 58, folder 520, GEB, RAC; and Abraham Flexner to James Bertam, May 5, 1919, box 59, folder 522, GEB, RAC.

6. Rayford Logan, in Ridgely Torrence, *The Story of John Hope*, with an introduction by Rayford Logan (New York: Macmillan, 1948; reprint, New York: Arno and The New York Times, 1969), iii; Torrence, *Story of John Hope*, 184; and Edward A. Jones, *A Candle in the Dark: A History of Morehouse College* (Valley Forge, Pennsylvania: Judson, 1967), 82.
7. Fosdick, Pringle and Pringle, *Adventures in Giving*, 197.
8. Myrdal, in his study *An American Dilemma*, noted that blacks of "mixed bloods" had "always been preferred by the whites in practically all respects." He added that these blacks "made a better appearance to the whites and were assumed to be mentally more capable." Gunnar Myrdal, *An American Dilemma: The Negro Problem and Modern Democracy*, vol. 2, with a new introduction by Sissela Bok (New York: Harper & Row, 1944, 1962; reprint, New Brunswick, NJ: Transaction Publishers, 1996), 696.
9. Jones, *Candle in the Dark*, 82.
10. Davis, *Clashing of the Soul*, xxvi, 60, 61, 68. Mulattos were free people of color, individuals who were of biracial ancestry, here black and white. The term also differentiated blacks with fairer hues from blacks of darker hue. These individuals, because of their skin tone and white paternal ancestry, lived better lives and had a higher social status than their darker counterparts; yet they maintained a lower class status than whites.
11. Davis, *Clashing of the Soul*, 119.
12. Jones, *Candle in the Dark*, 84.
13. Torrence, *Story of John Hope*, 133.
14. "The Significance of the Niagara Movement," *Voice of the Negro*, August 1905, 600.
15. John Hope, Conference on Negro Education, GEB, RAC, 18.
16. Kelly Miller, "Washington's Policy," *Boston Evening Transcript*, September 18–19, 1903, and in *Booker T. Washington and His Critic: Problems in American Civilization*, edited and with an introduction by Hugh Hawkins (Boston: D. C. Hearth, 1962), 51.
17. Davis, *Clashing of the Soul*, 120; Torrence, *Story of John Hope*, 135. Although Hope spoke to church groups, he also made speeches at secular functions.
18. John Hope, quoted in Torrence, *Story of John Hope*, 135–136.
19. Davis, *Clashing of the Soul*, 138.
20. Ibid., 129, 133; "A Negro Educator," Interview with John Hope, box 65, folder 3, Hope Records, AUC.
21. David Levering Lewis, *The Fight for Equality and the American Century, 1919–1963* (New York: Henry Holt, 2000), 137.
22. Wallace Buttrick to John Hope, June 19, 1906, box 58, folder 520, Ga 157 Morehouse College, 1903–1910, GEB, RAC.
23. Malcolm MacVicar, quoted in Davis, *Clashing of the Soul*, 132.
24. Ibid., 133.

25. John Hope to W. E. B. Du Bois, January 17, 1910, real 2, frame 152, Du Bois Papers, Auburn Avenue Research Library on African-American Culture and History, Archives Department (hereafter, designated as Du Bois Papers and AARL); Davis, *Clashing of the Soul*, 162.
26. John Hope, Biographical Sketch, box 65, folder 3, Hope Records, AUC.
27. Davis, *Clashing of the Soul*, 163.
28. Torrence, *Story of John Hope*, 132–133. See Lewis, *W. E. B. Du Bois*, 297–342.
29. Lewis, *W. E. B. Du Bois*, 253.
30. See Correspondence, W. E. B. Du Bois and Hope in Du Bois Papers, AARL.
31. Mark Bauerlein, *Negrophobia, A Race Riot in Atlanta, 1906* (San Francisco: Encounter Books, 2001), 433; Clifford M. Kuhn, Harlon E. Joye, and E. Bernard West, *Living Atlanta: An Oral History of the City, 1914–1948*, foreword by Michael Lomax (Athens, Georgia: University of Georgia Press, 1990), 37; and Lewis, *W. E. B. Du Bois*, 333. Franklin noted other cities had race riots around this time as well: Springfield, Ohio (1904), Brownsville, Texas (1906), and Springfield, Illinois (1908). John Hope Franklin, *From Slavery to Freedom: A History of American Negroes*, 2nd ed. (New York: Alfred A. Knopf, 1964), 433–435.
32. Gary M. Pomerantz, *Where Peachtree Meets Sweet Auburn: The Saga of Two Families and the Making of Atlanta* (New York: A Lisa Drew Book/Scribner, 1996), 73.
33. Franklin, *From Slavery to Freedom*, 433.
34. Davis, *Clashing of the Soul*, 167.
35. Bauerlein, *Negrophobia*, 289; Davis, *Clashing of the Soul*, 168; and Kuhn, Joyce, and West, *Living Atlanta*, 37.
36. Jones, *Candle in the Dark*, 87, 88; Davis, *Clashing of the Soul*, 190; Lewis, *W. E. B. Du Bois*, 404; and Torrence, *Story of John Hope*, 158.
37. Torrence, *Story of John Hope*, 159; Davis, *Clashing of the Soul*, 145.
38. Davis, *Clashing of the Soul*, 143; Torrence, *Story of John Hope*, 159.
39. Robert R. Moton to Wallace Buttrick, October 9, 1906, box 58, folder 520, Ga 157 Morehouse College, 1903–1910, GEB, RAC.
40. Ibid.; Torrence, *Story of John Hope*, 157–158.
41. Buttrick to Moton, November 13, 1906, box 58, folder 520, Ga 157 Morehouse College, 1903–1910, GEB, RAC; Torrence, *Story of John Hope*, 157–158.
42. Jones, *Candle in the Dark*, 88.
43. Michael Bieze, *Booker T. Washington and the Art of Self-Representation* (New York: Peter Lang, 2008), 123.
44. Booker T. Washington to Andrew Carnegie, November 13, 1909, in Louis Harlan, ed., *The Booker T. Washington Papers, 1909–1911* (Chicago: University of Illinois Press, 1981), 600.

45. Davis, *Clashing of the Soul*, 190; Jones, *Candle in the Dark*, 88; and Torrence, *Story of John Hope*, 159.
46. John Hope to W. E. B. Du Bois, January 17, 1910, reel 2, frame 153, W. E. B. Du Bois Papers, AARL.
47. Ibid.
48. Jones, *Candle in the Dark*, 89.
49. Ibid., 62.
50. Ibid., 91; Benjamin Brawley, *The History of Morehouse College* (Atlanta, Georgia: Morehouse College, 1917), 105.
51. Clarence A. Bacote, *The Story of Atlanta University: A Century of Service, 1865-1965* (New Jersey: Princeton University Press, 1969), 275; Davis, *Clashing of the Soul*, 188. See Lewis, *W. E. B, Du Bois*, 387.
52. Abraham Flexner to Hollis B. Frissell, November 3, 1915, box 353, folder 3651, GEB, RAC; Rufus Cole to Abraham Flexner, November 8, 1915, box 303, folder 3169, ibid.; Abraham Flexner to Wallace Buttrick, November 22, 1915, ibid.
53. Fosdick, Pringle, Pringle, *Adventures in Giving*, 197.
54. "Negro Education," Minutes of the Interracial Conference, General Education Board of the Rockefeller Foundation, November 29, 1915, GEB, RAC.
55. Ibid., 1.
56. Ibid., 7.
57. John Hope, ibid., 15.
58. Abraham Flexner, ibid., 15-16.
59. John Hope, ibid., 16-17.
60. Hollis Frissell, ibid., 18.
61. John Hope, ibid., 149; Abraham Flexner, ibid, 149. The exchange continues through page 174.
62. John Hope, ibid., 160.
63. Ibid., 168-174.

4 Layers of Complexity

1. Bacote, *Story of Atlanta University*, 5. *McGuffey's Reader* were primer series of readers for children created by William Holmes McGuffey in 1836. These readers were used in schools to emphasize morality and Americanism. Besides training students in English and grammar, these texts introduced poetry and the writings of statesmen, politicians, moralists, and religious leaders. Kevin Ryan and James Cooper, *Those Who Can, Teach*, 7th ed. (Boston: Houghton Mifflin, 1995), 153; *McGuffy's Reader*, 4th ed. (New York: American Book, 1879).
2. Bacote, *Story of Atlanta University*, 41-43. From the time the department opened in 1870 to its discontinuance in 1876, there

were only eight students who had registered for the courses. Having so few students was also the reason for closing the department.
3. Brawley, *History of Morehouse College*, 24–25. Brawley noted that Robert heard recitations for five hours a day and delivered two lectures a week on Biblical and Scientific subjects. They did not add a second teacher until 1876.
4. Ibid., 28; Bacote, *Story of Atlanta University*, 27; Jones, *Candle in the Dark*, 34; and Leroy Davis, *A Clashing of the Soul: John Hope and the Dilemma of African American Leadership and Black Higher Education in the Early Twentieth Century*, with a foreword by John Hope Franklin (Athens, Georgia: University of Georgia Press, 1998), 106.
5. Brawley, *History of Morehouse College*, 33–34, 36–37. The curriculum consisted of "arithmetic, algebra, geometry, geology, geography, botany, physiology, chemistry, physics, astronomy, literature, composition, history, civil government, Latin, review of English branches, mental philosophy, methods of teaching, and practice teaching." Lincoln University (1864), Wilberforce University (1866), Howard University (1868), Leland University and Benedict College (1870), and Fisk University (1871) also had college departments at this time.
6. Bacote, *Story of Atlanta University*, 41–43. From the time the Department opened in 1870 to its discontinuance in 1876, there were only eight students who had registered for the courses. Having so few students was also the reason for closing the department.
7. Bacote, *Story of Atlanta University*, 31, 34–35, 37, 44. Lucy Laney was one of the first graduates, who later became one of John Hope's teachers.
8. Brawley, *History of Morehouse College*, 28; Jones, *Candle in the Dark*, 35, 42.
9. Jones, *Candle in the Dark*, 42, 43, 46–47.
10. Read, *Story of Spelman College*, 86–89. In order to care for the sick students and provide courses in nursing training, they created the school infirmary and Atlanta physicians provided regular lectures in physiology and hygiene. All of the Atlanta physicians who worked in the infirmary were white. Black physicians who graduated from Rush, Harvard, Howard, or Meharry "were shut out from even the city hospital practice and clinics in Atlanta until 1953, and were not admitted to membership in medical societies in the South (or many in the North), and so had negligible opportunity to keep abreast of progress in medicine or surgery except inadequately through the printed page." Ibid., 139.
11. Ibid., 103.
12. Ibid., 114.
13. Historical Statement: Atlanta University, February 5, 1921, box 96, folder 6, Hope Records, AUC.

14. Edward A. Jones, *A Candle in the Dark: A History of Morehouse College* (Valley Forge, Pennsylvania: Judson, 1967), 66. See "Amended Charter of 1897," Appendix D, in Historical Statement: Atlanta University, February 5, 1921, box 96, folder 6, Hope Records, AUC, 318.
15. Judge J. H. Lumpkin, *Ex Parte Petition of Atlanta Baptist Seminary*, in Historical Statement: Atlanta University, February 5, 1921, box 96, folder 6, Hope Records, AUC, 319–320.
16. Jones, *Candle in the Dark*, 91.
17. College History, SCB, 5; Ron Chernow, *Titan: The Life of John D. Rockefeller, Sr.* (New York: Random House, 1998), 309.
18. Historical Statement: Spelman College, box 96, folder 6, Hope Records, AUC; Chernow, *Titan*, 240; Atlanta University, October 1929, *Spelman Messenger*, SCA; Florence M. Read, *The Story of Spelman College* (Princeton, New Jersey: Princeton University Press, 1961), 81–111. When Packard and Giles wrote to Rockefeller initially for money for the institution, they asked for permission to rename the seminary, "Rockefeller College," and if he did not want to use his name, perhaps they could use his wife's maiden of Spelman. Ibid., 80. Chernow noted that Rockefeller never allowed any institution to "stake a claim on him," especially since "Rockefeller had never matriculated and graduated from a college." Chernow, *Titan*, 309. Both the ABHMS and WABHMS boards agreed with the name change and agreed "that the institution was to be kept as a school for girls and women." Interestingly, the boards did not want either "Female" or "Baptist" in the institutions name. Regarding the denomination, the board felt the use of "Baptist" in the name would "repel desirable students." Read, *Story of Spelman College*, 84.
19. Chernow, *Titan*, 241; Read, *Story of Spelman College*, 199; and Lucy Tapley to Trevor Arnett, April 14, 1924, box 40, folder 366, Ga 10 Spelman College, GEB, RAC.
20. Benjamin Brawley, *History of Morehouse College* (College Park, Maryland: McGrath, 1917; reprinted 1970), 32.
21. James D. Anderson, "Philanthropic Control over Private Black Higher Education," in *Philanthropy and Cultural Imperialism*, ed. Robert F. Arnove (Bloomington, Indiana: Indiana University Press, 1980), 158; James D. Anderson, *The Education of Blacks in the South, 1860–1935* (Chapel Hill: University of North Carolina Press, 1988), 251.
22. Clarence A. Bacote, *The Story of Atlanta University: A Century of Service, 1865–1965* (New Jersey: Princeton University Press, 1969), 70.
23. Ibid., 70–76.
24. Ibid., 90. With the initial $8,000 appropriation, the State set up a committee to investigate Atlanta University. Upon its initial report, the committee indicated displeasure of the social equality of the

races (e.g., teachers eating and socializing with their students). Consequently, in 1887, the Glenn Bill was passed, "to regulate the manner of conducting educational institutions in the State, and to protect the rights of colored and white people, and to provide penalties for infractions of the provisions of this act."

25. Ibid., 90–92. Black communities and newspaper editorials also attacked the Glenn Bill.
26. Ibid., 76, 94, 100.The basic argument Atlanta University provided was that the resolution violated "the purposes of the founders, who from the beginning insisted upon the University being open to all students on a non-segregated basis; it would violate the principals of the AMA, which had contributed generously to its support; it would be in direct conflict with a pledge to the United States Government, which, through the Freedmen's Bureau, granted the funds for the original purchase of land for the University; it would alienate from its support a large number of Negro friends and other patrons throughout the country; it was repugnant to the principles of the trustees and faculty, who were unwilling to abandon a policy, which, in their opinion, had justified itself in the past." In 1891, the State College of Industry for Colored Youth (later known as Savannah State) was established.
27. Description of Boards Appropriation, Atlanta University, 1918, box 49, folder 444, Ga 80 Atlanta University, 1912–1918, GEB, RAC.
28. Edward T. Ware to the General Education Board, December 4, 1913, box 49, folder 444, Ga 80 Atlanta University, 1912–1918, GEB, RAC. Edward Ware was the son of Atlanta University's first president, Edmund Asa Ware.
29. E. G. Sage to Edward T. Ware, January 23, 1914, box 49, folder 449, Ga 80 Atlanta University, 1912–1918, GEB, RAC. Also see Description of Boards Appropriations, Atlanta University, 1918, box 49, folder 444, ibid.
30. William G. Willcox to Abraham Flexner, October 28, 1916, box 49, folder 449, Ga 80 Atlanta University, 1912–1918, GEB, RAC; E. C. Sage to Edward T. Ware, October 30, 1916, ibid. E. C. Sage was the secretary of the GEB; Abraham Flexner to William Willcox, November 3, 1916, ibid.
31. Anson Phelps Stokes to E. C. Sage, November 9, 1916, ibid. In response, Sage indicated he would "endeavor to present the facts in as thorough-going manner as may be possible," and that he would "particularly appreciate the cooperation of Dr. Thomas Jesse Jones" in his investigation. E. C. Sage to Anson Phelps Stokes, November 10, 1916, ibid.
32. Edward T. Ware to E. C. Sage, "Appeal to the General Education Board for a Grant to Help Meet the Current Expenses of Atlanta University for the Year 1917–1918," October 30, 1917, ibid.
33. Description of Board's Appropriations, 1918, ibid.

34. E. C. Sage to Edward Ware, September 24, 1918, ibid.
35. W. T. B. Williams, "Report on Atlanta University," April 9, 1918, ibid.
36. Abraham Flexner to Wallace Buttrick, November 27, 1918, box 59, folder 522, Ga 157 Morehouse College, GEB, RAC.
37. Ibid.
38. Buttrick to Flexner, December 3, 1918, box 59, folder 522, Ga 157 Morehouse College, GEB, RAC.
39. Bacote, *Story of Atlanta University*, 173.
40. Edward T. Ware to Wallace Buttrick, October 25, 1919, box 50, folder 445, Ga 80 Atlanta University, GEB, RAC.
41. Ware to Buttrick, October 25, 1919, ibid. In this request, though for $5,000, Ware indicated that Flexner and Hovey visited Atlanta University and found that the institution was "deficient in scholarship and that [their] students were weak and inaccurate in the simple fundamentals of Latin grammar." Consequently, Atlanta University obtained "the services of Professor E. M. Wollank," who had taught Latin in the South for 25 years. Wollank was a "German by birth and spent two years and a half in Berlin specializing in Latin, French, and Greek." One concludes that this request for $5,000 was to also assist with covering Wollank's salary. A few days later, Buttrick wrote to Ware, acknowledged receipt of the request, and stated that the GEB would give "careful consideration" of it. Buttrick to Ware, October 31, 1919, ibid.
42. Edward T. Ware to Wallace Buttrick, October 25, 1919, ibid.
43. Anderson noted that this was also the case with organizations such as the Rosenwald Fund. Anderson, *Education of Blacks in the South*, 159, 161.
44. John D. Rockefeller Sr., *Random Reminiscences of Men and Events* (Garden City, New York: Doubleday, Page, 1913), 182.
45. Ibid., 183.
46. M. W. Adams to the General Education Board, June 4, 1921, box 50, folder 445, Ga 80 Atlanta University, GEB, RAC; Wallace Buttrick to James R. Angell, June 6, 1921, ibid. At this time, Myron W. Adams was Atlanta University's treasurer. In 1922, he became acting president, and by 1924, he was the institution's president. James R. Angell was the president of the Carnegie Corporation.
47. Edward T. Ware to the General Education Board, October 10, 1921, bix 50, folder 445, Ga 80 Atlanta University, GEB, RAC.
48. M. W. Adams to the General Education Board, April 12, 1922, ibid.; E. C. Sage to Adams, April 19, 1922, ibid.; M. W. Adams, "Receipts and Expenses: Estimates Accompanying and Application," May 2, 1922, ibid., Sage to Adams, June 8, 1922, ibid.; Adams to the General Education Board, April 7, 1923, folder 446, box 50, Ga 80 Atlanta University, 1923–1928, ibid.; and Trevor Arnett to Adams, April 10, 1923, ibid.

49. Trevor Arnett to M. W. Adams, April 10, 1923, ibid.
50. Brawley, *History of Morehouse College*, 23, 24. Since President Robert knew whites in Augusta were in opposition and would not assist with Augusta Institute, he turned to black churches, such as Shiloh Baptist Missionary and William White's Harmony Baptist Church, for financial assistance.
51. Raymond B. Fosdick, Henry F. Pringle, and Katherine Douglas Pringle, *Adventures in Giving: The Story of the General Education Board* (New York: Harper & Row, 1962), 196.
52. John Hope to Wallace Buttrick, July 27, 1920, box 59, folder 523, Ga 157 Morehouse College, 1903–1963, GEB, RAC; Buttrick to Hope, July 30, 1920, ibid.; Jones, *Candle in the Dark*, 90, 106, 109, 343–347.
53. Chernow, *Titan*, 242, 309.
54. Read, *Story of Spelman College*, 77; Chernow, *Titan*, 239–240, 482.
55. John D. Rockefeller Jr. to General Education Board, March 23, 1906, in Report of Rockefeller Gift to Spelman, box 41, folder 372, Ga 10 Spelman College, GEB, RAC.
56. Ibid.
57. Read, *Story of Spelman College*, 79. Read detailed how influential Atlantans, such as Sidney Root, a trustee of both institutions, supported Packard and Giles's desire to have a separate school for girls. Henry Morehouse changed his mind and was in support of an independent school for females. He informed the WABHMS that if they raised the money, they could have the new site.
58. Chernow, *Titan*, 240, 241; College History, 2000–2001, SCB, 5; Willard Range, *The Rise and Progress of Negro Colleges in Georgia, 1865–1949* (Athens, Georgia: University of Georgia, 1951), 52; Read, *Story of Spelman College*, 81.
59. "John D. Rockefeller Was Greatest Benefactor of Atlanta University System," July 1937, *Atlanta University Bulletin*, 4. Rockefeller served on the board until 1907.
60. Chernow, *Titan*, 241, 482.
61. John D. Rockefeller Jr. to the General Education Board, March 23, 1906, box 39, folder 360, Ga 10 Spelman College, 1902–1965, GEB, RAC; Abraham Flexner to John D. Rockefeller Jr., September 21, 1914, box 40, folder 362, ibid.

5 Creating the Atlanta University System

1. Jackson Davis, "Recent Developments in Negro Schools and Colleges," May 25, 1927, box 315, folder 3296, Wallace Buttrick Papers, 1927–1952, RAC; "Leading Institutions," in ibid.; and "Summary: College Reports by Denomination and Control," in ibid.

2. Eric Anderson and Alfred A. Moss Jr., *Dangerous Donations: Northern Philanthropy and Southern Black Education, 1902–1930*, foreword by Louis R. Harlan (Missouri: University of Missouri Press, 1990), 101.
3. Jackson Davis, "Recent Development in Negro Schools and Colleges," May 25, 1927, box 315, folder 3296, Wallace Buttrick Papers, 1927–1952, RAC; "Leading Institutions," in ibid.; "Summary: College Reports by Denomination and Control," in ibid.; Negro Education Report, November 17, 1927, box 315, folder 3295, in ibid.; James D. Anderson, *The Education of Blacks in the South, 1860–1935* (Chapel Hill: University of North Carolina Press, 1988), 254–255; Anderson and Moss Jr., *Dangerous Donations*, 101; Dwight Oliver Wendell Holmes, *The Evolution of the Negro College* (New York: Arno and The New York Times, 1969), 174; and Clarence A. Bacote, *The Story of Atlanta University: A Century of Service, 1865–1965* (New Jersey: Princeton University Press, 1969), 256.
4. Negro Colleges in Atlanta, Georgia, 1907–1911, box 49, folder 443, Ga 80 Atlanta University, 1912–1918, GEB, RAC.
5. Ibid.
6. "Number and Percent of Blacks in Total Population of Southern States, 1870–1930," in Anderson, *Education of Blacks in the South*, 41. Anderson provided the population only in decades.
7. Clifford M. Kuhn, Harlon E. Joye, and E. Bernard West, *Living Atlanta: An Oral History of the City, 1914–1948*, foreword by Michael Lomax (Athens, Georgia: University of Georgia Press, 1990), 87, 93, 95.
8. Raymond B. Fosdick, Henry F. Pringle, and Katherine Douglas Pringle, *Adventures in Giving: The Story of the General Education Board* (New York: Harper & Row, 1962), 196. See H. J. Thorkelson, Memorandum of Interview with Doctor George R. Hovey, December 23, 1927, box 315, folder 3294, Wallace Buttrick Papers, GEB, RAC. This document detailed a conversation between Thorkelson, a GEB member, and Hovey, member of the ABHMS. Thorkelson indicated the status of the GEB's study, "of Negro colleges in the South," to Hovey and stated that the GEB's "major interest was in Virginia Union and Morehouse."
9. Henry E. Fisk to Wallace Buttrick, October 23, 1906, box 49, folder 442, Ga 80 Atlanta University, 1912–1918, GEB, RAC. Fisk asked if Buttrick had any suggestions regarding Atlanta University and possible consolidation with other institutions. However, correspondence indicated that there had been consideration of a consolidation of Fisk and Atlanta University. Buttrick expressed his delight in a "suggestion regarding the desirability" Fisk had "of a consolidation of [Atlanta University and Fisk]. No other information was forthcoming, and obviously this consolidation never occurred. Wallace Buttrick to Harvey Fisk, December 10, 1906, in ibid.

10. Edward T. Ware to E. C. Sage, January 26, 1914, box 49, folder 444, GEB, RAC.
11. Edward T. Ware and John Hope, "Course in Business Law and Ethics," January 14, 1915, box 58, folder 521, Ga Morehouse College, GEB, RAC; Edward T. Ware to Anson Phelps Stokes, January 27, 1915, box 49, folder 444, Ga 80 Atlanta University, 1912–1918, in ibid.; and Anson Phelps Stokes to Wallace Buttrick, February 1, 1915, in ibid.
12. Stokes to Buttrick, February 1, 1915, in ibid. The instructor for these lectures was Mr. Weltner, a Southerner who was the head of the Atlanta Prison Association. The quoted transitions are written as they appeared in Stokes's letter.
13. Ware to Stokes, January 27, 1915, in ibid.
14. Ibid.
15. Ibid.
16. Anson Phelps Stokes to Abraham Flexner, February 9, 1915, box 49, folder 444, Ga 80 Atlanta University, 1912–1918, GEB, RAC; Wallace Buttrick to Anson Phelps Stokes, February 9, 1915, box 58, folder 521, Ga 157 Morehouse College, 1912–1917, in ibid.
17. W. W. Brierley to M. W. Adams, November 28, 1924, in ibid.; Bacote, *Story of Atlanta University*, 174.
18. Bacote, *Story of Atlanta University*, 174.
19. Anson Phelps Stokes to Edward T. Ware, July 12, 1925, box 50, folder 446, Ga 80 Atlanta University, 1923–1928, GEB, RAC.
20. H. J. Thorkelson, Memorandum, October 30, 1925, in ibid. Thorkelson was the GEB's director of College and University Education. His memorandum recounted a conversation he had with Myron Adams. Adams informed Thorkelson that the Atlanta University's trustees formed a committee to discuss cooperation with the other institutions.
21. W. S. Richardson to Henry Sharpe, June 8, 1925, box 75, folder 536, GEB, RAC; Henry Sharpe to W. S. Richardson, June 9, 1925, in ibid.
22. W. S. Richardson to Wallace Buttrick, May 21, 1925, in ibid.
23. Peter Collier and David Horowitz, *The Rockefellers* (New York: Holt, Rinehart, and Winston, 1976), 157.
24. Marybeth Gasman, "A Word for Every Occasion: John D. Rockefeller Jr. and the United Negro College Fund, 1944–1960," *History of Higher Education Annual*, 2002.
25. Wallace Buttrick to John Hope, May 21, 1925, box 75, folder 536, GEB, RAC.
26. Wallace Buttrick to W. S. Richardson, May 22, 1925, in ibid.
27. M. W. Adams to the president of Morehouse College, January 22, 1926, box 89, folder 2, Hope Records, AUC.
28. Ibid.
29. Ibid.
30. Hope to Adams, January 23, 1926, in ibid.

31. Lucy Tapley to Trevor Arnett, February 25, 1925, Read Papers, SCA. Upon retirement, Tapley was named president emeritus. Florence M. Read, *The Story of Spelman College* (Princeton, New Jersey: Princeton University Press, 1961), 209.
32. "Death of Mr. Rockefeller Recalls His Many Benefactions to Spelman," May 1937, *Spelman Messenger*, 2; "John D. Rockefeller Was Greatest Benefactor of Atlanta University System," July 1937, *Atlanta University Bulletin*, 4. The Rockefeller family involvement has continued for over ten decades. Starting with John D. Rockefeller Sr., a Rockefeller has served on Spelman's board of trustees for over 100 years.
33. Trevor Arnett to Wickliffe Rose, March 20, 1925, Read Papers, SCA; Arnett to Wallace Buttrick, March 20, 1925, in ibid.; Wickliffe Rose to Arnett, March 23, 1925, in ibid.; and Buttrick to Arnett, March 24, 1925 in ibid.
34. Anderson and Moss Jr. used this term when explaining how several foundations, such as "the Southern Education Board, Jeanes Fund, Phelps-Stokes Fund, Julius Rosenwald Fund, worked closely with the GEB." They further explained that such foundations imitated the GEB's organization and responded to its initiatives. However, they all shared the same trustees in an "'interlocking directorate' of calculating altruism." Anderson and Moss Jr., *Dangerous Donations*, 5.
35. Memorandum of Conference Regarding Spelman College, May 26, 1927, box 41, folder 369, Ga 10 Spelman College, 1926–1965, GEB, RAC. This memorandum documented the conversation between Trevor Arnett, John D. Rockefeller Jr., and Wickliffe Rose. It revealed "the committee of trustees of Spelman College appointed to nominate a president... had come to a unanimous conclusion to recommend... Miss Florence M. Read." The memorandum also disclosed the majority of Spelman's support, in the past, came from John D. Rockefeller Sr. and his family, the GEB, and the WABHMS. However, "the [WABHMS] saw no way in which it could increase its contribution." This implied future fund for the institution would have to come from the Rockefellers and the GEB. Additionally, Trevor Arnett was the president of Spelman's Board of Trustees. See Trevor Arnett to Spelman Alumnae, Students, and Faculty, June 22, 1927, Read Papers, SCA. Arnett had also introduced Read to the WABHMS and the GEB's secretary, and Sage, ahead of time, and received approval of Read's nomination. Read, *Story of Spelman*, 209–212.
36. Jackson Davis, "Recent Development in Negro Schools and Colleges," May 25, 1927, box 315, folder 3296, Wallace Buttrick Papers, RAC; "Leading Institutions," in ibid.; "Summary, College Reports by Denomination and Control," in ibid. The enrollment in the 1921–1922 school year was 5,231; however, by the 1923–1924 school year, the enrollment had increased to 7,641.

37. Ibid., 2–3, 12–14. The five institutions in Atlanta (and enrollment) Davis referred to were: Morehouse College (291), Atlanta University (286), Clark College (207), Morris Brown College (169), and Spelman College (104).
38. Ibid., 15.
39. Ibid.
40. Ibid., 21–22, 26.
41. Jno. J. Tigert to Department of the Interior, March 15, 1928, in Arthur Klein, *Survey of Negro Colleges and Universities*, 2nd ed. (New York: Negro Universities Press, 1929; reprinted 1969), vi.
42. Read, *Story of Spelman College*, 210.
43. John Hope to Wickliffe Rose, October 21, 1927, box 89, folder 2, Hope Records, AUC.
44. Negro Education Report, November 17, 1927, box 315, folder 3295, Wallace Buttrick Papers, RAC.
45. Jackson Davis to W. T. B. Williams, December 20, 1927, box 50, folder 446, Ga 80 Atlanta University, GEB, RAC; Williams to Davis, December 11, 1927, in ibid. Williams initially wrote to Davis regarding the financial difficulties of Morris Brown. He said, "If Atlanta University, Morehouse, and possibly Spelman College, should unite in this move for federation of some kind and give Morris Brown the chance to come if she did not go in at the outset, [Morris Brown] would probably see the advantage of the move and join the others later." However, Morris Brown would not consider a move unless Atlanta University made room for them "on some portion of the land [Atlanta University] now owns." Although discussion of Morris Brown joining the affiliation is forthcoming in the next chapter, it is worthy to note here the beginnings of such a move and the issue of land.
46. M. W. Adams to Messrs. Trevor Arnett, Jackson Davis, H. L. Thorkelson, December 24, 1927, box 50, folder 446, Ga 80 Atlanta University, GEB, RAC.
47. H. J. Thorkelson to Thomas Appleget, January 24, 1928, box 43, folder 381, Ga 12 Atlanta Library for Negro Institution, 1928–1929, GEB, RAC.
48. Ibid.
49. Fosdick, Pringle, and Pringle, *Adventures in Giving*, 200.
50. H. J. Thorkelson to Thomas Appleget, January 24, 1928, box 43, folder 381, Ga 12 Atlanta Library for Negro Institution, 1928–1929, GEB, RAC.
51. Ibid.
52. M. J. Holmes to James H. Dillard, January 24, 1928, in ibid. The high school work at Atlanta University was discontinued in 1928. Historical Statement: Atlanta University, box 96, folder 6, Hope Records, AUC.
53. H. J. Thorkelson to Thomas Appleget, January 24, 1928, box 43, folder 381, Ga 12 Atlanta Library for Negro Institution, 1928–1929,

GEB, RAC; Appleget to John Rockefeller Jr., February 2, 1928, in ibid.; Thorkelson to Appleget, February 2, 1928, in ibid.; John D. Rockefeller Jr., to Wickliffe Rose, February 8, 1928, in ibid.; Rose to Rockefeller Jr., February 10, 1928, in ibid.; Trevor Arnett to John D. Rockefeller Jr., May 10, 1928, in ibid.; John D. Rockefeller Jr., to Trevor Arnett, May 17, 1928, in ibid.; Arnett to Rockefeller Jr., May 25, 1928, in ibid; and Memorandum Regarding Proposed Library for Negro Colleges of Atlanta, Georgia, September 26–27, 1928, in ibid. Apparently, the officers of the GEB felt a need to develop a clear strategy and rationale for the purpose of the land and library, as well as its importance, before addressing the issue with Rockefeller Jr.
54. John D. Rockefeller Jr., to Wickliffe Rose, February 8, 1928, in ibid.
55. Ibid.
56. John D. Rockefeller Jr., to Trevor Arnett, May 17, 1928, in ibid. The land was purchased by Rockefeller Jr.'s representative, under the guise of the Seaboard Realty Company, which Fosdick explained had been created solely for this purpose. Fosdick, Pringle, and Pringle, *Adventures in Giving*, 200.
57. Klein, *Survey of Negro Colleges and Universities*. Tigert indicated, "The State departments of education in 19 States, 79 negro [*sic*] colleges and universities, the Association of Colleges for Negro Youth, the Phelps-Stokes Fund, and the educational boards and foundations of seven church bodies cooperated in arranging for the study and in furnishing information." Tigert to Department of the Interior, March 15, 1928, in ibid., vi.
58. Ibid., 2–3.
59. Ibid., 245. The nine black colleges in Georgia were: Clark University, Morris Brown University, Morehouse College, Atlanta University, and Spelman College (Atlanta); Paine College (Augusta); Georgia State Industrial College (Savannah); State Agricultural and Mechanical School for Negroes (Forsyth); and Georgia Normal and Industrial College (Albany).
60. "Morehouse College," Klein, *Survey of Negro Colleges and Universities*, 284; "Enrollment of Students in Negro Colleges," Table I, Appendix, in ibid., 946; and "Different Sources of Income of Negro Colleges, with Percentage of Total Income from Each Source," Table 5, Appendix, in ibid., 955.
61. "Spelman College," Klein, *Survey of Negro Colleges and Universities in ibid.,* 305–306; "Enrollment of Students in Negro Colleges," Table I, Appendix, in ibid., 946; and "Different Sources of Income of Negro Colleges, with Percentage of Total Income from Each Source," Table 5, Appendix, in ibid., 955.
62. "Atlanta University," in ibid., 294; "Enrollment of Students in Negro Colleges," Table I, Appendix, in ibid., 946; and "Different Sources of Income of Negro Colleges, with Percentage of Total Income from Each Source," Table 5, Appendix, in ibid., 954.

63. Historical Statement: Overlapping of Work, box 96, folder 6, Hope Records, AUC; Bacote, *Story of Atlanta University*, 299.
64. Ridgely Torrence, *The Story of John Hope*, with an introduction by Rayford Logan (New York: Macmillan, 1948; reprint, New York: Arno and The New York Times, 1969), 292–293.
65. Ibid., 293.
66. Trevor Arnett to John Hope, August 15, 1928, box 43, folder 381, Ga 12 Atlanta Library for Negro Institutions, 1928–1929, GEB, RAC; Interviews with President Florence Read of Spelman College and President John Hope of Morehouse College regarding Library at Atlanta, Georgia, September 5, 1928, in ibid.
67. Trevor Arnett to Florence Read, October 26, 1928, in ibid.
68. Florence Read to Trevor Arnett, November 2, 1928, in ibid.
69. "Morehouse-Spelman Summer School," April 1929, *Spelman Messenger*, 30; Read, *Story of Spelman College*, 194.
70. James H. Dillard to John Hope, December 7, 1928, box 73, folder 4, Hope Records, AUC. See Read, *Story of Spelman College*, 194.
71. John Hope to James Dillard, December 29, 1928, box 73, folder 4, Hope Records, AUC.
72. Bacote, *Story of Atlanta University*, 260; John Hope to Wallace Buttrick, July 27, 1920, box 59, folder 535, Ga 157 Morehouse College, 1903–1963, GEB, RAC; Buttrick to Hope, July 30, 1920, in ibid.; and Edward A. Jones, "Morehouse College Endowment," *A Candle in the Dark: A History of Morehouse College* (Valley Forge, Pennsylvania: Judson, 1967), 343–347.
73. John Hope to W. S. Richardson, August 18, 1928, box 75, folder 536, GEB, RAC.
74. John Hope to Wallace Buttrick, July 27, 1920, box 59, folder 523, Ga 157 Morehouse College, GEB, RAC; Buttrick to Hope, July 30, 1920, in ibid; "Morehouse College Endowment," Appendix, in Jones, *Candle in the Dark*, 343–347; General Education Board Agreement with Spelman College, May 14, 1929, box 41, folder 369, Ga 10 Spelman College, 1927–1929, GEB, RAC; and Read, *Story of Spelman*, 212–213, 229. Julius Rosenwald personally pledged $100,000 and arranged for a gift of another $100,000 from the Julius Rosenwald Fund. The WABHMS gave $25,000 toward the endowment. Read, *Story of Spelman*, 213.
75. Read, *Story of Spelman College*, 229.
76. Bacote, *Story of Atlanta University*, 261.
77. Ibid.
78. Atlanta University, Memorandum, January 15–17, 1929, box 50, folder 447, Ga 80 Atlanta University, 1929, GEB, RAC.
79. Read, *Story of Spelman College*, 230.
80. Atlanta University Board of Trustees Minutes, February 25–26, 1929, Hope Records, AUC. The representatives from Atlanta

University were Myron Adams, James Weldon Johnson, Willis D. Weatherford, and Will W. Alexander. John Hope and Florence Read were the representatives from Morehouse and Spelman, respectively, and as a trustee for both Morehouse and Spelman, George Rive Hovey was in attendance. Read was appointed secretary at this meeting. See Bacote, *Story of Atlanta University*, 267; Leroy Davis, *A Clashing of the Soul: John Hope and the Dilemma of African American Leadership and Black Higher Education in the Early Twentieth Century*, with a foreword by John Hope Franklin (Athens, Georgia: University of Georgia Press, 1998), 305; Read, *Story of Spelman College*, 233; and Torrence, *Story of John Hope*, 300.

81. Atlanta University Board of Trustees Minutes, February 25–26, 1929, Hope Records, AUC, 1–2.
82. Ibid., 2–3.
83. Holmes, *Evolution of the Negro College*, 192.
84. Atlanta University Board of Trustees Minutes, February 25–26, 1929, Hope Records, AUC, 3.
85. John Hope, quoted in Torrence, *Story of John Hope*, 301.
86. Atlanta University Board of Trustees Minutes, February 25–26, 1929, Hope Records, AUC, 3–4.
87. Ibid., 5.
88. Charter of Atlanta University, April 1, 1929, State of Georgia, box 89, folder 1, Hope Records, AUC. See Bacote, *Story of Atlanta University*, 267; Lewis, *W. E. B. Du Bois*, 297; Jones, *Candle in the Dark*, 121; Holmes, *Evolution of the Negro Colleges*, 194; Read, *Story of Spelman College*, 235; and Torrence, *Story of John Hope*, 301.
89. Charter of Atlanta University, April 1, 1929, State of Georgia, box 89, folder 1, Hope Records, AUC. As a new organization, the new Board of Trustees for this system consisted of nine elected individuals. The charter outlined that the Board of Trustees of Atlanta University had to reorganize and select three members, which the president represented one. Additionally, the new Board had to include three members nominated by Morehouse College, which the president represented one, and three nominated by Spelman, which the president represented one.
90. Charter of Atlanta University, April 1, 1929, State of Georgia, box 89, folder 1, Hope Records, AUC.
91. Atlanta University: Affiliation in University Plan, box 96, folder 6, Charter of Atlanta University, April 1, 1929, State of Georgia, box 89, folder 1, Hope Records, AUC; "By-Laws of the Corporation," Trustees of the Atlanta University, box 90, folder 1, in ibid.
92. Davis, *Clashing of the Soul*, 305.
93. Memorandum, Atlanta University, January 15–17, 1929, box 50, folder 447, Ga 80 Atlanta University, 1929, GEB, RAC. It was

stated in this memorandum that "there was a general agreement that under John Hope a plan of coordination could be worked out." Also, see Charter of Atlanta University, April 1, 1929, State of Georgia, box 89, folder 1, Hope Records, AUC; Bacote, *Story of Atlanta University*, 268; Davis, *Clashing of the Soul*, 297, 305; Jones, *Candle in the Dark*, 113; Read, *Story of Spelman College*, 234–235; and Torrence, *Story of John Hope*, 301–302.

94. Bacote, *Story of Atlanta University*, 268–269; Davis, *Clashing of the Soul*, 305; Jones, *Candle in the Dark*, 117, 121; Read, *Story of Spelman College*, 234; and Torrence, *Story of John Hope*, 301–302.
95. John Hope, quoted in Torrence, *Story of John Hope*, 301.
96. Kuhn, Joye, and West, *Living Atlanta*, 155; John Hope Franklin, *From Slavery to Freedom: A History of American Negroes*, 2nd ed. (New York: Alfred A. Knopf, 1964), 539; Holmes, *Evolution of the Negro College*, 195; Jones, *Candle in the Dark*, 114; Julian B. Roebuck and Komanduri S. Murty, *Historically Black Colleges and Universities: Their Place in American Higher Education* (Westport, Connecticut: Praeger, an imprint of Greenwood Publishing Group), 54; and Read, *Story of Spelman College*, 229.
97. Minutes of the Trustees of Morehouse College and Atlanta University, box 73, folder 2, Hope Records, AUC. The date was not provided, however, it was written after Hope's death in 1936. See Atlanta University, Memorandum, January 15–17, 1929, box 50, folder 447, Ga 80 Atlanta University, 1929, GEB, RAC.
98. Fosdick, Pringle, and Pringle, *Adventures in Giving*, 200. See Bacote, *Story of Atlanta University*, 260–270; Franklin, *From Slavery to Freedom*, 539; Holmes, *Evolution of the Negro Colleges*, 195; Jones, *Candle in the Dark*, 114–117; Kuhn, Joye, and West, *Living Atlanta*, 155; Read, *Story of Spelman*, 229; and Roebuck and Murty, *Historically Black Colleges and Universities*, 54.
99. M. W. Adams to Graduate Students and Friends, April 17, 1929, box 89, folder 2, Hope Records, AUC.
100. Jones, *Candle in the Dark*, 117.
101. "Three Atlanta Colleges Combine," *Afro American*, April 13, 1929, Baltimore, box 61, folder 1B, Hope Records, AUC. See "Three Great Schools Form a Merger," April 5, 1929, *Dallas Express*, Dallas, Texas, in ibid.; "The New University," *The Independent*, April 11, 1929, in ibid.; "Educating Our Colored People to Higher Efficiencies of Citizenship," *Constitution*, April 12, 1929, Atlanta, Georgia, in ibid.; and "Higher Education and the Negro," *New York Telegram*, April 16, 1929, in ibid.
102. Sam W. Small, "Educating Our Colored People to Higher Efficiencies of Citizenship," *Constitution*, April 12, 1929, box 61, folder 1B, Hope Records, AUC.

6 Germinating a Black Intelligentsia

1. "A Negro Educator," an Interview with John Hope, April 8, 1931, box 65, folder 3 Hope Records, AUC. The interviewer is unknown.
2. "3 Atlanta Colleges Combine," *Afro American*, Baltimore, April 13, 1929; "Higher Education and The Negro," *New York Telegram*, April 16, 1929; "3 Negro Colleges Will Be Linked in Atlanta System," *Atlanta Journal*, April 5, 1929, 6; and "What the Merging of the Three Colleges Means to Atlanta," *The Independent*, April 11, 1929, Newspaper Clippings Regarding the Affiliation of Atlanta University, Morehouse and Spelman Colleges, Historical, Personal, and Family Files, 1917–1954, Hope Records, box 61, folder 1B, Hope Records, AUC.
3. H. S. Murphy, Editorial, "The New University", *The Independent*, April 11, 1929, ibid.
4. Excerpts from *The Landmark*, April, 1933, box 65, folder 1, Hope Records, AUC.
5. Phineas Fogg, "A New University Leader," *New Chronicle*, May 2, 1929, box 61, folder 1F, Hope Records, AUC.
6. W. E. B. Du Bois, "Postscripts," June 1929, *Crisis*, Hope Records, AUC.
7. Ridgely Torrence, *The Story of John Hope*, with an introduction by Rayford Logan (New York: Arno and The New York Times, 1948. Reprint, New York: Arno and The New York Times, 1969), 302; Clarence A. Bacote, *The Story of Atlanta University: A Century of Service, 1865–1965* (New Jersey: Princeton University Press, 1969), 270; and Edward A. Jones, *A Candle in the Dark: A History of Morehouse College* (Valley Forge, Pennsylvania: Judson, 1967), 116, 120.
8. Charter of Atlanta University, April 1, 1929, State of Georgia, box 89, folder 1, Hope Records, AUC.
9. Torrence, *Story of John Hope*, 302. See Bacote, *Story of Atlanta University*, 270; Leroy Davis, *A Clashing of the Soul: John Hope and the Dilemma of African American Leadership and Black Higher Education in the Early Twentieth Century*, with a foreword by John Hope Franklin (Athens, Georgia: University of Georgia Press, 1998), 316.
10. Jones, *Candle in the Dark*, 120; Florence M. Read, *The Story of Spelman College* (Princeton, New Jersey: Princeton University Press, 1961), 239; and Bacote, *Story of Atlanta University*, 270.
11. Bacote, *Story of Atlanta University*, 270; Davis, *Clashing of the Soul*, 311.
12. Jones, *Candle in the Dark*, 116; Bacote, *Story of Atlanta University*, 271.
13. Bacote, *Story of Atlanta University*, 280; Read, *The Story of Spelman*, 239.

14. "Death of Mr. Rockefeller Recalls His Many Benefactions to Spelman," May 1937, *Spelman Messenger*, 2; "John D. Rockefeller Was Greatest Benefactor of Atlanta University System," July 1937, *Atlanta University Bulletin*, 4. The Rockefeller family involvement continued throughout the twenty-first century; one of the last trustees was Valerie Rockefeller Carnegie. Laura Rockefeller Chasin is a Spelman College Life Trustee, "Spelman Photo Album: Presidents, Trustees, and Spelman Family," Winter/Spring 2003, *Spelman Messenger*, 16.
15. President Hoover to John Hope, July 16, 1931, box 111, folder 17, Hope Records, AUC.
16. James A. Blaisdell to John Hope, May 10, 1929, box 89, folder 2, Hope Records, AUC. Blaisdell was the president at Claremont College. In this letter, he requested a copy of the arrangement to see how the Atlanta affiliation differed from theirs. George Johnson to John Hope, July 30, 1930, box 96, folder 1, Hope Records, AUC; Hope to Johnson, August 6, 1930, ibid. Johnson was the dean of Lincoln University and requested a copy of the policy outlining how Atlanta University was reorganized. Vivian E. Cook to John Hope, March 17, 1931, box 89, folder 2, ibid.; and Hope to Cook, March 23, 1931, ibid. Cook was the chairman for the Committee on Standards at the National Association of College Women and inquired about the "educational, social, and cultural environment" for the females in the affiliation. Accordingly, Hope responded and explained the organization of the affiliation, and that "Spelman was exclusively for women." He furthered by saying that the few graduate women at Atlanta University "had separate rooms."
17. "Three Great Schools Form a Merger," April 5, 1929, *Dallas Express*, Newspaper Clippings Regarding the Affiliation of Atlanta University, Morehouse and Spelman Colleges, Historical, Personal, and Family Files, 1917–1954, box 61, folder 1B, Hope Records, AUC.
18. Read, *Story of Spelman College*, 235; Raymond B. Fosdick, Henry F. Pringle, and Katherine Douglas Pringle, *Adventures in Giving: The Story of the General Education Board* (New York: Harper & Row, 1962), 276–278.
19. Fosdick, Pringle, and Pringle, *Adventures in Giving*, 279.
20. Ibid., 280–281. At one time, only the faculty and students from Agnes Scott and Emory were in an exchange program. Several institutions in Atlanta, black and white, are members of the Atlanta Regional Consortium for Higher Education (ARCHE), which allows students to take courses not available at their institutions. "Cross-Registration," Agnes Scott College, accessed July 15, 2001, http://www.agnesscott.edu.
21. Jackson Davis, Conference with L. H. Foster, June 17, 1930, box 50, folder 448, Ga 80 Atlanta University, 1930, GEB, RAC.
22. Torrence, *Story of John Hope*, 302–303.

23. Jackson Davis's Conference with L. H. Foster, June 17, 1930, box 50, folder 448, Ga 80 Atlanta University, 1930, GEB, RAC; Memorandum, July 11, 1930, ibid. This memorandum documented a conversation between members of the GEB and President Fountain of Clark College.
24. James P. Brawley, *The Clark College Legacy: An Interpretive History of Relevant Education, 1869–1975*, (Princeton, New Jersey: Princeton University Press, 1969), 104.
25. Jones, *Candle in the Dark*, 125; John Hope Franklin, *From Slavery to Freedom: A History of American Negroes*, 2nd ed. (New York: Alfred A. Knopf, 1964), 536.
26. Franklin, *From Slavery to Freedom*, 536.
27. Bacote, *Story of Atlanta University*, 279; Atlanta University, Program of Atlanta University for the Years 1930–1936, box 96, folder 6, Hope Records, AUC, 11.
28. Edwin R. Embree to Dean Sage, October 30, 1929, box 96, folder 6, Hope Records, AUC.
29. Ibid.
30. Edwin Embree to Trevor Arnett, October 30, 1929, box 50, folder 447, Ga 80 Atlanta University, 1929, GEB, RAC; Jackson Davis to Trevor Arnett, November 4, 1929, ibid.; John Hope Interview with Trevor Arnett, November 9, 1929, ibid.; John Hope to Edwin Embree, November 14, 1929, box 90, folder 3, Hope Records, AUC; Trevor Arnett to Dean Sage, November 15, 1929, box 50, folder 447, Ga 80 Atlanta University, 1929, GEB, RAC; Florence Read to Trevor Arnett, November 21, 1929, box 89, folder 10, Hope Records; Edwin Embree to John Hope, December 7, 1929, box 96, folder 6, ibid.; and Edwin Embree to Trevor Arnett, December 12, 1929, box 50, folder 447, Ga 80 Atlanta University, 1929, GEB, RAC.
31. Read, *Story of Spelman College*, 241.
32. John Hope to Edwin Embree, February 22, 1930, box 96, folder 6, Hope Records, AUC.
33. Atlanta University, Program of Atlanta University for the Years 1930–1936, box 96, folder 6, Hope Records, AUC, 12. This amount is equitable to $90 million today.
34. Read, *Story of Spelman College*, 242.
35. John Hope to Edwin Embree, February 22, 1930, box 96, folder 6, Hope Records, AUC.
36. Ibid.
37. Embree to Hope, March 7, 1930, box 96, folder 6, Hope Records, AUC.
38. Davis, *Clashing of the Soul*, 332–333.
39. Bacote, *Story of Atlanta University*, 279; Read, *Story of Spelman College*, 239; and "Professor Clarence Bacote Received First Appointment to Graduate School Faculty," July, 1941, *Atlanta University Bulletin*, 13. Bacote also received fellowships from the GEB for advanced study.

40. Read, *Story of Spelman College*, 239.
41. Bacote, *Story of Atlanta University*, 284–296; Davis, *Clashing of the Soul*, 319, 331–333; and Read, *Story of Spelman College*, 239, 242. Though Atlanta University did not have graduate courses in fine arts, at this time, Hope had created a laboratory school that operated with the Department of Education. Hale Woodruff taught college and high school art courses at the Laboratory High School. Bacote, *Story of Atlanta University*, 293, 296.
42. W. E. B. Du Bois to John Hope, October 14, 1932, reel 36, frame 791, Du Bois Papers, AARL; Hope to Du Bois, November 17, 1932, reel 36, frame 793, ibid.; Du Bois to Hope, November 28, 1932, reel 36, frame 794, ibid.; Du Bois to Hope, December 7, 1932, reel 36, frame 794, ibid.; and Hope to Du Bois, December 28, 1932, reel 36, frame 798, ibid.
43. John Hope to W. E. B. Du Bois, November 17, 1932, reel 36, frame 793, Du Bois Papers, AARL; Forecast of Proposed Scientific Survey of the Economic Condition of the American Negro, reel 36, frame 788, ibid.; and Additional Memorandum to President Hope on the Proposed Scientific Survey of the Economic Condition of the American Negro, reel 36, frame 789, ibid.
44. Dean Sage to Trevor Arnett, January 19, 1931, box 46, folder 297, Atlanta University, RAC.
45. Trevor Arnett to Earnest M. Hopkins, June 2, 1930, box 43, folder 382, Ga 12 Atlanta Library for Negro Institutions, 1928–1929, GEB, RAC. See Hopkins to Arnett, May 27, 1939, ibid. Hopkins was the president of Dartmouth College and a GEB member.
46. Trevor Arnett to John Hope, June 6, 1930, box 43, folder 382, Ga 12 Atlanta Library for Negro Institutions, 1928–1929, GEB, RAC.
47. Hope to Arnett, July 9, 1930, box 43, folder 382, ibid.
48. Ibid.
49. John Hope to Trevor Arnett, August 14, 1930, box 50, folder 448, Ga 80 Atlanta University, 1930, GEB, RAC.
50. Jackson Davis, Conference with L. H. Foster, June 17, 1930, box 50, folder 448, Ga 80 Atlanta University, 1930, GEB, RAC; Memorandum, July 11, 1930, ibid. This memorandum documented a conversation between members of the GEB and W. A. Fountain, president of Morris Brown.
51. Jackson Davis, "Report on Atlanta University," July 22, 1930, ibid.
52. James P. Brawley, *The Clark College Legacy: An Interpretative History of Relevant Education, 1869–1975* (Princeton, New Jersey: Princeton University Press), 6–7; Jackson Davis, Report on Atlanta University, July 22, 1930, box 50, folder 448, Ga 80 Atlanta University.
53. Jackson Davis, Report on Atlanta University, ibid.

54. Ibid.; Arthur Klein, *Survey of Negro Colleges and Universities*, 2nd ed. (New York: Negro Universities Press, 1929; reprinted 1969), 259.
55. Jackson Davis, Report on Atlanta University, July 22, 1930, box 50, folder 448, Ga 80 Atlanta University, 1930, GEB. RAC.
56. John Hope to Trevor Arnett, November 8, 1930, ibid. Also see John Hope, Florence Read, Trevor Arnett, and W. S. Richardson, Memorandum, October 25, 1930, ibid. This memorandum explained the meeting that took place and the discussion among black ministers and their training at Gammon Seminary. Particularly, Hope indicated that there were not enough educated black ministers to lead the present situation of the black community. Moreover, Hope mentioned that denominational control "made it difficult for the president to act independently and to get and retain able members of the faculty." What was needed was an institution "free of such control in close connection with and in the atmosphere of liberal thought to maintain an institution for the education of Negro ministers of all denominations."
57. Bacote, *Story of Atlanta University*, 281; Fosdick, Pringle, and Pringle, *Adventures in Giving*, 201.
58. John Hope to Trevor Arnett, August 14, 1930, box 50, folder 448, Ga 80 Atlanta University, 1930, GEB, RAC.
59. John Hope to Trevor Arnett, August 21, 1930, box 43, folder 382, Ga 12 Atlanta Library for Negro Institutions, 1928–1929, GEB, RAC.
60. Jackson Davis, Atlanta University, November 6–8, 1930, box 50, folder 448, Ga 80 Atlanta University, 1930, GEB, RAC.
61. Ibid.
62. Ibid.
63. Ibid.
64. Ibid.
65. Ibid.
66. W. W. Brierley to John Hope, November 7, 1930, box 156, folder 15, Hope Records, AUC. The $450,000 was broken down as follows: $150,000 for the tract of land and $300,000 for construction and equipment, including books. See W. W. Brierley to Florence Read, June 6, 1930, box 43, folder 382, Ga 12 Atlanta Library for Negro Institutions, 1928–1929, GEB, RAC.
67. Trevor Arnett to Ernest Hopkins, June 2, 1930, box 43, folder 382, Ga 12 Atlanta Library for Negro Institutions, 1928–1929, GEB, RAC.
68. John Hope to Trevor Arnett, November 19, 1930, box 43, folder 382, Ga 12 Atlanta Library for Negro Institutions, 1928–1929, GEB, RAC.
69. Jackson Davis, Atlanta University, November 6–8, 1930, box 50, folder 448, Ga 80 Atlanta University, 1930, GEB, RAC.

70. "Who We Are," Association of American Colleges and Universities, accessed March 21, 2013, www.aacu.org/membershop/index.cfm. The association was founded in "1915 and comprised of institutions of higher educaton dedicateds to ensuring that the advantages of a liberal edication are available to all students regardless of background, enrollment path, academic specialization, or intended career."
71. Read, *Story of Spelman College*, 241; "The Atlanta University Affiliation," reprint from *Bulletin of the Association of American Colleges*, xix, May 1933, AUC. SACS is the regional body for the accreditation of degree-granting higher education institutions in the Southern states.
72. Conference between Edwin R. Embree of the Rosenwald Fund and Trevor Arnett, December 31, 1930, Box 43, folder 382, Ga 12 Atlanta Library for Negro Institutions, 1928–1929, GEB, RAC; Edwin R. Embree to Trevor Arnett, February 9, 1931, box 41, folder 370, Ga 10 Spelman College, GEB, RAC.
73. Bacote, *Story of Atlanta University*, 304; Read, *Story of Spelman College*, 284.
74. Dean Sage to Trevor Arnett, January 19, 1931, box 46, folder 297, Atlanta University, Rockefeller Family Archives, RAC.
75. Ibid.
76. Trevor Arnett to John D. Rockefeller Jr., January 20, 1931, box 46, folder 297, Atlanta University, Rockefeller Family Archives, RAC.
77. Ibid.
78. John D. Rockefeller Jr. to Trevor Arnett, February 4, 1931, box 46, folder 297, Atlanta University Messrs. Rockefeller Papers, RAC. Also see Arnett to Rockefeller Jr., February 5, 1931, ibid.; Dean Sage to John D. Rockefeller Jr., February 6, 1931, ibid.; Arnett to Rockefeller Jr., February 27, 1931, ibid.; Trevor Arnett to Thomas M. Debevoise, February 18, 1931; Arnett to Debevoise, February 27, 1931, ibid.; and Rockefeller Jr. to Arnett, July 3, 1933, ibid.
79. Rockefeller Jr. to Trevor Arnett, February 4, 1931, ibid. Rockefeller Jr. provided no explanation for the anonymity.
80. Interviews: President John Hope of Atlanta University with Mr. Trevor Arnett, January 20, 1932, box 41, folder 371, Ga 10 Spelman College, GEB, RAC. Also see Davis, *Clashing of the Soul*, 318; Jones, *Candle in the Dark*, 119, 121; Read, *Story of Spelman College*, 238; and General Education Board Agreement with Morehouse College, May 20, 1932, box 59, folder 527, Ga 157 Morehouse College, GEB, RAC.
81. Bacote, *Story of Atlanta University*, 299–300; Davis, *Clashing of the Soul*, 318; Trevor Arnett to John D. Rockefeller Jr., May 10, 1932, Read Papers, SCA; Read, *Story of Spelman College*, 244, 286–287; and Jones, *Candle in the Dark*, 118.
82. Hope to Arnett, December 6, 1932, box 156, folder 5, Hope Records, AUC; John Hope to Trevor Arnett, December 6, 1932, box 156, folder 5, Hope Records, AUC; Arnett to Hope, December

9, 1932, ibid.; "The Atlanta University Affiliation," May, 1933, reprinted from *Bulletin of the Association of American Colleges*, AUC; Jones, *Candle in the Dark*, 121; and Read, *Story of Spelman College*, 241.
83. Jones, *Candle in the Dark*, 117–118; Davis, *Clashing of the Soul*, 335. See The American Baptist Home Mission Society to Morehouse, September 11, 1935, Appendix, in Jones, *Candle in the Dark*, 356.
84. M. S. Davage to John Hope, November 1, 1935, box 156, folder 7, Hope Records, AUC; John Hope to Leo Favrot, November 9, 1935, box 50, folder 453, Ga 80 Atlanta University, GEB, RAC; Favrot to Hope, November 13, 1935, box 156, folder 7, Hope Records, AUC; Hope to Favrot, November 23, 1935, ibid; Hope to Favrot, November 24, 1935, ibid; Hope to Favrot, November 25, 1935, ibid.; Favrot to Hope, November 25, 1935, ibid.; Trevor Arnett to Hope, November 25, 1935, ibid.; Favrot to Hope, November 26, 1935, ibid.; and Arnett to Hope, June 4, 1935, ibid.
85. Hope to Favrot, November 9, 1935, box 50, folder 453, Ga 80 Atlanta University, GEB, RAC.
86. Ibid.
87. "President Hope is Buried on University Campus: Great Throng Witnesses Commitment Services," *Atlanta University Bulletin*, July 1936, 5–8.
88. John D. Rockefeller 3rd to Florence M. Read and Samuel Archer, February 21, 1936, box 46, folder 297, Atlanta University, Messrs. Rockefeller Papers, RAC.
89. John D. Rockefeller Jr. to Florence M. Read, March 12, 1936, box 46, folder 297, Atlanta University, Messrs. Rockefeller Papers, RAC. In 1937, Rockefeller Jr., sent Read a check for $5,000 adding to the funds generated for the John Hope Memorial Fund, because he was "highly appreciative of Dr. Hope's character and his contribution to education." W. S. Richardson to Florence Read, May 24, 1937, box 46, folder 297, Atlanta University, Messrs. Rockefeller Papers, RAC; and Florence Read to John D. Rockefeller Jr., May 26, 1937, ibid.
90. Bacote, *Story of Atlanta University*, 314; Read, *Story of Spelman College*, 243; and "Expressions of Appreciation of Dr. Hope from Letters and Telegrams from His Friends," *Atlanta University Bulletin*, July 1936, 13.
91. "Editorial Comment on Occasion of the Death of Dr. Hope," ibid., 11. Other individuals in this section who expressed comments on John Hope included Louie Newton in the *Atlanta Constitution*, February 24, 1936; W. E. B. Du Bois in the *Pittsburgh Courier*, March 28, 1936. Editorials were also included from such newspapers and magazines as *Atlanta Constitution*, February 23, 1936; *Chattanooga News*, February 23, 1936; *Houston Informer*, February 28, 1936; *National Baptist Voice*, February 29, 1936;

Atlanta World, March 8, 1936; *Tuskegee Messenger*, March–April, 1936; and *Opportunity*, May 1936.
92. "Expressions of Appreciation of Dr. Hope from Letters and Telegrams from His Friends," *Atlanta University Bulletin*, July 1936, 13–16.
93. Jackson Davis, quoted ibid., 13.
94. Brawley, *Clark College Legacy*, 118.
95. Jones, *Candle in the Dark*, 120; Read, *Story of Spelman College*, 238; Fosdick, Pringle, and Pringle, *Adventures in Giving*, 204; and Bacote, *Story of Atlanta University*, 396–397. Though some overlapping continued with general courses, the colleges emphasized specific major fields. Though Spelman and Morehouse both emphasized liberal arts, Morehouse focused on chemistry, biology, and economics; Morris Brown emphasized rural education, and Clark emphasized physics and accounting.

7 Conclusion

1. "Minutes adopted by the Trustees of Morehouse College and Atlanta University," 1937, box 73, folder 2, Hope Records, AUC.
2. History of Camp John Hope, Camp John Hope FAA-FCCLA, accessed November 25, 2012, http://campjohnhope.com/Home/tabid/56/Default.aspx.
3. John Hope Settlement House, accessed November 25, 2012, http://www.johnhope.org.
4. Hope-Hill Elementary School, accessed November 25, 2012, http://www.atlanta.k12.ga.us/page/6865.
5. John Hope College Preparatory High School, accessed April 3, 2012, http://www.jhcp.k12.il.us/.
6. "Dr. John Hope Lived a Fruitful and Abundant Life; Was First President of Atlanta University System," *Atlanta University Bulletin*, July 1936, 3; Edward A. Jones, *A Candle in the Dark: A History of Morehouse College* (Valley Forge, Pennsylvania: Judson, 1967), 105.
7. "The Spingarn Medal," NAACP, accessed November 28, 2012, http://www.naacp.org/pages/springarn-medal.
8. "The Pre-Eminent Educator," *The Sphinx: Official Organ of AΦA, Inc.*, May 1944, box 70, folder 1, Hope Records, AUC.
9. Roy E. Finkenbine, "Law, Reconstruction, and African American Education," in *Charity, Philanthropy, and Civility in American History*. Edited by Lawrence J. Friedman and Mark D. McGarvie (New York: Cambridge University Press).175.
10. For other examples of black college presidents who understood the complexity of working with philanthropists, see Wayne J. Urban, *Black Scholar: Horace Mann Bond, 1904–1972* (Athens: University of Georgia Press, 1992); Patrick J. Gilpin, Marybeth Gasman, and David Levering Lewis, *Charles S. Johnson: Leadership beyond the*

Veil in the Age of Jim Crow (New York: SUNY, 2003); and Michael Bieze, *Booker T. Washington and the Art of Self-Representation* (New York: Peter Lang, 2008).
11. Tananarive Due, *The Living Blood* (New York: Pocket Books, 2001).
12. Elizabeth A. Lyon and Dan Durett, "Atlanta University District," *National Register Nomination Form*, January 1, 1976, Office of Historic Preservation, Department of Natural Resources, Atlanta, Georgia.
13. Allan Nevins, *John D. Rockefeller: The Heroic Age of American Enterprise*, 2 vols. (New York: Charles Scribner's Sons, 1940), 485.
14. "Expenditures—Negro Education," Appendix III, in Raymond B. Fosdick, Henry F. Pringle, and Katherine Douglas Pringle, *Adventures in Giving: The Story of the General Education Board* (New York: Harper & Row, 1962), 329–332.
15. Eleanor Lee Yates, "Capital Campaigns," *Black Issues in Higher Education*, July 5, 2002, 23. In 2001, Spelman's endowment was ($229 million), only second to Howard University ($308 million). Morehouse's endowment was fourth ($101 million), after Hampton University ($175 million). See Kimberly Davis, "The Richest Black Colleges," *Ebony*, September 2002, 84–94. In 2002, Spelman's endowment decreased to $215 million. Spelman College Annual Report, 2001–2002, *Inside Spelman*, Summer 2003, 5–9.
16. *Us News & World Report*, Historically Black Colleges and Universities, accessed November 25, 2012, http://colleges.usnews.rankingsandreviews.com/best-colleges/rankings/hbcu; Sonya A. Donaldson, "50 Best Colleges for African Americans," *Black Enterprise*, January 2003, 80.
17. "America's Best Colleges 2003," *US News & World Report*, accessed July 13, 2012, www.usnews.com/usnews/edu/college/rankings/rankindex_brief.php.

Appendix A

1. Fisk University was founded by the AMA and Western Freedmen's Aid Commission in 1866. General C. B. Fisk, agent for the Freedmen's Bureau in Tennessee and adjoining states, took interest in black's education; the institution is named in honor of him. "History of Fisk," *Fisk University News*, October 1924, reel 13, frame 693, Du Bois Papers and AARL.
2. Julius Rosenwald to Abraham Flexner, January 15, 1917, box 138, folder 1273, Fisk University, 1917–1918, GEB, RAC.
3. Flexner to Rosenwald, January 17, 1917, ibid.
4. Raymond B. Fosdick, Henry F. Pringle, and Katherine Douglas Pringle, *Adventures in Giving: The Story of the General Education Board* (New York: Harper & Row, 1962), 190; *General Education*

Board: An Account of Its Activities, 1902–1914 (New York: General Education Board, 1915), 209.
5. "Fisk University the First Million-Dollar Endowment for College Education of the Negro in the History of America," October 1924, *Fisk University News*, reel 13, frame 665, Du Bois Papers, AARL.
6. Paul D. Cravath to Fayette McKenzie, April 16, 1925, box 138, folder 1276, Fisk University, 1923–1925, GEB, RAC. The GEB appropriated $500,000 toward $1 million endowment campaign. The Carnegie Corporation gave $250,000 to the fund. The Board of Trustees raised $250,000 in the North, and the citizens in Nashville paid $35,000. At this time, $11,000 more was pledged for liquidating the indebtedness. Blacks paid $12,204.32. Fisk University, box 138, folder 1277, Fisk University, 1923–1925, GEB, RAC
7. David Levering Lewis, *Harlem Renaissance Reader*, edited and with an introduction by David Levering Lewis (New York: Penguin Books USA Inc., 1994), xxiv.
8. Ibid., xv.
9. Ibid. It should be noted the term "Talented Tenth" was originally created by Henry L. Morehouse and later popularized by W. E. B. Du Bois in his book, *Souls of Black Folks* (1903).
10. Lewis, *Harlem Renaissance Reader*, xxiii.
11. John Hope Franklin, *From Slavery to Freedom: A History of American Negroes*, 2nd ed. (New York: Alfred A. Knopf, 1964), 491.
12. Ibid., xviii.
13. Leroy Davis, *A Clashing of the Soul: John Hope and the Dilemma of African American Leadership and Black Higher Education in the Early Twentieth Century*, with a foreword by John Hope Franklin (Athens, Georgia: University of Georgia Press, 1998), 276–277; Eric Anderson and Alfred A. Moss Jr., *Dangerous Donations: Northern Philanthropy and Southern Black Education, 1902–1930*, foreword by Louis R. Harlan (Missouri: University of Missouri Press, 1990), 214; and David Levering Lewis, *The Fight for Equality and the American Century, 1919–1963* (New York: Henry Holt, 2000), 142–143.
14. James D. Anderson, "Philanthropic Control over Private Black Higher Education," in *Philanthropy and Cultural Imperialism*, ed. Robert F. Arnove (Bloomington, Indiana: Indiana University Press, 1980), 168; Anderson, *The Education of Blacks in the South, 1860–1935* (Chapel Hill: University of North Carolina Press, 1988), 264–269.
15. F. A. McKenzie to Wallace Buttrick, June 3, 1924, box 138, folder 1276, Fisk University, 1923–1925, GEB, RAC. Paul Cravath was the president of Fisk's Board of Trustees.
16. F. A. McKenzie to Paul D. Cravath, April 16, 1925, ibid.
17. Anderson, *Education of Blacks in the South*, 270.
18. Davis, *Clashing of the Soul*, 277.

19. Paul D. Cravath to F. A. McKenzie, April 16, 1925, box 138, folder 1276, Fisk University, 1923–1925, GEB, RAC; Paul D. Cravath to Wallace Buttrick, April 24, 1925, ibid.
20. Fosdick, Pringle, and Pringle, *Adventures in Giving*, 179.
21. Davis, *Clashing of the Soul*, 287–288. John W. Davis, Mordecai Johnson's roommate at Morehouse, was the president of West Virginia Institute, later West Virginia State College.
22. Fosdick, Pringle, and Pringle, *Adventures in Giving*, 207. Howard was founded in 1867 by an act of Congress as a comprehensive university. The institution is named after General Oliver Otis Howard, commissioner of the Freedmen's Bureau. Levrin Hill, ed., *Black American Colleges & Universities: Profiles of Two-Year, Four- Year, & Professional Schools* (Detroit, Michigan: Gale Research, 1994), 697–715; Julian B. Roebuck and Komanduri S. Murty, *Historically Black Colleges and Universities: Their Place in American Higher Education* (Westport, Connecticut: Praeger, an imprint of Greenwood Publishing Group), 73.
23. Fosdick, Pringle, and Pringle, *Adventures in Giving*, 207–208.
24. An Official Statement from the Trustees of Howard University, 1925, reel 15, frame 686, Du Bois Papers, AARL.
25. Fosdick, Pringle, and Pringle, *Adventures in Giving*, 205.
26. Ibid., 205–207.

Bibliography

Major Works Cited Primary Sources

Booker T. Washington Papers, 1909–1911, vol. 10. Edited by Louis Harlan. Chicago: University of Illinois Press, 1981.
Edwin Embree Papers, Rockefeller Archive Center, Sleepy Hollow, New York. *General Education Board Archives, Series 1.1,* Early Southern Program. The Rockefeller Archives Center, Sleepy Hollow, New York.
General Education Board: An Account of Its Activities, 1902–1914. New York: General Education Board, 1915.
John Hope Presidential Records, Atlanta University Center Robert W. Woodruff Library, Atlanta, Georgia.
John D. Rockefeller Jr., Personal Papers, Series I Correspondence, 1901–1906, Rockefeller Archive Center, Sleepy Hollow, New York.
"Negro Education." Minutes of the Interracial Conference, General Education Board of the Rockefeller Foundation, Rockefeller Archive Center, Sleepy Hollow, New York.
Office of the Messrs. Rockefeller General Files, 1891–1961, Rockefeller Archive Center, Sleepy Hollow, New York.
Office of the President: Florence M. Read Collection, 1927–1952 (Unprocessed), Spelman College Archives, Atlanta, Georgia.
Wallace Buttrick Papers, Rockefeller Archive Center, Sleepy Hollow, New York.
Wickliffe Rose Papers, Rockefeller Archive Center, Sleepy Hollow, New York.
William Edward Burghardt Du Bois Papers, Auburn Avenue Research Library, Atlanta, Georgia.

Articles, Books, Essays, and Institutional Materials Primary Sources

Atlanta University Board of Trustees Minutes, February 1929, Atlanta University Presidential Records—John Hope Records, Atlanta University Center Robert W. Woodruff Library, Atlanta, Georgia.

The Atlanta University Bulletin, July 1936, Atlanta University Center Robert W. Woodruff Library, Atlanta, Georgia.

The Atlanta University Bulletin, July 1937, Atlanta University Center Robert W. Woodruff Library, Atlanta, Georgia.

The Atlanta University Bulletin, July 1941, Atlanta University Center Robert W. Woodruff Library, Atlanta, Georgia.

The Bulletin of the Association of American Colleges, May 1933, Spelman College Archives, Atlanta, Georgia.

Carnegie, Andrew. "The Best Fields of Philanthropy." *North American Review* 149 (397) (December 1889): 682–699. Cornell University Library Making of America Collection. Accessed April 11, 2001. http://cdl.library.cornell.edu/.

———. "Wealth." *North American Review* 148 (391) (June 1889): 653–665.

Du Bois, W. E. B. *The Education of Blacks: Ten Critiques, 1906–1960*. Edited by Herbert Aptheker. New York: Monthly Review Press, 2001.

———. *The Souls of Black Folks*. With an introduction by Herb Boyd. New York: The Modern Library, Modern Library Edition, 1996.

———. "The Jubilee of the New South." *The Century Magazine*, January 1896, 470.

Ernst, Joseph W., ed. *"Dear Father"/"Dear Son:" Correspondence of John D. Rockefeller and John D. Rockefeller, Jr.* New York: Fordham University Press in Cooperation with Rockefeller Archive Center, 1994.

Klein, Arthur. *Survey of Negro Colleges and Universities*, 2nd ed. New York: Negro Universities Press, 1929; reprinted 1969.

Lyon, Elizabeth A., and Dan Durett. "Atlanta University District." *National Register Nomination Form*, January 1, 1976. Office of Historic Preservation, Department of Natural Resources, Atlanta, Georgia.

Rockefeller, John D., Sr. *Random Reminiscences of Men and Events*. Garden City, New York: Doubleday, Page & Company, 1913.

"The Significance of the Niagara Movement." *Voice of the Negro*, August 1905, 600.

Spelman College Annual Report, 2001–2002, *Inside Spelman*, Summer 2003.

Spelman Messenger, April 1929, Spelman College Archives, Atlanta, Georgia.

Spelman Messenger, May 1937, Spelman College Archives, Atlanta, Georgia.

University Library Making of America Collection. Accessed April 11, 2001. http://cdl.library.cornell.edu/.

Secondary Sources

Association of American Colleges and Universities. "Who We Are." Accessed March 21, 2013, www.aacu.org/membershop/index.cfm.

Alderson, Bernard. *Andrew Carnegie: The Man and His Work.* New York: Doubleday, Page, 1908.

Anderson, Eric, and Alfred A. Moss Jr. *Dangerous Donations: Northern Philanthropy and Southern Black Education, 1902–1930.* Foreword by Louis R. Harlan. Missouri: University of Missouri Press, 1990.

Anderson, James D. *The Education of Blacks in the South, 1860–1935.* Chapel Hill: University of North Carolina Press, 1988.

———. "Philanthropic Control over Private Black Higher Education." In *Philanthropy and Cultural Imperialism.* Edited by Robert F. Arnove. Bloomington: Indiana University Press, 1980, 147–177.

Aptheker, Herbert. *Afro-American History, the Modern Era: A Pioneering Chronicle of the Black People in Twentieth-Century America.* Secacus, New Jersey: Citadel, 1971.

Ausubel, David P. "Ego Development among Segregated Negro Children." In *Health and Segregation.* Edited by Martin M. Grossack. New York: Springer, 1963, 33–40.

Bacote, Clarence A. *The Story of Atlanta University: A Century of Service, 1865–1965.* Princeton, New Jersey: Princeton University Press, 1969.

Barzun, Jacques, and Henry F. Graff. *The Modern Researcher.* New York: Harcourt Brace Jovanovich, 1992.

Bateman, Bradley W. "Clearing the Ground: The Demise of the Social Gospel Movement and the Rise of Neoclassicism in American Economics." *History of Political Economy*, Winter 1998.

Bauerlein, Mark. *Negrophobia: A Race Riot in Atlanta, 1906.* San Francisco: Encounter Books, 2001.

Bennett, Lerone. *Before the Mayflower: A History of Black America*, 4th ed. Chicago: Johnson, 1969.

Bieze, Michael. *Booker T. Washington and the Art of Self-Representation.* New York: Peter Lang, 2008.

Bond, Horace Mann. *The Education of the Negro in the American Social Order.* New York: Octagon Books, 1970.

Brawley, Benjamin. *History of Morehouse College.* Atlanta, Georgia: Morehouse College, 1917. Reprint, College Park, Maryland: McGrath, 1970.

Brawley, James P. *The Clark College Legacy: An Interpretative History of Relevant Education, 1869–1975.* Princeton, New Jersey: Princeton University Press, 1977.

Brubacher, John S., and Willis Rudy. "Professional Education." In Goodchild and Wechsler, *The History of Higher Education*, 379–393.

Carnegie Foundation for the Advancement of Teaching. *Missions of the College Curriculum.* San Francisco: Jossey-Bass, 1977.

Chernow, Ron. *Titan: The Life of John D. Rockefeller, Sr.* New York: Random House, 1998.

Cohen, Michael D., and James G. March. *Leadership and Ambiguity*, 2nd ed. Boston: Harvard Business School Press, 1974.

Collier, Peter, and David Horowitz. *The Rockefellers*. New York: Holt, Rinehart, and Winston, 1976.

Cremin, Lawrence A. "The Education of the Educating Profession." In Goodchild and Wechsler, *The History of Higher Education*, 403–415.

Curti, Merle. "The History of American Philanthropy as a Field of Research." *American Historical Review* 62 (1957): 352–363.

Curti, Merle, and Roderick Nash. *Philanthropy in the Shaping of American Higher Education*. New Jersey: Rutgers University Press, 1965.

Dart, Bob. "An SOS for Rosenwald Schools: Black Education Sites to be Placed on the Endangered List." *Atlanta Journal Constitution*, June 6, 2002, A10.

Davis, Kimberly. "The Richest Black College: Spelman Scores Big Financial, Academic, and 'Sisterhood' Gains." *Ebony Magazine*, September 2002, 84–94.

Davis, Leroy, Jr. *A Clashing of the Soul: John Hope and the Dilemma of African American Leadership and Black Higher Education in the Early Twentieth Century*. With a foreword by John Hope Franklin. Athens, Georgia: University of Georgia Press, 1998.

Dictionary of American Negro Biography. Edited by Rayford Logan and Michael R. Winston. New York: W. W. Norton, 1982.

Donaldson, Sonya A. "50 Best Colleges for African Americans." *Black Enterprise*, January 2003, 76–83.

Due, Tananarive. *The Living Blood*. New York: Pocket Books, 2001.

Fanon, Frantz. *Black Skin, White Masks*. Translated by Charles Lam Markmann. New York: Grove, 1967.

———. *The Wretched of the Earth*. Translated by Constance Farrington. New York: Grove, 1963.

Farnham, Christie Anne. *The Education of the Southern Belle: Higher Education, and Student Socialization in the Antebellum South*. New York: New York University Press, 1994.

Finkenbine, Roy E. "Law, Reconstruction, and African American Education." In *Charity, Philanthropy, and Civility in American History*. Edited by Lawrence J. Friedman and Mark D. McGarvie. New York: Cambridge University Press, 2003, 161–178.

Fisher, John E. *The John F. Slater Fund: A Nineteenth Century Affirmative Action for Negro Education*. Lanham, Maryland: University Press of America, 1986.

Fleming, Alice. *Ida Tarbell: First of the Muckrakers*. New York: Thomas Y. Crowell, 1971.

Fosdick, Raymond B. *John D. Rockefeller, Jr.: A Portrait*. New York: Harper, 1956.

Fosdick, Raymond B., Henry F. Pringle, and Katherine Douglas Pringle. *Adventures in Giving: The Story of the General Education Board*. New York: Harper & Row, 1962.

Franklin, John Hope. *From Slavery to Freedom: A History of American Negroes*, 2nd ed. New York: Alfred A. Knopf, 1964.

Gall, Meredith D., Walter R. Borg, and Joyce P. Gall. *Educational Research: An Introduction*, 6th ed. White Plains, New York: Longman, 1996.

Gasman, Marybeth. "A Word for Every Occasion: John D. Rockefeller, Jr. and the United Negro College Fund, 1944–1960." *History of Higher Education Annual*, 2002, 67–70.

Gasman, Marybeth, and Katherine Sedgwick. *Uplifting a People: Essays on African American Philanthropy and Education*. New York: Peter Lang, 2005.

Geiger, Roger L. "Research, Graduate Education and the Ecology of American Universities: An Interpretive History." In Goodchild and Wechsler, *The History of Higher Education*, 273–289.

General Education Board: An Account of Its Activities, 1902–191. New York: General Education Board, 1915.

Geertz, Clifford. "Deep Play on the Balinese Cockfights." *Daedelus* 101 (Winter 1972):1–37.

Gilpin, Patrick, J. Marybeth Gasman, and David Levering Lewis. *Charles S. Johnson: Leadership Beyond the Veil in the Age of Jim Crow*. New York: SUNY, 2003.

Goodchild, Lester F., and Harold S. Wechsler, ed. *The History of Higher Education*, 2nd ed. ASHE Reader Series. Boston: Pearson Custom, 1997.

Grossack, Martin. "Introduction: Segregation and Its Meaning." In *Mental Health and Segregation*. Edited by Martin M. Grossack. New York: Springer, 1963, 1–4.

Hacker, Louis M. *The World of Andrew Carnegie, 1865–1901*. Philadelphia and New York: J. B. Lippincott, 1968.

Harr, John Ensor, and Peter J. Johnson. *The Rockefeller Conscience: An American Family in Public and in Private*. New York: Charles Scribner's Sons, Macmillan, 1991.

"History: Almost Two and a Half Centuries of History." Brown University. Accessed August 18, 2012, http://www.brown.edu/about/history.

Hill, Levrin, ed. *Black American Colleges & Universities: Profiles of Two-Year, Four- Year, & Professional Schools*. Detroit, Michigan: Gale Research, 1994.

Holbrook, Stewart H. *The Age of the Moguls*. Garden City, New York: Doubleday, 1952.

Holmes, Dwight Oliver Wendell. *The Evolution of the Negro College*. New York: Arno and The New York Times, 1969.

Hunter-Gault, Charlayne. *In My Place*. New York: Farrar Straus Giroux, 1992.

Jones, Edward A. *A Candle in the Dark: A History of Morehouse College*. Valley Forge, Pennsylvania: Judson, 1967.

Kuhn, Clifford M., Harlon E. Joye, and E. Bernard West. *Living Atlanta: An Oral History of the City, 1914–1948*. With a foreword by Michael Lomax. Athens, Georgia: University of Georgia Press, 1990.

Lagerman, Ellen Condliffe. "Surveying the Professions." In Goodchild and Wechsler, *The History of Higher Education*, 394–402.

Leslie, W. Bruce. "The Age of the College." In Goodchild and Wechsler, *The History of Higher Education*, 333–361.

Lewis, David Levering. *The Fight for Equality and the American Century, 1919–1963*. New York: Henry Holt, 2000.

———. *Harlem Renaissance Reader*. Edited and with an introduction by David Levering Lewis. New York: Penguin Books USA, 1994.

———. *W. E. B. Du Bois: Biography of a Race, 1868–1919*. New York: Henry Holt & Company, 1993.

McGuffy's Reader, 4th ed. New York: American Book, 1879.

Miller, Kelly. "Washington's Policy." In *Booker T. Washington and His Critics: The Problem of Negro Leadership*. Edited and with an introduction by Hugh Hawkins. Boston: D. C. Heath, 1962, 49–54.

Morris, Robert C. *Reading, 'Riting, and Reconstruction: The Education of Freedmen in the South, 1861–1870*. Chicago: University of Chicago Press, 1976; reprinted 1981.

Myrdal, Gunnar. *An American Dilemma: The Negro Problem and Modern Democracy*. Vol. 2. With an introduction by Sissela Bok. New York: Harper & Row, 1944, 1962. Reprint, New Brunswick, New Jersey: Transaction, 1996.

Nevins, Allan. *John D. Rockefeller: The Heroic Age of American Enterprise*. 2 Vols. New York: Charles Scribner's Sons, 1940.

Newman, John Henry. *The Idea of a University*. Edited and with an introduction by Martin J. Svaglic. Notre Dame, Indiana: University of Notre Dame Press, 1982.

Pomerantz, Gary M. *Where Peachtree Meets Sweet Auburn: The Saga of Two Families and the Making of Atlanta*. New York: A Lisa Drew Book/Scribner, 1996.

Range, Willard. *The Rise and Progress of Negro Colleges in Georgia, 1865–1949*. Athens, Georgia: The University of Georgia, 1951.

Read, Florence M. *The Story of Spelman College*. Princeton, New Jersey: Princeton University Press, 1961.

Rockefeller Foundation. "Rockefeller Brothers Fund." Accessed April 23, 2001. http://www.rbf.org.

Roebuck, Julian B., and Komanduri S. Murty. *Historically Black Colleges and Universities: Their Place in American Higher Education*. Westport, Connecticut: Praeger, 1993.

"Roger Williams University." Tennessee State University, Library and Archives [digital]. Accessed August 16, 2012, ww2.tnstate.edu/library/digital/roger.htm.

Rose, Kenneth. "John D. Rockefeller, The American Baptist Education Society, and the Growth of Baptist Higher Education in the Midwest,"

12. The Rockefellers Archives. Accessed July 10, 2012. www.rockarch.org/publications/resrep/rosel.pdf.

———. "The Rockefeller Foundation: A History; Introduction." Accessed April 23, 2001. http://rockfound.org.

Rovaris, Dereck Joseph. "Developer of an Institution: Dr. Benjamin E. Mays, Morehouse College President, 1940–1967." PhD diss., University of Illinois at Urbana-Champaign, 1990.

Ryan, Kevin, and James Cooper. *Those Who Can, Teach*, 7th ed. Boston: Houghton Mifflin, 1995.

Schama, Simon. *Dead Certainties: Unwarranted Speculations*. New York: Vintage Books, 1991.

Stanfield, John H. *Philanthropy and Jim Crow in American Social Science*. Westport, Connecticut: Greenwood, 1985.

Torrence, Ridgely. *The Story of John Hope*. With an introduction by Rayford Logan. New York: Arno and The New York Times, 1948. Reprint, New York: Arno and The New York Times, 1969.

Urban, Wayne J. *Black Scholar: Horace Mann Bond, 1904–1972*. Athens, Georgia: University of Georgia Press, 1992.

US News & World Report. "America's Best Colleges 2003." Accessed July 13, 2003, www.usnews.com/usnews/edu/college/rankings/rankindex_brief.php.

Veysey, Laurence. *The Emergence of the American University*. Chicago: University of Chicago Press, 1965.

Washington, Booker T., W.E. Burghardt DuBois, Charles W. Chesnutt, Wilford H. Smith, H.T. Kealing, Paul Laurence Dunbar, and T. Thomas Fortune, *The Negro Problem*. With a preface by August Meier. New York: Arno Press and The New York Times, 1969.

Watkins, Williams H. *The White Architects of Black Education: Ideology and Power in America, 1985–1954*. New York: Teachers College, Columbia University, 2001.

Watson-Moore, Yolanda. "Training the Head, the Hand, and the Heart: The Evolution of the Academic Curriculum of Spelman College (1881–1953)." PhD diss., Georgia State University, 2000.

Webster's II, New Riverside University Dictionary. Boston: Houghton Mifflin, Riverside, 1984.

West, Cornell. *Race Matters*. Boston: Beacon, 1993.

Wharton, Vernon L. "Jim Crow Laws and Miscegenation." In *The Origins of Segregation*. Edited and with an introduction by Joel Williamson. Boston: D. C. Heath, 1968, 14–20.

White, Jr., Ronald C. *Liberty and Justice for All: Racial Reform and the Social Gospel*. With a foreword by James M. McPherson. New York: Harper & Row, 1990.

William H. Watkins, William H. *The White Architects of Black Education: Ideology and Power in America, 1865–1954*. New York: Teachers College, Columbia University, 2001.

Woodson, Carter G. *The Education of the Negro Prior to 1861: A History of the Education of the Colored People in the United States from the Beginning of Slavery to the Civil War.* Washington, DC: Associated Publishers, 1969.

———. *The Mis-Education of the Negro.* With an introduction by H. Khalif Khalifah. Newport News, Virginia: United Brothers & Sisters Graphics & Printing, 1992.

Woodward, C. Vann. "Folkways, Stateways, and Racism." In *The Segregation Era, 1863–1954.* Edited by Allen Weinstein and Frank Otto Gatell. New York: Oxford University Press, 1970, 72–92.

———. "Why Negroes Were Segregated in the South." In *The Origins of Segregation,* 50–53..

Yates, Eleanor Lee. "Capital Campaigns." *Black Issues in Higher Education,* July 5 2002.

Index

AAC&U (Association of American Colleges and Universities), 164, 256n70
Abercrombie, Daniel Webster, 217n47
Abernathy, Ralph David, 198
ABHMS. *See* American Baptist Home Mission Society
abolitionists, 40–41, 62
Adams, Myron W.: on Atlanta institutions cooperation, 133–134, 141, 249n80; on Atlanta University funding, 118; as Atlanta University president, 118, 129, 140, 241n46; Atlanta University System creation and, 140, 144–147; on Hope as Atlanta University president, 146–147; photographs of, 145; retirement from Atlanta University, 146–147
Advance, The, 89
Africa, 55, 203
African Methodist Episcopal Church, 131, 160, 220n74
agency, black leadership and, 3–4, 211–212n6
Agnes Scott College, 2, 153, 162, 252n20
agricultural education. *See* rural and agricultural education
Alexander, Will W., 6, 142, 169, 249n80
AMA. *See* American Missionary Association

American Baptist Home Mission Society (ABHMS): Atlanta race riots and, 86; Atlanta University funded by, 110; on education for black women, 37; growth and development of, 89; Hope as president of, 82–90; on liberal arts *vs.* industrial education, 81; Morehouse funded by, 119, 136; name change to Morehouse College, 89–90; National Theological Institute's merge with, 35; overlapping curricular structures at, 102–109; Roger Williams University funded by, 24–25, 26; on Spelman Seminary name, 239n18
American Creed, 71
American Dilemma, An: The Negro Problem and Modern Democracy (Myrdal), 19, 235n8
American Missionary Association (AMA): Atlanta University funded by, 31, 33–34, 114, 240n26; Ayer School and, 31–32, 33, 103; black education and support from, 31–33; Daniel Hand Education Fund and, 54; Fisk University funded by, 32, 259n1; opposition to social equality in, 114, 240n26; post–Civil War Southern schools and, 31–32; Washburn Memorial Orphan Asylum and, 32, 103

272 Index

Anderson, Eric, 4
Anderson, James D., 211–212n6, 221n76, 233n81
"And There Was Light" motto, 36, 223n101
Angell, James R., 241n46
Ansa, Tina McElroy, 207
Appleget, Thomas, 134, 135
Archer, Samuel, 169
Armwood, Blanche, 205
Arnette, Trevor, 118, 129–130, 136, 138, 158–159, 161, 164–165, 171–172, 245n35
Arrington, Marvin S., Sr., 199
Association of American Colleges and Universities (AAC&U), 164, 256n70
Atlanta Baptist Female Seminary (Spelman Seminary/Spelman College): curriculum at, 38, 109, 224n108; establishment and growth of, 38–41, 223n103, 224n108; funding for, 38–41, 54, 111–112, 118, 239n18; graduates of, 152; motto of, 38; name change to Spelman Seminary, 41, 109; overlapping curricular structures at, 102–109; Packard and Giles on education for, 37–40, 120–121, 223n104, 224n108, 239n18, 242n57, 245n35, 248n74; Rockefeller, Sr.'s support and funding of, 39–41, 64, 119–121, 152; studies and surveys on, 62
Atlanta Baptist Seminary (Atlanta Baptist College/Morehouse College): black faculty at, 26–27; funding sources for, 111–113, 118; Hope as teacher at, 26–27; name change to Morehouse College, 109; Sale as president of, 27, 83
Atlanta Compromise speech (Washington), 25, 26
Atlanta Constitution, 147, 257n91
Atlanta Cotton States and International Exposition, 25, 28
Atlanta, Georgia: black college enrollment in, 123, 131; black colleges in, 123, 131; as black education center, 36, 123, 124, 131; black-owned businesses in, 124; black population in, 124, 162; race relations, post-WWI, 6
Atlanta institutions: enrollment in, 102, 141–142; funding sources for, 109–113; overlapping curricular structures among, 102–109; struggles and challenges of, 101–102, 109, 121; *See also* Atlanta University; Clark University; Morehouse College; Morris Brown College; Spelman College
Atlanta Regional Consortium for Higher Education (ARCHE), 252n20
Atlanta School of Social Work, 6, 163, 173
Atlanta University: affiliation and collaboration ideas for, 74, 123–140, 144n9, 151–152; AMA funding for, 31, 33–34, 114, 240n26; Carnegie funding for, 118; coeducation facilities for women at, 37; curriculum of, 162, 241n41; early establishment of, 31, 33–35; endowment campaign for, 157–159; faculty of, 33, 157–158, 241n41; financial instability of, 74, 126–127, 137–138, 140, 155–156; financial support for, 110; first master's degree awarded at, 152; funding and endowments for, 111–121, 126–127, 137–138, 155–156, 165, 240n26, 241n41; GEB funding for, 74, 112–113, 115–120, 126–127, 137–138,

Index   273

161, 164–165, 180, 241n41; graduate programs at, 135, 142, 144, 152, 155, 162, 167, 254n41; graduates of, 152, 162, 216n44, 238n6; growth and expansion of, 162–165; Hope as president of, 78, 145–147, 154–157; Hope's grave at, 169, 170; Hope's Six-Year Plan for, 156–158, 165, 189–195; motto for, 33, 222n89; Oglethorpe Practice School, 114, 143; overlapping curricular structures at, 102–109; Peabody funding for, 114; primary and grammar schools at, 114–115; Rockefeller family support and funding for, 180, 242n59; Rosenwald funding for, 155–156, 165; Slater funding for, 114; social equality at, 26, 33–34, 114, 239–240nn24–26; state appropriations for, 114–115, 239–240n24; studies and surveys of, 62, 74, 75, 115–116, 130–132, 137, 240n31; successes and importance of, 33–34, 157–158, 247n59; undergraduate programs at, 151–152; Ware (Edward) as president, 75, 115–121, 125, 126, 240n28

Atlanta University Bulletin, 170, 172

Atlanta University Center: college curriculum for schools in, 258n95; creation of, 154–173, 175; graduates of, 179; Morris Brown accepted into, 166–168

Atlanta University Center Robert W. Woodruff Library, 9, 10

Atlanta University Conference of Negro: Problem, 225n220

Atlanta University System: affiliation agreement for, 144–145; creation of, 140–147; exchange programs in, 158, 162,

252n20; financial challenges of, 155–156; GEB funding for, 155, 180; graduate programs in, 142–143; graduates of, 179, 197–209, 217n44, 238n7; Great Depression's impact on, 154–155, 157, 167; Hope as president of, 140–141, 145–147, 149–150, 177; ideas to expand, 162–163; as milestone in black higher education, 33–34, 149–151, 178; as model for cooperation, 153; policies and guidelines for, 142–144; race relations and, 152–153; societal reaction to, 147

Augusta, Georgia, 21–22, 216n32

Augusta Institute (Morehouse College): curriculum of, 238n3; faculty at, 37; financial instability and changes at, 36–37; founding of, 34–36, 103; motto of, 36, 223n101; move to Atlanta, 36; opposition to black education at, 21, 35–36, 242n50; Robert as president of, 35–38, 224n108, 238n3, 242n50

Augusta Manufacturing Company, 21, 216n32

Ausubel, David P., 18, 215n22

Ayer, Frederick (Ayer School), 31–32, 33, 103

Bacote, Clarence A., 33, 140, 157–158, 171, 218n57, 222n89, 253n39

Bailey, Joseph A., 152

Baldwin, William H., Jr., 65, 219n64, 233n81

Banks, Angela M., 209

Barksdale, Mary, 205

Bates College, 177

Bauerlein, Mark, 43

Benedict College, 238n5

Bennett College (Bennett Seminary), 223n103

274 Index

Bennett, Lerone, Jr., 201, 214n17
"Best Fields of Philanthropy, The" (Carnegie), 51, 228n21
Bethune, Mary McLeod (Bethune-Cookman College), 171
Biggins, J. Veronica, 206
Bishop, Sanford D., Jr., 203
"black codes," 14
black colleges and universities: in Atlanta, 123; defined and described, 27–28, 219n65; denominational control of, 34–36, 110, 123, 160, 224n108; early Southern schools, 30–34; enrollment rates in, 44, 102, 123, 130, 131, 141–142; faculty at, 26–27, 32–33, 37, 41, 157–158, 162, 241n41; financial instability of, 36–37, 74, 126–127, 137–138, 140, 155–156; funding challenges faced by, 109–110; funding sources for, 111–113; goals of and changes to, 109; Harlem Renaissance, 184; historically black colleges and universities (HBCUs), 219n65; improvements needed in, 73–74; inequity and lack of college-level programs, 27–28, 101–102; medical schools, 74, 163, 238n10; quality of conditions at, 44, 72–73; segregation and, 17, 27–28, 43–44, 67, 110, 114–115, 149; in Southern cities, 123, 131; studies and surveys on, 42–43, 71–75, 130–132, 136–137, 147n57, 225n123, 243n8; WWI and financial difficulties for, 44–45; *See also* specific colleges by name
black higher education: complexity and challenges of, 101–102; Fisk University as model for, 183–184; GEB and, 67–75, 134–135, 180–181, 229n25; Great Depression and, 154–155, 157, 167; inequity in and blacks' limited access to, 27–28, 30–31, 41, 69–70, 211–212n6, 221n80; need and desire for, 70–72, 91–93, 130; need for in South, 28–29, 34; "Negro problem," and, 28–29, 42, 55, 72, 150; societal views on in post-Civil War South, 17–20; whites' opposition to, 21, 35–36, 152–153, 242n50; *See also* General Education Board (GEB)
black leadership: agency and, 3–4, 211–212n6; higher education to create, 33–34; Hope as leader, 90–91, 146; philanthropists' relationship with, 45, 88, 90–91, 127–128, 178–181
black ministers: on education for women, 224n108; need for more, 73, 102, 255n56; teacher training for, 35, 217n52
black philanthropy: emergence of, 29; Fisk University funded by, 260n6; as funding source for black colleges, 110; Morehouse College funded by, 119; for teacher training, 70
black self-identity: skin tone and social stratification, 18–19, 235nn8,10; whites' social dominance and inferiority feelings, 18–19, 215n22
Black Skin, White Masks (Fanon), 18
black teachers and teacher training: at Atlanta University, 103, 237–238n2; funding for, 54, 114, 143; need for, 31, 69–70, 73–74, 102, 110–111, 136; Oglethorpe Practice School for, 114, 143; philanthropic and missionary funding for, 53, 56, 73–74, 102; white teachers *vs.*, 32–33
Blackwell, Traci Lynn, 209

black women: colleges for, 223n103, 228n23, 242n57; missionary work for, 37; Packard and Giles on education for, 37–40, 120–121, 223n104, 224n108, 239n18, 242n57, 245n35, 248n74
Blaisdell, James A., 252n16
Blake, Renee, 200
Blayton, Jesse B., 158
Bowman, Nelson, III, 205
Boys Club of America, 176
Boys Scouts, 176
BP (British Petroleum), 50
Bragg, Janet, 205
Braithwaite, William Stanley, 158
Brawley, Benjamin, 238n3
Brawley, James P., 154
Brazeal, Aurelia, 206
Brewer, Rosalind Gates, 208
Brittain, M. L., 162
Bronner, Nathaniel H., 201
Brown, Benjamin, 199
Brown Daily Herald, 24
Brown University: first black PhD graduate at, 200; Hope as student at, 24–25, 26, 71, 81, 170, 217n47; Hope's honors and degrees from, 24, 177
Bryant, Linda Goode, 208
Bucknell University, 177
Bunyan, John, 227n9
Burns, Lugenia (Mrs. John Hope), 5, 6, 24, 80, 86, 128–129
business monopolies, 49–50
Butler, Selena Sloan, 205
Buttrick, Wallace, 30, 66, 67, 72, 74, 78, 83, 87–88, 125, 127–128, 130, 144n9, 230n32, 241n41
Butts, Calvin O., III, 22
Butts, James and Nannie, 22

Cain, Herman, 203
Calvin Resolution, 114
Camp John Hope FAA-FCCLA Center, 175, 176

Candle in the Dark (Jones), 79
Carnegie, Andrew: Atlanta University funded by, 112, 113, 118–119; "The Best Fields of Philanthropy," 51, 228n21; birthdate of, 227n13; business tactics and corporate greed of, 50; contributions to higher education by, 56; "The Gospel of Wealth," 51; Hope's criticism of, 86–87; philanthropic motives of, 50–51, 55–56; public libraries and, 55–56, 86–87; racial views of, 86–87; wealth of, 56
Carnegie Corporation of New York, 56, 230n39, 241n46, 260n6; Fisk University funded by, 260n6
Carnegie Endowment for International Peace, 56
Carnegie Foundation, 19, 47, 56–57
Carnegie Foundation for the Advancement of Teaching, 56
Carnegie free and public libraries, 55–56, 86–87
Carnegie Institute of Pittsburgh, 56
Carnegie Institute of Washington, 56
Carnegie, Valerie Rockefeller, 252n14
Carver, Wayman, 198
Charleston, South Carolina, 21
Chasin, Laura Rockefeller, 252n14
Chatard, Peter, 202
Chernow, Ron, 15, 233n79, 239n18
Chevron, 50
CIC (Commission on Interracial Cooperation, 6
Civil War, 3, 13–17, 20, 27, 29, 31–32, 39, 47, 53, 149, 183
Claflin University, 54
Clansman, The: An Historical Romance of the Ku Klux Klan (Dixon), 86

Claremont Colleges, 2, 153, 252n16
Clark, Bishop D. W., 160
Clark College Legacy, The (Brawley), 154
Clark, Renita Barge, 209
Clark University (Clark College): curriculum at, 258n95; founding of and success of, 160, 180; Gammon Theological Seminary and, 131, 160–163, 173, 255n56; graduates of, 197–200, 217n44, 238n7; on joining Atlanta institutions affiliation, 123, 131, 133, 153–154, 159–162; name change of, 172
classical education. *See* liberal arts education
Cleage, Pearl, 207
Clendenon, Don, 202
Coca-Cola Company, 124
Coles, Julius, 203
College-Bred Negro, The (Du Bois), 71, 225n26
Collier, Peter, 128
Collins, Marva, 199
Columbia University, 229n24
Commission on Interracial Cooperation (CIC), 6
conditional grants, 117–119, 241n43
Cook, Samuel DuBois, 201
Cook, Vivian E., 252n16
Cornell, Ezra (Cornell University), 52, 227–228n20, 228nn22–23
cotton, 216n32
Coulter, Richard, 34–35, 223n98
Cravath, Paul, 185, 260n15
Crisis, The, 150
curriculum: Atlanta institutions overlapping structure of, 102–109; German university model for, 52–53, 228n21, 229n24; postindustrial changes in, 52–53; standardization in, 57; utility, in curricular focus on, 52–53, 228nn21–22, 229n24
Curry, Jabez L. M., 65, 230n27, 230n32

Dallas Express, 153
Dangerous Donations (Moss and Anderson), 4
Daniel Hand Education Fund for Colored People, 47, 54
Daniels, Grandison, 31
Dart, John, 216n45
Dartmouth College, 33, 254n45
Darwin, Charles, 48
data collection methods, 8–11
Davage, M. S., 167
Davenport, Chester A., 202
Davidson, Robert C., Jr., 203
Davis, Abraham, 202
Davis, Amanda, 200
Davis, Betty, 209
Davis, Cassi, 209
Davis, Jackson: on Atlanta University System expansion ideas, 162–164; on Clark University in affiliation, 160, 161; on cooperation among white institutions, 133, 154; on Hope's death, 172; at Interracial Conference on Negro Education, 91; on Morris Brown College, 160–161, 246n45; photographs of, 66; study on black colleges by, 130–132, 137, 160–161
Davis, John W., 261n22
Davis, Kimberly B., 208
Davis, Leroy, Jr., 78, 185, 217n49, 225n119
Davis, Ruth A., 206
Dawson, Harold A., Sr., 202
Dawson, Phire, 209
democracy, 19, 116, 180; *See also* social equality in education
DeVard, Jerri, 207
Diallo, Dazon Dixon, 209
Dillard, James H., 91, 97, 139, 230n32
Dillard University, 187, 201, 203, 206, 224n106
Dixon, Thomas, 86
Dobbs, Mattiwilda, 205

double consciousness, 18
Du Bois, Edward, 81
Du Bois, W. E. B.: as Atlanta University faculty, 10, 41–43, 71–72, 158; on Atlanta University growth and expansion, 150; background and achievements of, 10, 41–43, 77, 225n121; on black higher education, 10, 40–42, 72, 225n22, 225n119; *The College-Bred Negro,* 71, 225n124; commitment to of black education, 28; criticism of, 42; on double consciousness, 18; on Hope's death, 257–258n91; Hope's friendship with, 6, 41–42, 77, 84–85, 88–89, 225n119; on industrial education, 81–82; on inequity for blacks in education, 40–41, 225n119; on McKenzie at Fisk, 185; on "Negro problem," 42, 225n120; at Niagara Movement meeting, 12, 81, 84–85; *The Philadelphia Negro,* 42, 225nn122–123; published works of, 42, 71, 225nn122–126, 260n9; on sociological studies, 42, 225n122–123; *The Souls of Black Folks,* 42, 260n9; studies on black colleges by, 71–72; studies on education by, 123–124; on "Talented Tenth" term, 260n9; *W. E. B. Du Bois Papers,* 10

Early, Mary Frances, 198
economic recessions, 154–155, 157, 167
Edelman, Marian Wright, 206
Edmonds, Mary McKinney, 206
educational foundations: black education and support for, 54–55; Daniel Hand Education Fund for Colored People, 47, 54; establishment of, 53–62; Peabody Education Fund, 47, 53–54, 114, 211n6, 229–230nn26–27; Phelps-Stokes Fund, 47, 54–55, 72, 125, 136, 211–212n6, 245n34; Rockefeller's support in creating, 57–60, 232n58; Slater Fund, 47, 54, 114, 161, 190, 211n6, 230n32; *See also* Carnegie, Andrew; Rockefeller family and foundations
E. G. Folsom Commercial College, 15
elementary and secondary education: at Atlanta University, 246n52; high schools and secondary schools, 67–69; illiteracy among blacks and, 17, 27, 149; Southern Education Board and, 68, 72, 245n34; at Spelman College, 137
Eliot, Charles, 228nn22–23
Embree Edwin R.: on Atlanta institutions future, 155–156; as GEB president, 63–64; Hope on Six-Year Plan to, 156–158, 165, 189–195; on Hope's death, 171; on Rockefeller Sr.'s endeavors, 63–64; on visits to Atlanta institutions, 165
Emory University, 2, 153, 162, 199, 204, 252n20
endow *vs.* engender, 5
Everett, Ralph B., 204
ExxonMobil, 50

Family Career and Community Leaders of American (FFA-FCCLA), 176
Fanon, Frantz, 18
farm demonstrations, 68, 71, 110, 114, 227n20
Farnham, Christie Anne, 221n76
Farris, Christine King, 205
Favrot, Leo, 168, 171
Federal Bureau of Education, 72
FFA-FCCLA (Family Career and Community Leaders of American), 176

278 Index

FFA (New [Future] Farmers of America, 176
FHA (New Homemakers of America), 176
Fifteenth Amendment, 14
First Baptist Church (Medford, Massachusetts), 38
Fisk, Clinton B., 32, 259n1
Fisk, Henry E., 144n9
Fisk Herald, 185
Fisk University: establishment of, 32, 259n1, 260n6; funding and endowments for, 74, 183–184, 186, 260n6; GEB funding for, 74, 183–184; Johnson as president of, 186; liberal arts curriculum at, 183; McKenzie as president of, 91, 183–186; Meharry Medical College merger with, 186; as model for black education, 183–184; as part of Atlanta institutions affiliation, 144n9; SACS ratings for, 165; studies and surveys on, 37, 73, 131; white *vs.* black presidents at, 185–186
Fleming, Alice, 226–227n9
Flexner, Abraham *(Flexner Report),* 57, 73, 91–93, 98, 116–117, 171, 183, 241n41
Florence Read Presidential Papers, 10
Florida Baptist Academy, 74
Floyd, Virginia Davis, 207
Foreman, Clark, 162
"Forward Atlanta" campaign, 124
Fosdick, Raymond B., 61, 79, 127, 134, 146, 231n53, 247n56
Foster, Henry W., Jr., 201
Fountain, W. A., 161, 162, 254n50
4-H Clubs, 176
Fourteenth Amendment, 14
Franklin, John Hope, 44, 77–78, 85–86, 154–155, 157, 167, 217–218n52, 225n130, 236n31
Franklin, Michael Robert, 204

Freedmen's Bureau, 29, 31, 32, 33–34, 110, 240n26, 259n1
Friendship Baptist Church, 31, 36–38, 200–201, 223n101
Frissell, Hollis, 91–96
Frissell, Sidney, 91
Fuller, Tia, 209

Gammon Theological Seminary, 131, 160–163, 173, 255n56
Gasman, Marybeth, 4–5, 128
Gates, Frederick T., 9, 58, 63–64, 65, 87, 232n58
General Education Board (GEB): as administrator for philanthropic funds, 65, 69, 74, 232n58; on affiliations for white institutions, 154–155; Atlanta Baptist Seminary funding for, 112–113, 118; on Atlanta Institutions collaboration, 115, 123–127, 133; Atlanta institutions funded by, 111–121; Atlanta University funded by, 74, 112–113, 115–120, 126–127, 137–138, 161, 164–165, 180, 241n41; Atlanta University System funded by, 155, 180; on black higher education, 67–75, 134–135, 180–181, 229n25; charter membership of, 64; conditional grants for black colleges, 117–119; criticism of, 64–65, 178–179; Du Bois and, 72, 123–124; Embree as president of, 63–64; establishment of, 59, 64–75; Fisk University funded by, 74, 183–184, 186, 260n6; goals and purpose of, 59, 64, 66–69; Hope's relationship with, 78, 79, 90, 127–128; on industrial education, 70–72, 180; initial members of, 65–66; Interracial Conference on Negro Education, 90–100; on liberal arts education, 124; on library for Atlanta

institutions, 161, 166–167, 178, 246–247n53, 255n66; Morehouse College funded by, 74, 112–113, 139–140, 234n98; organizational structure of, 130; principles and policies of, 91, 93, 126–127; racial views of, 180; Rockefeller Sr.'s funding for, 59, 63–69; Rose as president of, 229n25; on social equality and segregation, 67–71, 92; Southern Education Board and, 68, 72, 245n34; Spelman College funded by, 212–213, 234n98, 245n35; studies and surveys commissioned by, 74–75, 93, 123–127, 130–132, 133
George Peabody College for Teachers, 53, 229n26
George Peabody Fund: establishment of, 53–54; Peabody, George Foster, 53, 65
Georgia: black colleges in, 136, 247n59; miscegenous unions in, 22; segregation and black higher education in, 110, 115; state funding for black education in, 28–32, 102, 114; *See also* Atlanta, Georgia; Atlanta institutions
Georgia FFA-FCCLA, 176
Georgia Institute of Technology, 2, 153–154, 162
Georgia Normal and Industrial College, 247n59
Georgia State Council for Work among Negro Boys, 176
Georgia State Industrial College, 197, 247n59
German university model, 52–53, 228n21, 229n24
Gilded Age, 14
Giles, Harriet, 37–40, 120–121, 223nn104, 108, 239n18, 242n57, 245n35, 248n74
Gilman, Daniel C., 65
Girls Reserve, 176

Glenn Bill of 1887, 114, 239–240nn24–25
Gloster, Hugh M., Sr., 200
Gordon, Mary A., 208
"Gospel of Wealth, The" (Carnegie), 51
Gould, Jay, 47, 50, 227n13
"Great Black Migration," 184
Great Depression, 154–155, 157, 167
Gripper, Sheryl Riley, 207
Guy-Sheftall, Beverly, 206

Haley, George W., 201
Hall, James R., 202
Hamilton, Grace Towns, 198
Hammonds, Evelynn M., 207
Hampton Institute: agricultural *vs.* liberal arts education at, 70–71; funding and endowments for, 53, 54, 70, 259n15; philanthropists' visits to, 62; studies and surveys on, 131
Hand, Daniel, 54
Harkness, Edward, 165, 166
Harlem Renaissance, 184–185, 187
Harmon Award, 177
Harmony Baptist Church, 35, 242n50
Harris, Marcelite J., 206
Harr, John Ensor, 51
Hartsfield, William, 124
Harvard University, 42, 207, 228–229nn22–24, 238n10
Haygood, Bishop, 230n32
HBCUs. *See* black colleges and universities
Hefner, James A., 199
Henderson, Fletcher, 198
Henson, Lexius, 23, 27
Hepburn Act of 1906, 49
high school education. *See* elementary and secondary education
Hill, Charles Walter, 176
Hilliard, Earl F., 203

historically black colleges and universities (HBCUs), 219n65; *See also* black colleges and universities
historical timeline, xv–xx
History of Standard Oil, The (Tarbell), 49
Holmes, William, 26
Honeywood, Varnette, 207
Hoover, Herbert, 3, 152
Hope, Edward Swain, 80, 165, 217n46
Hope-Hill Elementary School, 176–177
Hope, James, 20–23, 216n32
Hope, John: as ABHMS president, 82–90; as Atlanta Baptist College president, 128; as Atlanta Baptist Seminary faculty, 26–27, 41; on Atlanta institutions collaboration ideas, 126, 132–133, 138, 142–143, 149–151, 162; Atlanta University fund-raising for, 158–159; as Atlanta University president, 78, 145–147, 154–157; Atlanta University System creation and, 145–147; awards and honors, 152–153, 175–177; background and upbringing of, 20–24, 79–80; on black identity, 24, 218n54; career and achievements of, 80–84, 217n51, 218n54; as CIC chairman, 6; commitment to black higher education, 79–80, 178, 180–181; contributions to black higher education, 169–172, 177; criticism of Carnegie by, 86–87; death and funeral services of, 169–172, 257–258n91; Du Bois' friendship with, 6, 41–42, 77, 84–85, 88–89, 225n119; educational philosophy of, 81–82; education of, 23–26, 81, 83, 170, 216nn44–45, 217nn45–47, 51–52; on federation for Atlanta institutions, 168–169; fund-raising skills of, 27, 82, 86–90; GEB's relationship with, 78, 79, 90, 127–128; humanitarian values of, 6–7; Industrial Era, role in, 14–15; at Interracial Conference on Negro Education, 90–91; leadership skills of, 90–91, 146; on liberal arts education, 24, 81–82, 217n48; on liberal arts *vs.* industrial education, 25–26; on living in The South, 180, 217n51, 218n54; memorial services for, 170; as Morehouse College president, 78, 118–119, 124, 138–140, 145, 146; NAACP and, 6, 12, 90, 177; at Niagara Movement meeting, 12, 81, 84–85; oratory and presentation skills of, 24, 25–26, 81, 82–83; people's respect for, 78–79; personal financial support for, 24, 127–128, 217n46; personal nature of, 10, 77–78; photographs of, 80, 145, 168; physical features and racial status of, 27, 79, 180, 216n34, 235n8; on race riots, 90; religious convictions of, 22–23; on segregation, 25–26; Six-Year Plan of, 156–158, 165, 189–195; on social equality and educational equity, 23, 25–26, 41–42, 77, 91–100; social racial activism of, 78; tributes to, 170–172; Washington's relationship with, 24–25, 88–90, 217nn51; youth projects and camps of, 175–177
Hope, Lugenia Burns, 5, 6, 24, 80, 86, 128–129
Hope, Mary Francis "Fanny" Taylor, 20–23, 216nn34, 37
Hopkins, Donald R., Sr., 202, 254n45
Hopkins, Johns (Johns Hopkins University), 52, 153, 227–228n20, 229n24

Horowitz, David, 128
Hovey, George Rive, 141, 241n41, 243n8, 248n80
Howard, M. William, Jr., 203
Howard, Oliver Otis, 29, 261n22
Howard University: curriculum and college departments at, 238n5; degree for hope from, 177; founding and naming of, 29, 261n22; funding and endowments for, 259n15; Johnson as president of, 186, 200, 261n21; medical programs at, 163, 238n10; protests at, 186; studies and surveys on, 73, 131; white *vs.* black presidents at, 186

Independent, The, 149
industrial education: GEB support of, 70–72, 180; inequity in education and, 233n81; liberal arts education *vs.*, 47–48; rural and agricultural education, 69–71, 110, 114, 227n20, 258n95; at Tuskegee and Hampton Institutes, 81; Washington on, 24–25, 81–82
industrialization, 13–14, 179–180
industrial philanthropists: benefits *vs.* and detriments of, 102; blacks leaders' relationship with, 45, 88, 90–91, 127–128, 178–181; business tactics and corporate greed of, 49–50; college presidents correspondence with, 124–144, 144n20, 243n9; emergence of, 44–45, 47; examples set by, 51–52; focus on black higher education by, 47–53, 180; Gould, Jay, 47, 50, 227n13; on liberal arts education for blacks, 47–48; "Millionaires' Special" train trip, 62–63; Morgan, J. P., 47, 50, 227n13; philanthropic giving defined, 178; philanthropic motives and influence of, 7, 49–52, 130, 178–179; segregationist views of, 49; Social Darwinism and Social Gospel and, 48–50, 55; Vanderbilt, Cornelius, 47; *See also* Carnegie, Andrew; Rockefeller, John D., Jr.; Rockefeller, John D., Sr.
inferiority feelings, of blacks, 18–19, 215n22
institutional segregation, 19, 214n17
"interlocking directorate," 130, 245n34
Interracial Conference on Negro Education, 90–100

Jackson, Alexine Clement, 206
Jackson, Maynard H., 202
Jackson, Samuel L., 204, 207
Jackson, Sibyl Avery, 207
Jackson, Traci S., 208
Jackson, Yvonne R., 206
Jack, T. H., 162
Jarvis, Kristen, 209
Jeanes, Anna T., 69, 211n6
Jefferson, Alexander, 198
Jennings, Robert R., 204
Jesup, Morris K., 65
Jeter, Howard E., 203
Jewish students, views of, 228n23
Jim Crow laws, 2, 5, 14, 17, 20, 43, 180, 214n17
John Hope College Preparatory High School, 177
John Hope Memorial Fund, 257n89
John Hope Presidential Records, 10
John Hope Settlement House, 176
John Hope, S.S. (ship), 177
Johns Hopkins Hospital, 227–228n20
Johns Hopkins Medical School, 227–228n20
Johns Hopkins University, 52, 153, 227–228n20, 229n24
John Slater Fund, 47, 54, 114, 161, 190, 211n6, 230n32

Johnson, Adrienne-Joi, 209
Johnson, Arthur E., 203
Johnson, Charles Spurgeon, 184–185, 186
Johnson C. Smith University, 165, 200
Johnson, George, 252n16
Johnson, Henry C. "Hank," 200
Johnson, James Weldon, 142, 197, 249n80
Johnson, Jeh, 204
Johnson, Mordecai, 186, 200, 261n21
Johnson, Otis, 199
Johnson, Peter J., 51
Johnson, Robert Edward, 201
Jones, Clara Stanton, 205
Jones, Edward A., 79, 222n97, 223n101
Jones, Tayari, 209
Jones, Thomas Jesse, 72–73, 91, 115–116, 130, 185–187; at Interracial Conference on Negro Education, 91
Jordan, David Starr, 228n21
Julius Rosenwald Fund: Atlanta University funded by, 155–156, 165; conditional grants from, 241n43; Embree as president of, 171; establishment of, 47, 55, 211–212n6; Fisk University funded by, 186; goals of, 55; Morehouse College funded by, 119

Keith, Leroy, Jr., 202
Kilgore, Thomas, Jr., 200–201
King, Alberta Williams, 205
King, Bernice, 208
King, Martin Luther, Jr., 201
King, Reatha Clark, 199
Klein, Arthur, 136–137, 247n57
Knowles High School, 143
Ku Klux Klan (KKK), 85, 86

Landers, Walt, 200
Landmark, The, 150
Lane College, 74, 173

Laney, Lucy Craft, 197, 217n44, 238n7
Langston, John Mercer, 33–34
Laura Spellman Rockefeller Foundation, 140
Laura Spellman Rockefeller Memorial, 59
Lee, Shelton "Spike," 204
Leland University, 238n5
Leon, Kenny, 199
Lewis, David Levering, 41, 83, 85, 184, 216n37, 225nn120-124
Lewis, Martha S., 198
liberal arts education: described, 221n76; at Fisk University, 183; industrial education *vs.*, 24–26, 47–48; missionary societies preference for, 29–30; at Morehouse College, 119, 124, 238n5, 258n95; philanthropists' views of, 47–48; societal views on for blacks, 29–30, 34; at Spelman College, 132, 258n95
libraries: Atlanta University System joint library, 134–135, 138, 159–161, 166–167, 178, 246–247n53, 56, 255n66; Carnegie and public libraries, 55–56, 86–87
Lincoln University, 164, 204, 238n5, 252n16
Lindsay, Reginald C., 203
Livingstone College, 74
Logan, Rayford, 158
Lomax, Michael L., 203
Lowery, Evelyn G., 199

MacVicar, Malcolm, 83–84
Mallett, Robert L., 204
Manley, Audrey F., 206
manual labor training.
  See industrial education
Marshall, Jacqueline Calhoun, 208
Marshall, Texas, 97–98, 131
Massey, Walter E., 202
Mauze, Abby Rockefeller, 231–232n52

Mayfield, Jody, 200
McCain, J. R., 162
McClure's Magazine, 49
McGee-Anderson, Kathleen, 207
McGuffey's Reader, 103, 237n1
McGuffrey, William Holmes, 237n1
McKenzie, Fayette A., 91, 183–186
McKinney, Richard I., 201
McMaster University, 177
Medical College of Georgia, 21
Medical Education in the United States and Canada (Flexner). *See* Flexner, Abraham
medical schools: at Atlanta University, 163; Meharry Medical College, 73, 163, 186, 238n10; need for black medical colleges, 74, 238n10; nursing training, 238n10
Meharry Medical College, 73, 163, 186, 238n10
middle class, postindustrial growth of, 52
migration, South to North, 184
Miller, Kelly, 82
"Millionaires' Special" train trip, 62–63
Milton, Lorimer, 158
miscegenous unions, 21, 216n37
missionary philanthropy: on black higher education, 101–102; competition among societies in, 34–36; denominational control of colleges and, 34–36, 160, 224n108; educational foundations established by, 29, 31, 53; as funding sources for black colleges, 110; listing of societies, 220n74; philanthropic motives of, 34, 102; WWI's impact on, 44–45
Moody, Cameron, 204
Moody, Charles David "C. D.", 204
Morehouse College: Atlanta University System creation and, 140–145; Augusta Institute and, 34–37, 223n101, 238n3; in early Atlanta institutions collaboration, 123–140; elected into AAC&U, 164; faculty of, 162; funding and endowments for, 118–119, 136, 139–140, 181, 259n15; GEB funding for, 74, 112–113, 139–140, 234n98; graduates of, 200–205; Hope as president of, 78, 118–119, 124, 138–140, 145, 146; liberal arts education at, 119, 124, 238n5, 258n95; as main Georgia black college, 247n59; SACS ratings for, 165; studies and surveys on, 136; successes of, 89–90, 140, 180–181; *See also* Atlanta Baptist Seminary; Augusta Institute
Morehouse, Henry L., 38, 39–41, 83, 88, 89, 109, 121, 242n57, 260n9
Morehouse-Spelman Summer School, 139
Morgan, J. P., 47, 49–50, 227n13
Morgan, Thomas J., 30, 83
Morrill Land Grant Act of 1862, 110, 227n20
Morris Brown College: establishment of, 160–161; Fountain as president of, 161, 162, 254n50; funding sources for, 160–161; on joining Atlanta institutions affiliation, 123, 131, 154, 159–168, 246n45
Moses, Edwin C., 204
Moss, Alfred A., Jr., 4
Moss, Otis, Jr., 202
Moton, Robert R., 87, 91
Mott, John R., 171
Mount Holyoke, 32, 130
"muckrakers," 227n9
mulattos, 79–80, 216nn34, 37, 235n10
Murphy, H. S., 149, 232n58
Myrdal, Gunnar, 18–19, 235n8

NAACP. See National Association for the Advancement of Colored People
Nabrit, James M., 200
Nabrit, Samuel M., 200
Nashville, Tennessee: black college enrollment in, 131, 141; as black education center, 36; Hope's speeches in, 25, 26; Meharry Medical College, 73, 163, 186, 238n10; Roger Williams University, 24–25, 26, 81, 83, 217n51, 217–218n52; Vanderbilt University, 24, 53, 94; See also Fisk University
Nathan, Winfred, 158
National Association for the Advancement of Colored People (NAACP), 6, 12, 85, 90, 177, 184; founding of, 85, 90; Hope's involvement with, 6, 12, 90, 177; leaders of, 197, 201; Talented Tenth and, 184
National Theological Institute, 35, 223n98
National Urban League, 184
"negrophobia," 43, 85–86
Negrophobia: A Race Riot in Atlanta (Bauerlein), 43
"Negro problem", 28–29, 42, 55, 72, 150
Nevin, Allan, 62
New Chronicle, The, 150
New [Future] Farmers of America (FFA), 176
New Homemakers of America (FHA), 176
Newman, John Henry, 221n76
New Negro Movement, 185
New Orleans, Louisiana, 123, 131, 141
New Orleans University, 37, 186–187, 224n106
Newton, George M., 21–22, 216n37
Newton, Georgia "Sissie," 79–80, 217n44

Newton, Louie, 257n91
Niagara Movement meeting, 12, 81, 84–85
North Carolina College for Women, 62
Northern Methodist Church, 160, 162
Norwood, Luella F., 158
Nunn, Bill G., III, 204
nursing training, 238n10

Oberlin College, 32, 33
Ogden, Robert C., 62–63, 65, 67, 68
Oglethorpe Practice School, 114, 143
Oppenheimer, Dean, 162
Origin of the Species (Darwin), 48
orphans, 32
Owens, Major R., 202

Packard, Sophia, 37–40, 120–121, 223nn104, 108, 239n18, 242n57, 245n35, 248n74
Page, Walter H., 65
Paine College, 247n59
Payne, Bruce, 91
Peabody Education Fund, 47, 53–54, 114, 211n6, 229–230nn26–27
Peabody, George Foster, 53, 65
Pettigrew, Roderic I., 203
Phelps-Stokes, Caroline, 54
Phelps-Stokes Fund, 47, 54–55, 72, 125, 136, 211–212n6, 245n34
Philadelphia Negro, The (Du Bois), 42, 225nn122–123
philanthropic foundations, emergence of, 47; See also educational foundations
philanthropic giving, 178
Philanthropy and Jim Crow in American Social Science (Stanfield), 17, 214n17
philanthropy, types of, 29; See also black philanthropy; industrial philanthropists; missionary societies

Phillips, Charles, 24–25
Phillips, Daniel W., 24–25, 217n52
Pilgrim's Progress (Bunyan), 227n9
Plessy v. Ferguson (1896), 41
Pomerantz, Gary M., 85
Pratt, Tanya Walton, 208
Progressive Era, 48, 184–185
Prothrow-Stith, Deborah, 207
Providence Journal, 24, 218n54
Providence, Rhode Island, 176
public education: blacks' limited access to, 27–28, 41, 69–70, 211–212n6; states' refusal to fund for blacks, 28–32, 102, 114
Pulliam, Keshia Knight, 209

quadroons, 21, 216n34
Quarles, Frank, 31, 36, 37, 38, 223n101

race relations: Hoover on importance of improving, 152–153; Interracial Conference on Negro Education for, 90–100; miscegenous unions and, 21, 216n37; in post-Civil War South, 17–18
race riots, 43, 85–86, 90, 185, 225n127, 236n31
racial segregation. *See* segregation
racism and inequality. *See* segregation; white superiority views
Random Reminiscences (Rockefeller), 51
Ray, Tanika, 209
Read, Florence M.: on Atlanta institutes joint library, 159–161, 166–167, 178; on Atlanta institutions collaboration, 138–139, 141, 248–249n80; Atlanta University System creation and, 141, 144–145; background of, 10, 130; on education for black women, 233n104, 242n57; on Hope's death, 169; photographs of, 145; on Quarles, 223n101; as Spelman College president, 10, 130, 132, 178, 245n35
Reagon, Bernice Johnson, 206
Recent Developments in Negro Schools and Colleges study, 130, 136
Reconstruction Era: flaws of, 13–15; segregation and, 19–21
Reed College, 130
Reid, Ira De A., 158
Reid, Jacque, 200
research, focus on: Carnegie organizations created for, 56; German university model and, 52–53, 228n21, 229n24; graduate programs and, 229n24; Rockefeller funding for, 56–57
Rhode Island, 176
Richardson, LaTanya, 207
Richardson, W. S., 127, 128, 139, 255n56
Richmond, Virginia, 131
riots, 43, 85–86, 90, 185, 225n127, 236n31
Robert, Joseph T., 35–38, 224n108, 238n3, 242n50
Robinson, Jo Ann, 198
Robinson, Rubye, 206
Robinson, Shaun, 208
Rockefeller Brothers Fund, 231n52
Rockefeller Conscience, The (Harr and Johnson), 51
Rockefeller, Eliza Davison, 15, 16
Rockefeller family: Atlanta Female Baptist Seminary funded by, 9, 112, 119–121, 130, 245n35; on black higher education, 40–41; immense giving of, 231–232nn48–49; Morehouse College funding for, 124; Spelman College funding for, 124, 145n32

Rockefeller family and foundations: anonymous and confidential giving of, 40, 127–128; on confidential giving, 120
Rockefeller Foundation, 59, 231n48
Rockefeller Foundation Fellows, 231n48
Rockefeller Hall, 111, 121
Rockefeller Institute for Medical Research, 59, 232n58
Rockefeller, John D., III, 169
Rockefeller, John D., Jr.: on Atlanta institutions affiliation, 134, 135–136; on black higher education, 62–63, 74; father's influence on, 61–63; foundations and institutes created by, 57–61, 232n58; funding for black colleges by, 119–120, 139–140; on GEB as funds administrator, 73, 232nn58, 233n39; on Hope's death, 170; Hope's relationship with, 127–128, 257–258n91; Morehouse College funded by, 139–140; motives for giving, 128, 180; photographs of, 61; racial views of, 128; Spelman College funding for, 130, 245n32
Rockefeller, John D., Sr.: as ABHMS benefactor, 38–39, 232n58; Atlanta Baptist Female Seminary funded by, 39–41; background and upbringing of, 15–17; birthdate of, 227n13; on black higher education, 32, 39–40, 55, 62–63, 119–120; business tactics and corporate greed of, 49–50, 59; on conditional grants, 117; educational foundations established by, 58–60; education of, 15–16; foundations and institutes created by, 57–60, 63–64, 232n58; Gates as advisor to, 9, 58, 63–64, 65, 87, 232n58; GEB funded by, 59, 63–69; Industrial Era and, 14–17, 213–214n2; Morehouse College and, 39–40; parents' influence on, 15, 16; philanthropic motives of, 48, 51–52, 120; photographs of, 57, 58; racial views of, 49; *Random Reminiscences*, 51; religious convictions of, 16–17, 60; Spelman Seminary funding for, 39–41, 64, 119–121, 152; Standard Oil Company and, 17, 49–50, 213–214n2; students funded by, 232nn49; wealth of, 41, 57, 213–214n2
Rockefeller, Laura Spelman, 40–41, 59–60, 140
Rockefeller Sanitary Commission for Eradication of the Hookworm Disease, 59
Rockefeller, William Avery, 15, 16
Rogers, James, 166
Roger Williams University: establishment of, 25, 26, 217–218n52; Hope's teaching career at, 24–25, 26, 81, 83, 217n51
Rooks, Noliwe, 209
Roosevelt, Theodore, 226–227n9
Root, Sidney, 242n57
Rose, Kenneth W., 65–66
Rosenwald Fund. *See* Julius Rosenwald Fund
Rosenwald, Julius, 55, 113, 183, 248n74
Rose, Wickliffe, 53–54, 91, 132–136, 229n25
Roundtree, Dovey Johnson, 205
rural and agricultural education: at black colleges and universities, 70–71, 258n95; farm demonstrations, 68, 71, 110, 114, 227n20; GEB funding for, 68–71; at Hampton Institute, 70–71
Rush University, 238n10
Rutland, Eva, 205

Index 287

SACS (Southern Association of Colleges and Secondary Schools), 165, 167, 256n71
Sage, E. C., 91, 115–116, 125, 155–156, 165, 240n31
Sale, George, 27, 83
Satcher, David, 202
Savannah College of Industry for Coloreds Youth (Savannah State University), 114, 197, 240n26
Seaboard Realty Company, 247n56
secondary education. *See* elementary and secondary education
Sedgwick, Katherine, 4–5
Seele, Pernessa C., 199
segregation: Atlanta University System and changes to, 180; Hope on, 25–26; industrial philanthropists' support of, 49, 92; institutional segregation, 19, 214n17; Jim Crow laws, 2, 5, 14, 17, 20, 43, 180, 214n17; in post-Civil War South, 17–21, 26, 67; "separate but equal" doctrine and, 41; social inequity and limits in education, 27–28, 41, 43–44, 67, 110, 114–115, 211–212n6
"separate but equal" doctrine, 41
Sharpe, Henry D., 170
Shaw, Albert, 65
Shaw University, 74
Sherman Anti-Trust Act of 1890, 49–50
Shiloh Baptist Missionary, 242n50
Six-Year Plan (Hope), 156–158, 165, 189–195
Slater Fund, 47, 54, 114, 161, 190, 211n6, 230n32
Slater, John F., 54
slavery and slaves: black education prohibited during, 101–102; colleges founded for former slaves, 24, 183; Du Bois on, 225n123; education inequity due to, 14–15; education needed for former slaves, 32, 37, 102; emancipation and transitions from, 13–15, 28, 81, 101–102, 149; flaws in American society and, 11, 13–15; institutions founded by former slaves, 31, 223n101; opposition to, 35, 40–41, 62, 109; post-Civil War taxable value of slaves, 17; social stratification among blacks and, 18–19, 235nn8, 10; white dominance in society and, 43–44, 211–212n6
Sloan, Maceo K., 204
Small, Sam W., 147
Smith, Brenda V., 207–208
social equality in education: at Atlanta University, 26, 33–34, 114, 239–240nn24–26; GEB on, 67–71, 92; Hope on need for, 23, 25–26, 41–42, 77, 91–100; legislation against, 114; opposition to, 21, 35–36, 152–153, 242n50
Social Gospel ideology, 48–50, 55
Soloman, Edward Burr, 23–24, 217n46
Souls of Black Folks, The (Du Bois), 42, 260n9
Southern Association of Colleges and Secondary Schools (SACS), 165, 167, 256n71
Southern Education Board, 68, 72, 245n34
Southern U.S. states (The South): agrarian economy and industrialism in, 13, 14, 17–18; Civil War and Reconstruction Era in, 13–15; lack of state funding for black education in, 28–32, 102, 114; life and conditions for blacks in, 17–20; migration North from, 184; post-Civil War poverty in, 14; racial inequity in school funding in, 28, 218–219n64; segregation

and Jim Crow laws in, 2, 5, 14, 17–21, 26, 43, 67, 180, 214n17; societal dominance by whites in, 17–18, 214n17, 215n22; *See also* Georgia; Nashville, Tennessee
Speers, William E., 171
Spelman College: Atlanta institutions collaboration ideas and, 123–140; Atlanta University System creation and, 140–145; curriculum of, 238n10, 258n95; faculty of, 162; funding and endowments for, 74, 130, 180–181, 234n98, 245n35, 259n15; GEB funding for, 74, 130, 180, 234n98; graduates of, 205–209; liberal arts education at, 132, 258n95; nursing training, 238n10; Read as president of, 10, 130, 132, 178, 245n35; Rockefeller Hall at, 111, 121; Rockefeller Sr.'s funding for, 9, 112, 119–121, 130, 245n35; SACS ratings for, 165; secondary education programs at, 137; studies and surveys on, 136–137; successes of, 140, 164, 180–181, 247n59; Tapley as president of, 129, 245n31
Spelman, Laura (Mrs. John D. Rockefeller), 59–60, 140
Spelman, Lucy, 40
Spelman, Lucy Henry, 40
Spelman Seminary. *See* Atlanta Baptist Female Seminary
Spencer, Herbert, 48
Spingarn Medal, 177
Springfield Baptist Church, 35
Standard Oil Company, 17, 49–50, 213–214n2
Stanfield, John H., 17, 214n17
Stanford, Leland (Stanford University), 52, 228n21
State Agricultural and Mechanical School for Negroes, 247n59

Stokes, Anson Phelps, 54, 115–116, 125–126, 172, 240n31
Storer College, 84, 201
Storrs School, 31, 32, 33, 103
Straight University, 37, 186–187, 224n106
Stroud, Morris, 199
student tuition, 110
studies and surveys: Buttrick's study, 130; Davis's study, 130–132, 243n8; Du Bois's studies on, 42–43, 71–72, 225n123; GEB funding for, 74–75, 93, 123–127, 133; Jones's study, 72–73, 115–116, 130; Klein's study, 136–137, 147n57; Williams's study, 72, 75, 91, 116, 137, 246n45
Sullivan, Louis W., 202
Sullivan, Sharmell, 209
Survey of Negro Colleges and Universities (Klein), 136, 247n57
symbiosis, 179

Talented Tenth, 184, 260n9
Talladega College, 151, 165, 190
Talmadge, Eugene, 154
Tapley, Lucy, 129, 245n31
Tarbell, Ida, 49, 59, 227n9
Tate, Horace E., 198
Tate, James, 31
Taylor, Mary Francis "Fanny" (Mrs. James Hope), 20–23, 216nn34, 37
Thirteenth Amendment, 14
Thorkelson, H. J., 128, 134–135, 138, 243n8, 244n20
Thurman, Howard, 200
Thurman, Sue Bailey, 205
Tigert, John T., 132, 247n57
Tisdale, Danica, 209
Tobias, Channing, 175–176
Torrence, Ridgely, 20, 216n32, 216n37, 217n51, 218n54
Trevor Arnett Library, 134–135, 138, 159–161, 166–167, 178, 247n53, 247n56, 255n66

Truth, Sojourner, 40
Tucker, Henry St. George, 63, 67
Turney, Edmund, 35, 223n98
Tuskegee Institute: funding and endowments for, 53, 54, 56, 70; GEB funding for, 71, 233n83; Hope's offer of employment at, 24, 217n51; industrial education programs at, 81; philanthropists' visits to, 62; studies and surveys on, 131

Underground Railroad, 40
United States Maritime Commission, 177
United Way, 176
University Center of Georgia, idea for, 153–154
University of Chicago, 38–39, 119, 163, 232n58
University of Georgia, 110, 115, 153–154
University of Kentucky, 198
Up from Slavery (Washington), 81
Uplifting a People (Gasman and Sedgwick), 4–5
US Congress, 29, 49–50
US Supreme Court, 41, 50
utility, in curricular focus on, 52–53, 228nn21–22, 229n24

Vanderbilt, Cornelius, 47
Vanderbilt University, 24, 53, 94
Veysey, Laurence R., 47, 228–229nn22–24
Virginia State College, 165
Virginia Union University, 74, 165, 201, 243n8

WABHMS. *See* Women's American Baptist Home Mission Society
Walden University, 218n52
Walker, Alice, 206
Ward, Horace T., 198
Ware, Edmund Asa, 31–34, 103, 110, 114–115, 126

Ware, Edward, 75, 115–117, 125, 126
Warfield, Nima A., 205
Washburn Asylum, 32, 103
Washburn Memorial Orphan Asylum, 32, 103
Washington, Booker T.: death of, 90; Hope's relationship with, 24–25, 88–90, 217n51; on industrial education, 24–26, 81–82; on inequity in school funding, 218–219n64; personality of, 77; philanthropists' relationship with, 88, 90; Rosenwald and, 55; as Tuskegee Institute president, 24; *Up from Slavery*, 81
Washington, D.C.: as black education center, 123, 131, 141; National Theological Institute, 35, 223n98; *See also* Howard University
Washington, Renee Chube, 208
Watkins-Hayes, Celeste, 209
Watson-Moore, Yolanda, 224n108
Watts, Rolonda, 208
wealth, Social Darwinism to justify, 48–50, 55
Weatherford, Willis D., 142, 249n80
W. E. B. Du Bois Papers, 10
Weber, Max, 43
Weisiger, Kendall, 162
West Virginia State College (West Virginia Institute), 261n21
Where Peachtree Meets Sweet Auburn (Pomerantz), 85
White, Andrew D., 227n20, 228n22
white superiority and dominance: blacks' feelings of inferiority and, 18–19, 215n22; inequity in school funding and, 28, 218–219n64; "negrophobia" and whites' fear of blacks, 43,

85–86; Social Darwinism and Social Gospel ideologies and, 48–49; Social Darwinism and Social Gospel to justify, 48–50, 55; by Southern whites, 18; white societal dominance in South, 17–20, 43–44
White, Walter Francis, 197
White, William J., 34–35, 222n97, 224n108, 242n50
Whittaker, John, 158
Wilberforce, Ohio, 131
Wilberforce University, 42, 131, 154, 238n5
William E. Harmon Foundation, 177
Williams, Elynor A., 206
Williams, Hosea, 199
Williams, W. T. B., 72, 75, 91, 116, 137, 246n45
Willie, Charles Vert, 201
Wilson Avenue Baptist Church, 39
Wilson, John Silvanus, Jr., 204
Wollank, E. M., 241n41
women. *See* Atlanta Baptist Female Seminary; black women
women, black colleges for: at Cornell University, 228n23
Women's American Baptist Home Mission Society (WABHMS), 37–38, 223n104, 239n18, 242n57, 245n35, 248n74
Woodruff, Hale, 158, 254n41
Woodson, Carter G., 211–212n6
Woodward, C. Vann, 18
Worcester Academy, 23–24, 81, 217n45
World War I, 6, 44–45, 47, 116
Wright, Louis Tompkins, 197
Wright, Richard R., 197

Xavier University, 187

Yale University, 32, 33, 166, 222n89
Yancy, Dorothy, 200
Yates, Ella Gaines, 206
Young Men's Christian Association (YMCA), 6, 171, 175, 176